# Contents

| | |
|---|---|
| Acknowledgements | vii |
| Introduction | viii |
| Guided tour | x |
| Table of cases and statutes | xii |
| | |
| Chapter 1: Evidential issues within the trial process | 1 |
| Chapter 2: Witnesses | 27 |
| Chapter 3: Character evidence | 55 |
| Chapter 4: Hearsay | 85 |
| Chapter 5: Opinion and expert evidence | 113 |
| Chapter 6: Confession evidence | 129 |
| Chapter 7: Hazardous evidence | 155 |
| Chapter 8: Illegally and improperly obtained evidence | 173 |
| Chapter 9: Privilege, disclosure and public interest immunity | 191 |
| | |
| And finally, before the exam . . . | 221 |
| Glossary of terms | 243 |
| Index | 245 |

## What do you think of LawExpress?

We're really keen to hear your opinions about the series and how well it supports your studies. Your views will help inform the future development of Law Express and ensure it is best suited to the revision needs of law students.

Please log on to the website and leave us your feedback. It will only take a few minutes and your thoughts are invaluable to us.

## www.pearsoned.co.uk/lawexpressfeedback

# Acknowledgements

Our thanks go to all reviewers who contributed to the development of this text, including students who participated in research and focus groups which helped to shape the series format.

# Introduction

The law of evidence is an increasingly popular subject on LLB programmes, with many students finding it an enjoyable and challenging area. It also features in courses for other groups, such as trading standards officers and forensic scientists, who may be called upon to give evidence as part of their work. We are all familiar with the trial process from popular courtroom dramas, but the real law of evidence is considerably more complex than such fictional accounts suggest and requires an understanding of not only the various rules, but also the wider objectives of the trial process itself. The law of evidence is designed to ensure (as far as is possible) that the most unreliable evidence is not placed before the court and that any evidence which is admitted is subjected to thorough challenge by the other side. The result is a series of rules and principles which must be understood by students.

Evidence examinations usually consist of both essay and problem questions. Essays will require students to assess the effectiveness of particular legal provisions or to consider recent changes to the law. Such questions are particularly popular following the implementation of the Criminal Justice Act 2003, which has made significant changes to important areas such as character evidence and hearsay evidence. Problem questions seek to test students on particular evidential principles, usually to assess whether a particular item of evidence will be admissible or, alternatively, will fall under one of the exclusionary rules. Such questions often feature a number of witnesses, each designed to highlight a specific aspect of the rule in question. In all cases, the examiner is looking for answers which contain two key elements:

■ an accurate summary of the relevant legal principles;

■ some critical evaluation in the form of analysis (in the case of an essay question) or application (in the case of a problem scenario).

In both cases it is vital to produce structured answers which develop reasoned and balanced arguments, supported by authority. In addition, particularly in problem questions, you should be able to recognise the weaknesses and limitations of the facts as presented. An important aspect of answering such questions is to identify additional information which you might require and which might impact on the final outcome. This is only possible if you fully understand the relevant rules of evidence, and the examiner will reward you for displaying such an analytical approach.

Remember that this is a revision guide, not a core text, so it can never provide you with the depth of understanding which you will need to excel in examinations and it will be no substitute for structured reading around the various topics. What it can do, however, is to focus your revision on the key areas and highlight those additional points which examiners are looking for and which serve to make your paper stand out. The single most common failing in evidence examinations is that students write 'common-sense' answers, without sufficient reference to the cases and statutory provisions. The law of evidence is often intricate and finely balanced between statutory and common law principles and, to excel in examination, you must be able to cite the relevant authorities in support of your arguments. You should also recognise that an evidence examination requires you to present your arguments much as you would in court, identifying the key evidential issues and applying them to the facts of the various scenarios. Ultimately, there is no substitute for a firm grasp of the legal principles and this is essential if you are to achieve a high grade.

## 📖 REVISION NOTE

- The principal objective of the law of evidence is to ensure the integrity of the evidence which is presented to the court in an attempt to minimise the possibility of error and subsequent miscarriage of justice.

- The law of evidence is composed of a series of rules, both from statute and common law, which are mostly concerned with the admissibility of various forms of evidence.

- Writing examination answers in the law of evidence requires you to consider the strengths and weaknesses of the evidence and whether any of the evidential rules allow you to put forward the evidence that you want to adduce and to exclude the evidence which you don't wish the court to hear.

- In all cases, a grasp of both the rule itself and the supporting case law is essential to success.

**Before you begin, you can use the study plan available on the companion website to assess how well you know the material in this book and identify the areas where you may want to focus your revision.**

# Guided tour

How to use features in the book 📖 and on the companion website 🖱

## Understand quickly

📖 **Topic maps** – Visual guides highlight key subject areas and facilitate easy navigation through the chapter. Download them from the companion website to pin on your wall or add to your revision notes.

📖 **Key definitions** – Make sure you understand essential legal terms.

📖 **Key cases and key statutes** – Identify and review the important elements of essential cases and statutes you will need to know for your exams.

📖 **Read to impress** – These carefully selected sources will extend your knowledge, deepen your understanding, and earn better marks in coursework and exams.

📖 **Glossary** – Forgotten the meaning of a word? This quick reference covers key definitions and other useful terms.

🖱 **Test your knowledge** – How well do you know each topic? Test yourself with quizzes tailored specifically to each chapter.

🖱 **Podcasts** – Listen as your own personal Law Express tutor guides you through a step-by-step explanation of how to approach a typical but challenging question.

## Revise effectively

📖 **Revision checklists** – Identify essential points you should know for your exams. The chapters will help you revise each point to ensure you are fully prepared. Print the checklists from the companion website to track your progress.

📖 **Revision notes** – These boxes highlight related points and areas where your course might adopt a particular approach that you should check with your course tutor.

**Study plan** – Assess how well you know a subject prior to your revision and determine which areas need the most attention. Take the full assessment or focus on targeted study units.

**Flashcards** – Test and improve recall of important legal terms, key cases and statutes. Available in both electronic and printable formats.

# Take exams with confidence

**Sample questions with answer guidelines** – Practice makes perfect! Consider how you would answer the question at the start of each chapter then refer to answer guidance at the end of the chapter. Try out additional sample questions online.

**Assessment advice** – Use this feature to identify how a subject may be examined and how to apply your knowledge effectively.

**Make your answer stand out** – Impress your examiners with these sources of further thinking and debate.

**Exam tips** – Feeling the pressure? These boxes indicate how you can improve your exam performance when it really counts.

**Don't be tempted to** – Spot common pitfalls and avoid losing marks.

**You be the marker** – Evaluate sample exam answers and understand how and why an examiner awards marks.

# Table of cases and statutes

## Cases

Al-Khawaja and Tahery v UK (2009) 49 EHRR 1 109
Al-Khawaja and Tahery v UK (2012) 54 EHRR 23 109
Anderson v Weston (1840) 6 Bing NC 296 8, 223
Ashworth Hospital Authority v MGN Ltd [2002] UKHL 29
    (HL) 205, 238

Barnaby v DPP [2015] EWHC 232 (Admin) 102, 230
Barrow v R [1998] AC 846 (PC) 66
Beghal v Director of Public Prosecutions [2015] UKSC
    49 183, 197, 237
Benedetto and Labrador v R [2003] 1 WLR 1545 (PC)
    161, 234
Bishop Meath v Marquis of Winchester (1836) 3 Bing
    NC 183 (HL) 7, 8, 223
Blunt v Park Lane Hotel [1942] 2 KB 253 (CA) 194

Chard v Chard [1955] 3 All ER 721 (Probate, Divorce &
    Admiralty Div) 22, 224
Condron v United Kingdom (2001) 31 EHRR 1 51
Conway v Rimmer [1968] AC 910 (HL) 217, 239

Doe d Arundel (Lord ) v Fowler (1850) 14 QB 700 8, 223
Doe d Tatum v Catomore (1851) 16 QB 745 8, 9, 223
DPP v A and BC Chewing Gum Ltd [1967] 2 All ER 504
    (QB) 123.231
DPP v Marshall [1988] 3 All ER 683 (DC) 186, 236
DPP v P [1991] 3 All ER 337 (HL) 62, 63, 226
Duncan v Cammell Laird & Co. Ltd [1942] AC 624 (HL)
    216

Folkes v Chadd (1783) 3 Doug KB 157 117, 230
Foye v R [2013] EWCA Crim 475 25

Gage v HM Advocate [2011] HCJAC 40 (HC of Justiciary
    (Sc)) 179
Gatland v Metropolitan Police Commissioner [1968] 2
    All ER 100 (QB) 17, 224
Goodwin v United Kingdom (1996) 1 BHRC 81 (ECtHR)
    206, 238

Hales v Kerr [1908] 2 KB 601 (KBD) 61, 225
Hobbs v Tinling & Co. Ltd [1929] 2 KB 1 (CA) 59, 225
Holcombe v Hewson (1810) 2 Camp 391 11, 223

Jones v Owens (1870) 34 JP 759 177, 235
Joseph Constantine Steamship Line Ltd v Imperial
    Smelting Corp. Ltd [1942] AC 54 (HL) 14, 223

Khan v Royal Mail Group Ltd [2014] EWCA Civ 1082 18

Levison and another v Patent Steam Carpet Cleaning
    Co Ltd [1978] QB 69 (CA) 15, 223
Li Shu-Ling v R [1988] 3 All ER 138 (PC) 138, 232

M'Naghten's Case (1843) 10 Cl & Fin 200 16
Matto v Wolverhampton Crown Court (1987) The Times,
    27 May (DC) 182, 236
Mood Music Publishing Co. Ltd v De Wolfe Publishing
    Ltd [1976] Ch 119 (CA) 61, 226

Nicholas v Penny [1950] 2 All ER 89 (DC) 159, 234

O'Brien v Chief Constable of South Wales Police [2005]
    UKHL 26 63, 226
Oyarce v Cheshire County Council [2008] EWCA Civ
    434; [2008] ICR 1179 (CA) 18

Parkes v R [1976] 3 All ER 380 (PC) 138, 232

*R (on the application of D)* v *Camberwell Green Youth Court* [2005] UKHL 4 46

*R (on the application of Prudential plc)* v *Special Commissioner of Income Tax* [2013] UKSC 1 202, 237

*R* v *A (I)* [2015] EWCA Crim 118 38

*R* v *Abadom* [1983] 1 All ER 364 (CA) 122, 231

*R* v *Alladice* (1988) 87 Cr App R 380 (CA) 148, 234

*R* v *Andrews* [1987] AC 281 (HL) 100, 110, 229

*R* v *Bailey* [1993] 3 All ER 513 (CA) 181, 236

*R* v *Barker* [2010] EWCA Crim 4 43, 225

*R* v *Barnett* [2002] EWCA Crim 454 163, 234

*R* v *Barry* (1991) 95 Cr App R 384 (CA) 149, 234

*R* v *Beckles* [2005] 1 All ER 705 (CA) 52, 53, 225

*R* v *Brima* [2007] 1 Cr App R 316 (CA) 73, 227

*R* v *Bryce* [1992] 4 All ER 567 (CA) 185, 236

*R* v *Burge; R* v *Pegg* [1996] 1 Cr App R 163 (CA) 162

*R* v *Butler* (1986) 84 Cr App R 12 60, 225

*R* v *Butler* [2015] EWCA Crim 854 81

*R* v *Campbell* [2007] EWCA Crim 1472 75, 227

*R* v *Cannings* [2004] EWCA Crim 1 125, 231

*R* v *Carnall* [1995] Crim LR 944 (CA) 102, 229

*R* v *Castillo and Others* [1996] 1 Cr App Rep 438 95, 229

*R* v *Chopra* [2007] 1 Cr App R 225 (CA) 72, 227

*R* v *Christou* [1992] QB 979 (CA) 184, 236

*R* v *Clare and Peach* [1995] Crim LR 947 (CA) 120, 231

*R* v *Clark* [2003] EWCA Crim 1020) 126, 231

*R* v *Clarke & Hewins* (1999) 6 Archbold News 2 (CA) 9

*R* v *Clewes* (1830) 4 C & P 221 9

*R* v *Condron and Condron* [1997] 1 Cr App R 185 (CA) 51, 52, 225

*R* v *Conway (Patrick Peter)* [2015] EWCA Crim 1063 74, 227

*R* v *Cox* [1991] Crim LR 276 (CA) 141, 144, 232

*R* v *Cox and Railton* (1884) 14 QBD 153 (CCR) 201, 237

*R* v *DS and another* [2015] EWCA Crim 662 213

*R* v *Daye* [1908] 2 KB 333 (KBD) 5, 222

*R* v *Delaney* (1988) 153 JP 103 (CA) 181, 235

*R* v *Docherty* [2006] EWCA Crim 2716 97, 229

*R* v *Edwards* [1975] QB 27 17

*R* v *Edwards* [2001] EWCA Crim 2185 121, 231

*R* v *Edwards* [2005] EWCA Crim 1813 70, 227

*R* v *Emmerson* (1991) 92 Cr App R 284 (CA) 142, 233

*R* v *Essa* [2009] EWCA Crim 43 50, 215, 225, 239

*R* v *Foye* [2013] EWCA Crim 475 21, 25

*R* v *Fulling* [1987] 1 WLR 1196 (HL) 142, 152, 232

*R* v *Funderburk* [1990] 2 All ER 482 (CA) 36, 224

*R* v *Garrett* [2015] EWCA Crim 757 78, 228

*R* v *Garrod* [1997] Crim LR 445 (CA) 232

*R* v *Gilfoyle* [1996] 3 All ER 883 (CA) 104, 230

*R* v *Goldenberg* (1988) 88 Cr App R 285 (CA) 146, 233

*R* v *Grant* [1996] 1 Cr App R 73 (CA) 10, 223

*R* v *Gray* [2004] EWCA Crim 1074 66, 226

*R* v *Gray and others* [2014] EWCA Crim 2372 218, 239

*R* v *H and C* [2004] UKHL 3 218, 239

*R* v *Hanson* [2005] 2 Cr App R 299 (CA) 73, 74, 227

*R* v *Harden* [1963] 1 QB 8 (CA) 7, 222

*R* v *Harmes & Crane* [2006] EWCA Crim 928 188

*R* v *Harvey* [1988] Crim LR 241 (CA) 147, 233

*R* v *Harvey and others* [2014] EWCA Crim 54 98, 229

*R* v *Hasan* [2005] UKHL 22 135, 232

*R* v *Hayes* [1977] 2 All ER 288 (CA) 42, 225

*R* v *Hayter* [2005] UKHL 6 137, 232

*R* v *Hesse and another* [2015] EWCA Crim 884 76, 77, 228

*R* v *Horncastle* [2010] 2 AC 373 (SC) 109

*R* v *Hunt* [1987] AC 352 (HL) 18, 224

*R* v *Ibrahim* [2012] 4 All ER 225 (CA) 108, 230

*R* v *J* [2003] EWCA Crim 3309 151, 234

*R* v *Johnson* [2007] EWCA Crim 1651 76, 228

*R* v *Johnstone* [2003] UKHL 28 19, 224

*R* v *Jones and Jenkins* [2003] EWCA Crim 1966 161, 234

*R* v *Kearley* [1992] 2 AC 228 (HL) 92, 229

*R* v *Kelly* [2003] EWCA Crim 596 167, 235

*R* v *Kenny* [1994] Crim LR 284 (CA) 144, 233

*R* v *Khan* [2007] EWCA Crim 2331 194, 237

*R* v *King* [1983] 1 All ER 929 (CA) 200, 237

*R* v *Kiszko* (1992) *The Times,* 18 February (CA) 209, 238

*R* v *L* [2008] EWCA Crim 973 105, 230

*R* v *Lambert* [2002] 2 AC 545 (HL) 19, 224

*R* v *Land* [1998] 1 All ER 403 (CA) 118, 127, 230

*R* v *Leatham* (1861) 8 Cox CC 498 176, 235

*R* v *Looseley, Attorney-General's Reference (No. 3 of 2000)* [2001] UKHL 53 186, 187, 236

*R* v *Lucas* [1981] QB 720 (CA) 156, 162–4, 167, 234

*R* v *McCay* [1991] 1 All ER 232 (CA) 103, 230

*R* v *McGovern* (1990) 92 Cr App Rep 228 (CA) 145, 233

*R* v *Maguire and others* [1992] QB 936 (CA) 209, 238

*R* v *Makanjuola* [1995] 3 All ER 730 (CA) 160, 234

*R* v *Marcus* [2004] EWCA Crim 3387; [2005] Crim LR 384 165

*R* v *Marshall (Stewart)* [2014] EWCA Crim 2957 96, 229

xiii

# TABLE OF CASES AND STATUTES

R v Martin [1996] Crim LR 589 (CA) 97, 229

R v Mason [1988] 1 WLR 139 (CA) 182, 189, 236

R v Moghal (1977) 65 Cr App R 56 (CA) 103, 230

R v Moore [2013] EWCA Crim 85 188

R v MP [2015] EWCA Crim 924 71, 227

R v Moshaid [1998] Crim LR 420 (CA) 50, 52, 225

R v Mukadi [2004] Crim LR 373 (CA) 38, 225

R v Murphy [1980] QB 434 (CA) 120, 231

R v Musone [2007] EWCA Crim 1237 76, 228

R v Nethercott [2001] EWCA Crim 2535 10, 24

R v Northam (1968) 52 Cr App R 97 (CA) 145, 233

R v Nwankwo and another [2014] EWCA Crim 1205 48

R v O [2006] 2 Cr App R 27 (CA) 34, 224

R v O'Connor [1980] Crim LR 43 (CA) 159

R v Palmer and others [2014] EWCA Crim 1681 188

R v Paris (1992) 97 Cr App R 99 (CA) 143, 152, 233

R v Pattinson [1995] 1 Cr App R 578 (CA) 168, 170, 235

R v Phillips [2005] 2 Cr App R 528 (CA) 70, 227

R v Pritchard [2011] EWCA Crim 2749 35

R v Redgrave (1981) 74 Cr App R 10 (CA) 64, 226

R v Riat [2012] EWCA Crim 1509 109

R v Rowton (1865) 29 JP 149 (CCR) 64, 226

R v S (P) and another [2015] EWCA Crim 783 169

R v Samuel [1988] 2 All ER 135 (CA) 180, 189, 235

R v Sang [1980] AC 402 (HL) 188–90, 236

R v Sanghera [2001] 1 Cr App R 299 (CA) 179, 235

R v Seelig [1991] 4 All ER 429 (CA) 143, 152, 233

R v Sharp [1988] 1 All ER 65 (HL) 228

R v Silverlock [1894] 2 QB 766 (CCR) 119, 231

R v Singh (James Paul) [2007] EWCA Crim 2140 80, 228

R v Slater [1995] 1 Cr App R 584 (CA) 169

R v Sliogeris [2015] EWCA Crim 22 136, 232

R v Smith [1979] 3 All ER 605 (CA) 118, 230

R v Speed [2013] EWCA Crim 1650 69, 227

R v Spiby [1990] 1 Cr App R 186 (CA) 5, 222

R v Stevenson [1971] 1 WLR 1 6

R v Stott [2004] EWCA Crim 615 166, 235

R v Sunalla (Adel Abdulwaheb) [2014] EWCA Crim 1870 163, 235

R v Sutton [2007] EWCA Crim 1387 78, 228

R v Tahed [2004] EWCA 1220 39, 225

R v Taylor (Michelle); R v Taylor (Lisa) (1993) The Times, 15 June (CA) 210, 238

R v Thornton [1995] 1 Cr App R 578 (CA) 169

R v Tucker [2008] EWCA Crim 3063 213, 239

R v Turnbull [1977] QB 244 (CA) 155, 156, 167–70

R v Turner [1975] QB 834 (CA) 117, 127, 230

R v Valentine [1996] 2 Cr App R 213 (CA) 34, 224

R v Vye [1993] 3 All ER 241 (CA) 56, 65–7, 226

R v W (L) [2015] EWCA Crim 1021 146

R v Walker [1998] Crim LR 211 (CA) 147, 233

R v Walsh (1989) 91 Cr App R 161 (CA) 183, 189, 236

R v Ward [1993] 2 All ER 577 (CA) 211, 238

R v Ward and others [2001] Crim LR 316 (CA) 140, 232

R v Watkinson (24 July 1996, unreported) 147

R v Zoppola-Barraza [1994] Crim LR 833 (CA) 67, 226

Ratten v R [1972] AC 378 (PC) 91, 229

Rawlinson and Hunter Trustees SA (as trustee of the Tchenguiz Family Trust) and another v Director of the Serious Fraud Office [2014] EWCA Civ 1129 203, 238

Rush & Tompkins Ltd v Greater London Council [1989] AC 1280 (HL) 203, 238

Saifi, Re [2001] 4 All ER 168 (DC) 179, 235

Saunders v United Kingdom (1996) 23 EHRR 313 (ECtHR) 196, 237

Scott v London & St Katherine Docks Co. (1865) 3 H & C 596 (Exch) 23, 224

Secretary of State for Defence v Guardian Newspapers Ltd [1984] 3 WLR 986 (HL) 205, 238

Sheldrake v DPP; Attorney-General's Reference (No 4 of 2002) [2004] UKHL 43 20, 224

Soward v Leggatt (1836) 7 C & P 613 14, 223

Sparks v R [1964] AC 964 (PC) 90, 91, 228

Subramaniam v Public Prosecutor [1956] 1 WLR 965 (PC) 90, 91, 229

Teixeira de Castro v Portugal (1998) 28 EHRR 101 (ECtHR) 187

Three Rivers District Council v Bank of England [2004] UKHL 48 199, 237

Tobi v Nicholas (1988) 86 Cr App R 323 (DC) 101, 229

U (Serious Injury: Standard of Proof), Re [2004] EWCA Civ 567 126

Waugh v British Railways Board [1980] AC 521 (HL) 200, 237

Williams v DPP [1993] 3 All ER 365 (DC) 185, 236

Woolf v Woolf [1931] P 134 (CA) 9

Woolmington v DPP [1935] AC 462 (HL) 15, 16, 214, 224

# ■ Statutes

Children Act 1989 43
  Pt IV 196
  Pt V 196
  s. 96 44
  s. 96(1) 44
  s. 96(2) 44
  s. 96(2)(a), (b) 44
  s. 98 196
  s. 98(1)(a), (b) 196
Civil Evidence Act 1995
  s. 1 88, 93
  s. 1(1) 88
  s. 1(2) 89
  s. 3 123
Companies Act 1985
  s. 434 197
Contempt of Court Act 1981 204, 238
  s. 10 204–6
Coroners and Justice Act 2009 47
  s. 86 47
  s. 86(1), (2) 47
  s. 88 47
  s. 88(1), (2) 47
  s. 88(3)(a) 47, 48
  s. 88(3)(b) 47
  s. 88(3)(b) 47
  s. 88 (4)–(6) 48
Crime (International Co-operation) Act 2003
  s. 7 99
Criminal Attempts Act 1981 185
Criminal Evidence Act 1898 40
  s. 1(2) 198
Criminal Justice Act 1967
  s. 9 94
  s. 9(1), (2) 94
Criminal Justice Act 1988 158
  Sch. 13, para. 6 99
Criminal Justice Act 2003 viii, 32, 33, 55–60, 62, 63, 68, 72, 77, 82, 85–9, 99, 102, 105, 107, 109–11, 149, 227–9, 242
  s. 98 67
  s. 100 68
  s. 100(1) 68
  s. 101 68
  s. 101(1)(a) 68, 69
  s. 101(1)(b) 68, 69
  s. 101(1)(c) 68, 70, 71
  s. 101(1)(d) 68, 71–5, 81
  s. 101(1)(e) 68, 75–7
  s. 101(1)(f) 68, 77–9, 81
  s. 101(1)(g) 68, 79–81
  s. 101(3) 81
  s. 102 70
  s. 103 71, 73
  s. 103(1) 71
  s. 103(1)(a) 72, 75
  s. 103(1)(b) 72, 74
  s. 103(2) 72
  s. 103(2)(a) 72, 75
  s. 103(2)(b) 72
  s. 103(3) 72
  s. 105 77, 78
  s. 105(1)(a), (b) 77
  s. 106 79, 80
  s. 106(1) 79, 80
  s. 106(1)(a)–(c) 79
  s. 106(2), (3) 80
  s. 114 93, 99, 104, 150
  s. 114(1) 93, 94, 104
  s. 114(1)(a) 94, 95, 104
  s. 114(1)(b) 94, 99, 104
  s. 114(1)(c) 94, 105
  s. 114(1)(d) 94, 104, 105, 110
  s. 114(1)(e)–(i) 105
  s. 115(2) 89
  s. 116 95
  s. 116(1) 95
  s. 116(1)(a)–(c) 95
  s. 116(2) 95, 97, 99
  s. 116(2)(a) 95, 97, 110
  s. 116(2)(b) 95, 96, 97
  s. 116(2)(c) 95, 97
  s. 116(2)(d) 95, 97
  s. 116(2)(e) 95–8, 110
  s. 117 95, 98, 107
  s. 117(1) 98
  s. 117(1)(a)–(c) 98
  s. 117(2) 98, 99
  s. 117(2)(a) 98, 99
  s. 117(2)(b) 98, 99
  s. 117(2)(c) 98, 99
  s. 117(4) 99
  s. 117(4)(a), (b) 99

s. 117(5) 98, 99
s. 117(5)(a), (b) 99
s. 118 94, 99, 100, 110
s. 118(1) 100
s. 118(1)(a)–(c) 100
s. 119 105, 107
s. 119(1)(a), (b) 105
s. 119(2), (3) 106
s. 120 33, 106, 107
s. 120(1), (2) 33
s. 120(4)–(6) 106
s. 120(7) 106
s. 120(7)(a)–(c) 33, 106
s. 120(7)(d) 33, 34, 106
s. 120(7)(e)–(f) 33, 106
s. 121(1)(a), (b) 107
s. 124 107
s. 124(2)(a) 107
s. 124(2)(b) 108
s. 124(2)(c) 106, 108
s. 125 108
s. 125(1), (2) 108
s. 133 6
s. 134 6
s. 139 31
s. 139(1)(a), (b) 31
Criminal Justice and Public Order Act 1994 48, 49, 53, 139, 158, 220
s. 32 160
s. 32(1)(a), (b) 160
s. 34 48–50, 52, 53, 215, 225
s. 35 49, 198
s. 36 49, 53
s. 37 49
Criminal Procedure Act 1865
s. 3 105
s. 4 36, 105
s. 5 105
s. 8 7
Criminal Procedure and Investigations Act 1996 24, 49, 191–220
s. 3 211, 212
s. 3(1)(a), (b) 211
s. 3(2) 212
s. 3(2)(a), (b) 212
s. 5 214
s. 6A 214

s. 6A(1)(a)–(d) 214
s. 11 49, 214, 215
s. 12 214
Code of Practice 2.1 212
Homicide Act 1957 16
s. 2(2) 16, 21
Human Rights Act 1998 18, 19
Law of Property Act 1925 22
s. 184 22
Licensing Act 1964 186
Magistrates' Courts Act 1980 17
s. 101 16, 17
Mental Health Act 1983 45
Misuse of Drugs Act 1971 19
s. 5 19
s. 28 19
s. 28(3)(b)(i) 19
Obscene Publications Act 1959 123
Parochial Registers Act 1812 8
Perjury Act 1911
s.13 159
Police and Criminal Evidence Act 1984 131–52, 201, 232
s. 10 201
s. 10(1) 201
s. 10(2) 201, 202
s. 58 148, 180, 189
s. 76 11, 24, 129, 130, 136, 139, 140, 146, 147, 149–52, 175–8, 182, 188, 221, 222, 232
s. 76(1) 139, 140, 151
s. 76(2) 139, 141, 150, 178
s. 76(2)(a) 139, 141–5, 152, 232, 233
s. 76(2)(b) 139, 141, 145–8, 152, 233
s. 76(3) 140
s. 76(5) 152
s. 76(8) 142
s. 76A 149, 150
s. 76A(1) 149
s. 76A(2) 149, 150
s. 76A(3) 150
s. 77 150, 151
s. 77(1) 150
s. 77(2), (3) 151
s. 78 11, 24, 93, 129–31, 139, 146, 167, 173–5, 177–84, 186–90, 197, 221, 222, 235, 236
s. 78(1) 178
s. 80 41
s. 80(1) 41

s. 80(2) 41
s. 80(2)(a), (b) 41
s. 80(2A) 41
s. 80(3) 41
s. 80(3)(a), (b) 41
s. 80(4) 41
s. 80(5) 41
s. 82 134–7, 150, 173–5, 177
s. 82(1) 134
s. 82(3) 139, 188, 189
Codes of Practice 179–81, 183, 186, 189, 190, 234, 235
Codes A, B 133
Code C 133, 134, 144, 152, 164
Code C, para 12.8 152
Code D 133, 155, 164–7, 169
Codes E–H 133
Proceeds of Crime Act 2002
s. 329(1)(c) 78
Rehabilitation of Offenders Act 1974
s. 4 59
s. 4(1)(a) 59
s. 4(1)(b) 60
s. 7 59
s. 7(3) 60
s. 8 59, 60
Road Traffic Act 1988
s. 5(1) 20
s. 5(2) 21
s. 172 195
s. 172(1)(a), (b) 195
Road Traffic Regulation Act 1984
s. 89 158
Social Security Administration Act 1992
s. 111A 163
Terrorism Act 2000
s. 1 20
s. 11 21
s. 11(2) 20
Sched. 7 183, 184, 197, 198
Theft Act 1968
s. 31 196
s. 31(1), (2) 196
Trade Marks Act 1994
s. 92 20
s. 92(5) 20
Youth Justice and Criminal Evidence Act 1999 38, 39, 44
s. 16 44

s. 16(1) 44
s. 16(1)(a), (b) 44
s. 16(2) 44, 45
s. 16(2)(a), (b) 46
s. 17 45
s. 17(1)–(4) 45
s. 21 46
s. 21(1) 46
s. 24 46
s. 27 46
s. 38(4) 79
s. 41 37
s. 41(1) 37
s. 41(1)(a), (b) 37
s. 41(2) 37, 38
s. 41(2)(a) 37
s. 41(2)(b) 37, 38
s. 41(2)(c) 37
s. 41(3) 37, 225
s. 41(3)(b) 38
s. 41(3)(c) 38, 39
s. 42(1)(b) 38
s. 42(2)–(4) 40
s. 53 39, 40, 43, 44
s. 53(1)–(4) 40
s. 55 43
s. 55(1) 43

# ■ Statutory Instruments

Civil Procedure Rules 1998, SI 1998/3132 124, 125, 192, 207, 208
Pt 31 207
r. 31.6 207
Pt 35 208
r. 35.3 121
r. 35.11 208
r. 35.13 208
PD 35, para 2.2 124
Criminal Procedure Rules 2005, SI 2005/384 125
r. 33 2 121
r. 33.3 124
Employment Equality (Religion or Belief) Regulations 2003, SI 2003/1660
reg. 28 18

# ■ International Conventions

European Convention on Human Rights 1950 18, 19
Art. 6 18–21, 46, 51, 109, 187, 196, 196, 215, 217,
218, 224, 239

Art. 6(1) 51
Art. 6(2) 19, 21
Art. 6(3) 109
Art. 6(3)(a) 109
Art. 6(3)(d) 109
Art. 10 206, 207, 238
Art 10(1), (2) 206

# Evidential issues within the trial process

## Revision checklist

**Essential points you should know:**

- [ ] What, precisely, is meant by the term 'evidence'
- [ ] The different forms of evidence which may be presented at trial
- [ ] The evidential concepts of relevance, admissibility and weight, and the relationship between them
- [ ] The concepts of 'burden of proof' and 'standard of proof'
- [ ] The use of presumptions and judicial notice

# ■ Topic map

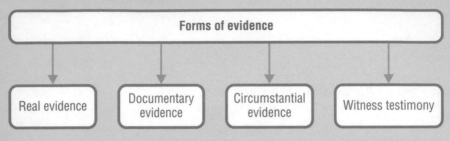

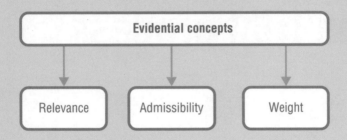

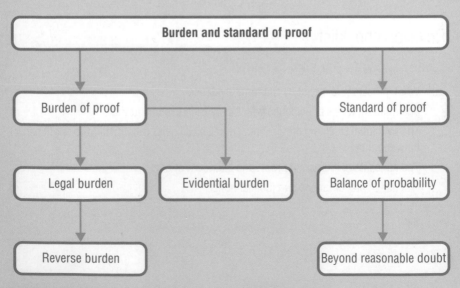

A printable version of this map is available from www.pearsoned.co.uk/lawexpress

# ■ Introduction

**'Evidence' is not just anything you think might help win the case.**

We are all familiar with the principle of evidence being used to prove whether someone has committed an offence, but this is not a haphazard process of each side putting before the court anything and everything that might help in winning the case. There are strict rules which govern what material may be adduced in evidence and the purpose for which it is put forward. Before examining the detailed law of evidence, however, you must understand some of the underlying principles affecting the presentation of evidence within the trial process.

## ASSESSMENT ADVICE

In an examination, it is unlikely that you would face a question on any single topic covered in this chapter (with the possible exception of burden and standard of proof), but you might be asked to outline two or more as parts of a 'discuss two from the following' style of question. In each case, the examiner will be looking for a firm grasp of the basic principles which will be used to underpin your understanding of other aspects of the law of evidence.

Because of the fundamental importance of these principles, you may also find that they feature as a small part of a question which centres on one of the more substantive topics, such as character or hearsay evidence. By recognising that such issues are a central feature of the trial process and mentioning them as they arise, you will be demonstrating your broader understanding of the law of evidence and the examiner will give you credit for this.

# ■ Sample question

Could you answer this question? Below is a typical essay question that could arise on this topic. Guidelines on answering the question are included at the end of this chapter, whilst a sample problem question and guidance on tackling it can be found on the companion website.

# ■ Facts in issue

The central task of the trial process is to determine the 'facts in issue' – the facts which each side must prove to win the case. To do this, each side must adduce evidence in support of their case. For example, in a criminal case, the prosecution must satisfy the various elements of the offence in question such as in a murder trial where it must be proved that the accused killed the victim with the requisite *mens rea* of 'malice aforethought'. In such a case, the prosecution must adduce sufficient evidence to convince the jury that the accused (rather than someone else) did kill the victim and that they did it with the intent to kill or to cause grievous bodily harm. Similarly, in a civil claim for negligence, the facts in issue may be the existence of a duty of care, the breach of that duty and the resultant damage.

# ■ Forms of evidence

When we hear the term 'evidence', our first thought is usually of the witness answering questions in court; however, this is only one form of evidence which may be presented to the court. There are a number of types of evidence, each with distinctive features. These include:

## Real evidence

**Real evidence** includes physical objects which may be produced in evidence, such as a murder weapon, an item of bloodstained clothing, illegal drugs or stolen goods. Frequently, such evidence requires additional evidence (such as witness testimony) to place it in its proper context. For example, a kitchen knife will require testimony from an expert witness to identify its significance as a murder weapon.

It is also possible to view some documents as real evidence, if the purpose of adducing them in evidence is not to show their contents (see documentary evidence below) but rather to illustrate their physical condition. For example, a partially burnt will may be adduced as evidence that an attempt was made to destroy it. Similarly, an automatic printout from a machine which operates without human involvement will be classed as real evidence.

**KEY CASE**

*R* v *Spiby* [1990] 1 Cr App R 186 (CA)

*Concerning: computer printouts as evidence*

**Facts**

The prosecution had adduced evidence of telephone calls relating to the sale of cannabis made by the accused from a hotel room. The calls were logged by the hotel's automated telephone system. D appealed on the basis that the record was hearsay evidence.

**Legal principle**

The court dismissed the appeal. As the machine logged the calls without any human involvement, the log was real evidence and, therefore, not covered by the hearsay rule. Taylor LJ: 'They did not depend for their content on anything that had passed through the human mind.'

# Documentary evidence

It is very common for evidence to be contained in documents (**documentary evidence**) and so the parties may wish to adduce such documents as part of their case. The definition of 'document' is extremely wide.

**KEY CASE**

*R* v *Daye* [1908] 2 KB 333 (KBD)

*Concerning: definition of 'document'*

**Facts**

A banker had received a sealed packet containing a formula. As part of its deliberations, the court was required to consider whether this constituted a 'document'.

**Legal principle**

Darling J: 'any written thing capable of being evidence is properly described as a document and . . . it is immaterial on what the writing may be inscribed. It might be inscribed on paper, as is the common case now; but the common case once was that it was not on paper, but on parchment; and long before that it was on stone, marble or clay . . . I should say it is a document no matter upon what material it be, provided it is writing or printing and capable of being evidence.'

In more modern times, the term 'document' has also been taken to include, for example, tape recordings (*R* v *Stevenson* [1971] 1 WLR 1).

In presenting documentary evidence, the question arises as to whether the original must be adduced or whether a copy will be sufficient.

---

**KEY STATUTE**

**Criminal Justice Act 2003, s. 133**

**Proof of statements in documents**

Where a statement in a document is admissible as evidence in criminal proceedings, the statement may be proved by producing either:

(a)  the document, or

(b)  (whether or not the document exists) a copy of the document or of the material part of it, authenticated in whatever way the court may approve.

---

Note also that the fact that the adduced document has been copied many times from the original does not affect its **admissibility**.

---

**KEY STATUTE**

**Criminal Justice Act 2003, s. 134**

In this Chapter – 'copy', in relation to a document, means anything on to which information recorded in the document has been copied, by whatever means and whether directly or indirectly; 'document' means anything in which information of any description is recorded.

---

## Execution of documents

Depending on the type of document that the party wishes to adduce in evidence, they may have to present evidence that the document has been properly executed (i.e. that it was written or signed by the person alleged to have done so). This may be achieved by evidence from the 'author' confirming that it was written by them, or from another person who observed the writing of the document. Alternatively, the disputed document may be compared with a known sample of handwriting from the person concerned. This may require expert evidence.

**KEY CASE**

*R* v *Harden* [1963] 1 QB 8 (CA)

*Concerning: verification of handwriting*

**Facts**

The defendant was accused of obtaining money by false pretences. In reaching their verdict, the jury were invited to compare various documents and cheques alleged to have been written by the accused.

**Legal principle**

The jury should not be invited to compare handwriting in documents unless expert evidence as to the genuineness of the handwriting had been called. Widgery JJ: '[the trial judge] erred in inviting the jury to reach their conclusions without the assistance of expert evidence.'

**KEY STATUTE**

**Criminal Procedure Act 1865, s. 8**

**Comparison of disputed writing with writing proved to be genuine**

Comparison of disputed writing with any writing proved to the satisfaction of the judge to be genuine shall be permitted to be made by witnesses; and such writings, and the evidence of witnesses respecting the same, may be submitted to the court and jury as evidence of the genuineness or otherwise of the writing in dispute.

## Documents and presumptions

There are a number of matters which may be presumed by the court when admitting documentary evidence. These include:

- A document which is more than 20 years old and has been in 'proper custody' for this time is presumed to have been properly executed.
- A document was created on the date which is written on it.
- Whereas alterations to a deed are presumed to have been made before it was executed, alterations to a will are presumed to have been made after execution.

**KEY CASE**

*Bishop Meath* v *Marquis of Winchester* (1836) 3 Bing NC 183 (HL)

*Concerning: 'proper custody'*

**Facts**

The documents in question were discovered amongst the papers of the deceased Bishop whereas they should have been passed to his successor.

**Legal principle**

The documents were found in a place in which and under the care of persons with whom papers of the Bishop might naturally and reasonably be expected to be found. It was not necessary that they should be found in the best and most proper place of deposit. 'It was not unreasonable that it should be found in the Bishop's mansion-house.'

---

**KEY CASE**

*Doe d Arundel (Lord)* v *Fowler* (1850) 14 QB 700

*Concerning: 'proper custody'*

**Facts**

Parish registers had been kept by the parish clerk at his house, when the Parochial Registers Act 1812 required such registers to be kept at the parson's house or in the church.

**Legal principle**

This did not constitute 'proper custody'.

---

**KEY CASE**

*Anderson* v *Weston* (1840) 6 Bing NC 296

*Concerning: date of creation*

**Facts**

The court was required to rule on the date on which a document had been created.

**Legal principle**

It was held that, in the absence of evidence to the contrary, the document would be taken to have been issued on the date stated on it.

---

**KEY CASE**

*Doe d Tatum* v *Catomore* (1851) 16 QB 745

*Concerning: presumed date of alteration*

**Facts**

The court was required to rule on the date on which a document had been altered.

**Legal principle**

It was held that, as a deed cannot be altered after execution without 'fraud or wrong', the presumption, if an alteration appears, is that it was made before execution. However, this does not apply in the case of a will, which may be altered by the testator without 'fraud or wrong'.

---

**□ REVISION NOTE**

When considering documentary evidence, you should also read the chapter on hearsay evidence, as there is an overlap between the two topics. You should also make clear this potential overlap in any answer which you write on the subject.

## Circumstantial evidence

**Circumstantial evidence** is a more difficult category of evidence to define but, in general terms, it refers to evidence from which facts in issue within the case may be inferred. Such evidence does not actually prove the offence but serves to increase the probability that the alleged conduct has taken place. For example, the fact that the murder victim's husband took out a large insurance policy on her life shortly before she died does not prove that he killed her. If coupled with evidence that the husband was having an affair and that the murder weapon was found in his car, the cumulative effect of such circumstantial evidence is to reduce the possibility of an alternative explanation. Recognised categories of circumstantial evidence include:

- motive – *R* v *Clewes* (1830) 4 C & P 221 (the defendant in a murder trial had hired the victim to commit another murder and faced being exposed);

- opportunity – *Woolf* v *Woolf* [1931] P 134 (CA) (evidence that a married man had shared a hotel room with another woman was taken as evidence supporting allegations of his adultery);

- evidence of planning or preparation for the crime – *R* v *Clarke & Hewins* (1999) (6 Archbold News 2 (in a case of murder by arson, where petrol had been poured through the victim's front door, evidence of the defendant's purchase of petrol before the fire was presented in support of the prosecution case);

- evidence that the accused has lied (**see Chapter 7**).

📖 REVISION NOTE

In considering circumstantial evidence, you might also wish to look at adverse inference and the so-called 'right to silence' (**discussed in Chapter 2**), as the failure of the accused to answer a question may be interpreted by the jury as circumstantial evidence of guilt.

## Witness testimony

This is the most recognisable form of evidence. A witness providing their evidence in person in court and various aspects of witness testimony are considered later (**see Chapter 2**). At the outset, however, it is important to note that the key advantages of such testimony are that it can be challenged by the other side and that the presence of a witness allows the jury to assess their demeanour.

# ■ Relevance, admissibility and weight

The law of evidence is governed by the three principles of relevance, admissibility and weight. The three concepts are distinct but interrelated.

## Relevance

The classic definition of **relevance** was restated in *R* v *Nethercott* [2001] EWCA Crim 2535 (CA):

> . . . any two facts to which it is applied are so related to each other that according to the common course of events one either taken by itself or in connection with other facts proves or renders probable the past, present or future existence or non-existence, of the other.

**KEY CASE**

*R* v *Grant* [1996] 1 Cr App R 73 (CA)

*Concerning: relevance*

**Facts**

The accused was found with a quantity of cocaine and £900 cash on his person. He was charged with possession with intent to supply. He admitted the possession but denied the (more serious) intent to supply.

**Legal principle**

On appeal, it was held that the possession of the £900 was relevant to a charge of possession with intent to supply. The accused had provided an innocent explanation for the presence of the money. It was for the jury to decide whether to believe him. Lord Taylor CJ: 'It is a matter for the jury to decide whether the presence of money, in all the circumstances, is indicative of an ongoing trading in the drugs.'

**KEY CASE**

*Holcombe* v *Hewson* (1810) 2 Camp 391

*Concerning: relevance*

**Facts**

The defendant publican claimed that he had broken a contract with the claimant brewer as he had been supplied with bad beer. The claimant wished to adduce evidence from other customers that his beer was good.

**Legal principle**

It was held that evidence that the claimant had supplied good beer to his other customers did not, necessarily, mean that he had supplied good beer to the defendant. For this reason such evidence was not relevant to the present case.

In this way, relevance is a relational concept – something can only be relevant *to something else* and so a relevant piece of evidence makes the existence of another fact either more or less likely.

As a general principle, all relevant evidence will be admissible, though this is subject to numerous exceptions, including those related to character evidence, hearsay evidence and opinion evidence, together with the exclusionary rules under section 76 and section 78 of the Police and Criminal Evidence Act 1984 (PACE). All of these are discussed in subsequent chapters.

# Admissibility

As indicated previously, evidence which is relevant is generally admissible, that is, it is allowed to be presented in court. This is entirely logical as clearly the court would not want to waste time on material which was not relevant to the case in question (see *Holcombe* v *Hewson* above). There are, however, a number of circumstances where evidence that is undeniably relevant will be held not to be admissible, primarily because it breaches one of the exclusionary rules of evidence which are intended to protect the jury from material which is unreliable in nature.

Make clear that you appreciate one of the key evidential distinctions between civil and criminal trials:

- In a civil trial the judge who hears the case does not need to be protected from questionable evidence as they are more than capable of assessing its impact.
- In a criminal trial, however, the jury which decides the verdict may need to be prevented from hearing evidence which may be unreliable but which may influence them unduly.

## Weight

The last of the three concepts is 'weight', that is the strength of a particular piece of evidence which is sometimes expressed in terms of its 'probative value'. In other words, how effective is the evidence in supporting the point for which it is adduced? For example, if one side produces an expert witness with 25 years' experience to support their argument and the other produces a new graduate, it might be assumed that the former will have greater weight. It is frequently stated that, whereas the judge in a criminal trial decides whether evidence is relevant and admissible, it is for the jury to decide what, if any, weight to attach to it. However, this ignores the fact that the judge's initial assessment of relevance will, in part, be based on the weight of the evidence.

! Don't be tempted to . . .

It is very easy to become confused over the relationship between the three principles of relevance, admissibility and weight. Remember that they are interrelated!

# ■ Burden and standard of proof

In both civil and criminal trials, each party may be required to prove certain facts. This obligation may be expressed in terms of a 'burden of proof' which rests upon the party concerned. Similarly, they are required to achieve a specified 'standard of proof' to satisfy the court of the fact in question.

## The evidential and legal burden of proof

The term 'burden of proof' may be said to comprise two elements: the 'evidential' burden and the 'legal' burden.

## The 'evidential' burden

This merely requires there to be at least some evidence in support of a particular point to make it worthy of consideration by the court. This evidence does not have to reach any particular standard but merely has to be sufficient to convince the judge that it should be heard. For this reason, the evidential burden is sometimes expressed in the old-fashioned term 'passing the judge'.

 **Make your answer stand out**

Some writers dispute whether the evidential burden is truly a 'burden of proof' at all, arguing that, as it only requires a party to produce *some* evidence in support of the fact in question, this falls short of what would ordinarily constitute 'proof'. For a discussion of this argument see Keane, A. (2014) *The Modern Law of Evidence,* 10th edn, OUP, p. 83.

## The 'legal' burden

This requires the party in question to adduce sufficient evidence on the issue in question to satisfy the court or, in a criminal trial, the jury. This expresses the general principle that 'he who asserts [a particular point] must prove'. There are, however, a number of complicating factors. First, the burden of proof does not relate to the case as a whole but, rather, to each individual element of the case. The way in which this works is slightly different in civil and criminal cases.

### The burden in civil cases

In civil cases (such as negligence or breach of contract) the only reason that the case reaches court is that the claimant and defendant put forward different versions of what has occurred. These competing versions are expressed in terms of claim and counterclaim. For example, A may claim that he has been injured as a result of B's negligent driving which resulted in a collision, when A was a passenger in the car. In response, B may argue that A contributed to his own injury by not wearing a seatbelt. This produces the following situation in relation to burden of proof:

| | |
|---|---|
| Burden and standard of proof A must prove (and so bears the burden of proof) | There was a collision<br>There was a duty of care owed by B<br>B breached that duty of care<br>The breach caused damage to A |
| B must prove (and so bears the burden of proof) | A was not wearing a seatbelt<br>The absence of a seatbelt increased the seriousness of A's injuries |

Note that only one party can have the burden of proof in relation to any single issue and so a case such as that outlined above involves both sides bearing a burden of proof in relation to the various issues in dispute. Also, this is usually expressed as a *positive,* rather than a *negative* obligation – that is the burden is on the party which seeks to prove the point, not the party which seeks to deny it.

---

**KEY CASE**

*Joseph Constantine Steamship Line Ltd* v *Imperial Smelting Corp. Ltd* [1942] AC 154 (HL)

*Concerning: burden of proof*

Facts

The charterers of a ship claimed against the ship owners for damages for failure to load a cargo, but the ship owners asserted that an explosion on the ship had frustrated the chartered voyage. The cause of the explosion could not be determined.

Legal principle

It was held that the ship owners, having established that the explosion had frustrated the contract, were not bound to prove further that the explosion had not been caused by them (a negative assertion). The burden of proof lay on the charterers to prove that the explosion was the fault of the ship owners (a positive assertion). Viscount Maugham: 'The plaintiff must prove that there was some negligent act or omission on the part of the defendant which caused or materially contributed to the injury.'

---

Further, this obligation is not affected by the form of words used by the parties and whether a positive assertion is expressed in negative terms.

---

**KEY CASE**

*Soward* v *Leggatt* (1836) 7 C & P 613

*Concerning: burden of proof*

Facts

In claiming breach of a covenant to repair, a landlord alleged that his tenant 'did not repair' (a negative proposition) whilst the tenant claimed that he did (a positive assertion).

Legal principle

It was held that, despite the form of words used, the burden of proof remained on the claimant to prove that the defendant had breached the covenant.

---

The rule is not always observed, however, and may be ignored where it is easier for one party to prove the issue than the other.

*Levison and another* v *Patent Steam Carpet Cleaning Co Ltd* [1978] QB 69 (CA)

*Concerning: burden of proof*

**Facts**

The claimants left a carpet worth £900 with the defendant cleaning company, which allowed it to be stolen. Under the terms of the cleaning contract, the company was only liable to pay damages of £44 unless they could be shown to have fundamentally breached the contract. This raised the question of whether it was for the claimant to show that there had been such a fundamental breach of contract or whether it fell to the defendant company to prove that there had been no such breach.

**Legal principle**

It was held that the burden of proof was on the defendant company to show that the loss had not occurred in consequence of a fundamental breach, as they were in a better position than the claimant to know what had happened to the carpet when it was in the company's possession. Orr LJ: 'however difficult it may sometimes be for a bailee to prove a negative, he is at least in a better position than the bailor to know what happened to the goods while in his possession.'

## The burden in criminal cases

In criminal cases, the basic rule is taken from the following decision.

*Woolmington* v *DPP* [1935] AC 462 (HL)

*Concerning: burden of proof*

**Facts**

The defendant was accused of murder, having shot his wife. In his defence, he alleged that the gun had been fired accidentally.

**Legal principle**

Viscount Sankey LC: 'Throughout the web of the English Criminal Law one golden thread is always to be seen, that it is the duty of the prosecution to prove the prisoner's guilt.'

The principle that the burden remains on the prosecution, often expressed in terms of the 'presumption of innocence', is viewed as a fundamental element of the criminal justice system and is seen as an attempt to acknowledge the inequality of bargaining power which lies at the heart of the criminal trial. The resources of the state and the prosecution far outweigh those of the accused and so it is considered an essential safeguard that the state bears the burden of proving the charge, rather than the accused having to prove their innocence.

## The 'reverse burden'

Despite the rule in *Woolmington* v *DPP*, there are circumstances where the burden of proof does pass to the accused. This is known as the '**reverse burden**' or 'reverse onus'.

---

**KEY DEFINITION: Reverse burden**

A situation where the burden of proof lies not with the prosecution but with the defence.

---

## Statutory exceptions

A number of statutes impose a burden of proof on the accused:

---

**KEY STATUTE**

**Homicide Act 1957, s. 2(2)**

**Persons suffering from diminished responsibility**

On a charge of murder, it shall be for the defence to prove that the person charged is by virtue of this section not liable to be convicted of murder.

---

**✎ EXAM TIP**

When discussing the reverse burden under the 1957 Act in cases of diminished responsibility, mention that there is a similar reverse burden on the accused to prove insanity under the common law rule in *M'Naghten's Case* (1843) 10 Cl & Fin 200.

---

**KEY STATUTE**

**Magistrates' Courts Act 1980, s. 101**

Where the defendant to an information or complaint relies for his defence on any exception, exemption, proviso, excuse or qualification, whether or not it accompanies the description of the offence or matter of complaint in the enactment creating the offence or on which the complaint is founded, the burden of proving the exception, exemption, proviso, excuse or qualification shall be on him; and this notwithstanding that the information or complaint contains an allegation negativing the exception, exemption, proviso, excuse or qualification.

### ✎ EXAM TIP

When raising section 101, remember to mention that in *R* v *Edwards* [1975] QB 27 the Court of Appeal held that the same principles applied in *all* criminal cases (not just in the magistrates' courts covered by the 1980 Act).

Section 101 applies in a range of situations where an offence is committed unless the contrary can be proved – in such cases the burden of proving the alternative version lies with the accused. This is usually expressed within the statute in terms such as 'unless', 'except' or 'other than'.

### KEY CASE

*Gatland* v *Metropolitan Police Commissioner* [1968] 2 All ER 100 (QB)

*Concerning: reverse burden of proof*

#### Facts

A lorry driver drove into a builder's skip which had been left in front of premises where the builders were working. The owners of the lorry claimed against the company which supplied the skip.

#### Legal principle

It was held that, although the burden of proving that the skip had been left in the highway and that it had endangered the driver lay with the prosecution, the burden of proving that it was there with 'lawful authority or excuse' lay with the defendant. Lord Parker CJ: 'It is, however, in every case for the prosecution to prove, not only that the article in question has been deposited on a highway, but also that in consequence thereof a user of the highway is injured or endangered.'

However, the courts have imposed limitations on this principle.

**KEY CASE**

*R* v *Hunt* [1987] AC 352 (HL)

*Concerning: reverse burden of proof*

**Facts**

The appellant had been convicted of possession of drugs contrary to the Misuse of Drugs Act 1971. At trial, it had been argued that the burden of proof lay with the appellant to show that the substances found in his possession fell within the exceptions provided by the Act.

**Legal principle**

It was held that, because it was an offence to possess morphine in one form but not an offence to possess it in another, this was an essential element of the offence. Therefore, it was for the prosecution to prove that the substance possessed was in the prohibited form, otherwise no offence was established. It was also stated that the courts should be slow to impose the burden of proving his innocence on the defendant in a criminal trial. Lord Ackner: 'The prosecution must always establish, by admission or otherwise, that the accused had in his possession a controlled drug.'

 Make your answer stand out

In discussing the concept of the reverse burden, point out that the law is not always consistent in applying such obligations. For example, in discrimination claims, provisions relating to reverse burden of proof do not apply to claims of victimisation on racial grounds: *Oyarce* v *Cheshire County Council* [2008] EWCA Civ 434, but do apply to claims of victimisation on religious grounds because of the difference in wording of regulation 28 of the Employment Equality (Religion or Belief) Regulations 2003. See, *Khan* v *Royal Mail Group Ltd* [2014] EWCA Civ 1082, para. 12.

**The reverse burden of proof and Article 6**

Following implementation of the Human Rights Act 1998 the courts have been required to consider whether the imposition of a burden of proof on the defendant is incompatible with the right to a fair trial under Article 6 of the European Convention on Human Rights (ECHR).

**KEY STATUTE**

**European Convention on Human Rights, Art. 6(2)**

Everyone charged with a criminal offence shall be presumed innocent until proved guilty according to law.

**KEY CASE**

*R v Lambert* [2002] 2 AC 545 (HL)

*Concerning: reverse burden of proof*

**Facts**

L was convicted of possession of a controlled drug, contrary to section 5 of the Misuse of Drugs Act 1971. His defence was based on section 28(3)(b)(i) of the Act, asserting that he did not believe or suspect, or have reason to suspect that the bag which he carried contained the drugs. The Act imposed a reverse burden on him in relation to this defence. On appeal against conviction, he argued that the imposition of the reverse burden contravened Article 6(2) (even though HRA 1998 was yet to come into force).

**Legal principle**

It was held that he could not rely on the Convention right as HRA 1998 was not in force. The effect of section 28 was to impose only an evidential burden on the accused, as the imposition of a legal burden under these circumstances would contravene Article 6(2). As a wider point of law, the imposition of a legal burden on the accused would always require a high degree of justification to be compatible with Article 6(2). In particular, it must be a reasonable and proportionate response to the mischief addressed by the offence which creates a 'pressing necessity' for a legal burden to be placed on the accused. Lord Hutton: 'The transfer of the onus satisfies the test that it has a legitimate aim in the public interest and that there is a reasonable relationship of proportionality between the means employed and the aim sought to be realised.'

 Make your answer stand out

The creative interpretation of statutes in order to ensure compatibility with ECHR by the judiciary has been an important aspect of the implementation of HRA 1998. This process of 'reading down' provisions to achieve compliance with the Convention rights is discussed in Young, A. L. 'Judicial Sovereignty and the Human Rights Act 1998', (2002) *CLJ*, 61(1), 53–65.

**KEY CASE**

*R v Johnstone* [2003] UKHL 28 (HL)

*Concerning: reverse burden of proof* ▶

## Facts

J was charged with an offence under section 92 of the Trade Marks Act 1994 relating to the production and sale of counterfeit CDs which involved reproducing the trademarks of the various artists. The defence relied on section 92(5) which provided:

'It is a defence for a person charged with an offence under this section to show that he believed on reasonable grounds that the use of the sign in the manner in which it was used, or was to be used, was not an infringement of the registered trade mark.'

## Legal principle

It was held that the imposition of a legal burden on the accused was compatible with Article 6. Lord Nicholls: 'Given the importance and difficulty of combating counterfeiting, and given the comparative ease with which an accused can raise an issue about his honesty, overall it is fair and reasonable to require a trader, should need arise, to prove on the balance of probability that he honestly and reasonably believed the goods were genuine.'

## KEY CASE

*Sheldrake* v *DPP; Attorney General's Reference (No. 4 of 2002)* [2004] UKHL 43 (HL)

*Concerning: reverse burden of proof*

### Facts

One of the appeals followed a conviction under section 1 of the Terrorism Act 2000 (membership of a proscribed organisation). Under section 11(2) it is a defence for a person charged under section 1 to prove:

'– that the organisation was not proscribed on the last (or only) occasion on which he became a member or began to profess to be a member, and

– that he has not taken part in the activities of the organisation at any time while it was proscribed.'

The second appeal related to a conviction under section 5(1) of the Road Traffic Act 1988 (driving or being in charge of a motor vehicle with alcohol concentration above prescribed limit). Section 5(2) provided a defence where the defendant could prove:

'that at the time he is alleged to have committed the offence the circumstances were such that there was no likelihood of his driving the vehicle whilst the proportion of alcohol in his breath, blood or urine remained likely to exceed the prescribed limit.'

Both appellants argued that the reverse burden contravened Article 6.

**Legal principle**

It was held that, in relation to section 11, this would be incompatible with Article 6 if interpreted as imposing a legal burden and therefore should be 'read down' so as to impose only an evidential burden on the accused. Lord Rodger: 'Simply placing the onus of proving this defence on the defendant involves no violation of his Article 6(2) convention rights.'

In relation to section 5(2) it was held that, even if this provision did contravene Article 6, that this was proportionate and directed towards a legitimate objective.

 Make your answer stand out

The potential conflict between the imposition of a reverse burden and the rights of the accused under Article 6 has provoked fierce debate. For discussion of some of the issues following the decision in *Sheldrake,* see McKinnon, G. (2003) 'Drink Driving, the Reverse Onus of Proof, and Human Rights', 167 *JPN* 527. For a broader analysis see Howes, V. (2004) 'Reverse Burden of Proof: An Overview of Recent Development', 168 *JPN* 227. See also judicial consideration of the reverse burden imposed under section 2(2) of the Homicide Act 1957. See also *R v Foye* (2013) 177 JP 449.

# Presumptions and judicial notice

There are a number of examples within the law of evidence of facts which may be presumed unless the contrary is proved. In this sense, they are said to be **rebuttable presumptions**.

**KEY DEFINITION: Rebuttable presumption**

A fact which the court will accept without evidence but which can be disputed.

## The presumption of marriage

Once a man and woman have undertaken a marriage ceremony and then cohabit, there is a presumption that they are married (i.e. that the marriage ceremony was valid and that the couple had the necessary capacity to marry).

# The presumption of death

Where an individual has been missing for a period of seven years, there is a presumption of death.

**KEY CASE**

*Chard* v *Chard* [1955] 3 All ER 721 (Probate, Divorce & Admiralty Div)

*Concerning: presumption of death*

**Facts**

A man sought to remarry some 16 years after his first wife had last been seen alive.

**Legal principle**

It was held that, where due inquiries had been made to locate an individual but had failed to do so, there was a presumption of their death if they had not been heard of for seven years by persons who would have been likely to have heard from them if they had still been alive. Sachs J: 'it appears accepted that there is a convenient presumption of law applicable to certain cases of seven years' absence where no statute applies.'

In addition, there are a number of statutory presumptions of death.

**KEY STATUTE**

**Law of Property Act 1925, s. 184**

*Presumption of survivorship in regard to claims to property*

In all cases where, after the commencement of this Act, two or more persons have died in circumstances rendering it uncertain which of them survived the other or others, such deaths shall (subject to any order of the court), for all purposes affecting the title to property, be presumed to have occurred in order of seniority, and accordingly the younger shall be deemed to have survived the elder.

# The presumption of legitimacy

Where a child is born to (or conceived by) a married woman, there is a presumption that the husband is the child's father, even where the couple do not live together.

# Res ipsa loquitur

In actions for negligence, it may be possible to assert the principle of *res ipsa loquitur*.

---

**KEY DEFINITION: Res ipsa loquitur**

'The thing speaks for itself' – passes the burden of proof to the defendant to show that the events were not their responsibility.

---

**KEY CASE**

*Scott* v *London & St Katherine Docks Co.* (1865) 3 H& C 596 (Exch)

*Concerning: res ipsa loquitur*

**Facts**
The claimant customs officer entered the defendant's premises and was injured by some bags of sugar which fell from a crane. The cause of the accident was unclear.

**Legal principle**
Erle CJ: 'Where the thing is shown to be under the management of the defendant, or his servants, and the accident is such as, in the ordinary course of things, does not happen if those who have the management of the machinery use proper care, it affords reasonable evidence, in the absence of explanation by the defendant, that the accident arose from want of care.'

---

# The presumption of regularity

This covers two related presumptions: first, that a mechanical device which is usually in working order (e.g. a set of traffic lights) will operate properly at the time in question. Secondly, that an individual acting in an official capacity has been properly appointed and is acting properly.

# ■ Putting it all together

## Answer guidelines

See the essay question at the start of the chapter.

### Approaching the question

This is a relatively straightforward essay which requires you to consider the concepts of relevance, admissibility and weight. The examiner will be looking for a confident discussion which, crucially, offers more than mere description. Always remember that analysis, even if relatively basic, will significantly increase the overall mark.

### Important points to include

- It is important to emphasise that the concepts of relevance, admissibility and weight are interrelated.
- All relevant evidence is admissible unless it falls under one of the exclusionary rules.
- Relevance may be difficult to define, but refer to the test in *R* v *Nethercott.*
- Note that admissibility concerns not only issues of resources and court time (by excluding unrelated or irrelevant material) but also evidence which may be unreliable (such as questionable confessions and hearsay evidence).
- Whereas relevance and admissibility in a criminal trial are matters for the judge, weight is a matter for the jury who decide how persuasive a particular piece of evidence may be.
- The three concepts interact to safeguard the operation of the justice system and the integrity of the trial process.

 Make your answer stand out

- Mention that the test for relevance in *R* v *Nethercott* is different from that employed in the Criminal Procedure and Investigations Act 1996 relating to unused material which should be disclosed to the defence (**see Chapter 9**).
- Outline the exclusionary rules under section 76 and section 78 of PACE which are key mechanisms by which evidence may be held inadmissible (**see Chapters 6 and 8**).

## READ TO IMPRESS

Coe. P. (2013) Court of Appeal: justifying reverse burdens of proof: a tale of diminished responsibility and a tangled knot of authorities. *Foye* v *R* [2013] EWCA Crim 475.(2013) *Journal of Criminal Law* 77: 360.

Howes, V. (2004) Reverse burden of proof: an overview of recent development. *JPN*, 168: 227.

McKinnon, G. (2003) Drink driving, the reverse onus of proof, and human rights. *JPN*, 167: 527.

Redmayne, M. (2006) The structure of evidence law. *OJLS*, 26: 805.

Samuels, A. (2005) What do the prosecution have to prove?. *JPN*, 169: 834.

Williams, B. (2004) Evidence and the onus of proof. *Taxation*, 16 September: 365.

**www.pearsoned.co.uk/lawexpress**

Go online to access more revision support including quizzes to test your knowledge, sample questions with answer guidelines, podcasts you can download, and more!

# Witnesses

## Revision checklist

**Essential points you should know:**

- [ ] The stages of witness testimony
- [ ] Competence and compellability of witnesses
- [ ] Unfavourable and hostile witnesses
- [ ] Previous statements
- [ ] The 'right to silence'

# ◼ Topic map

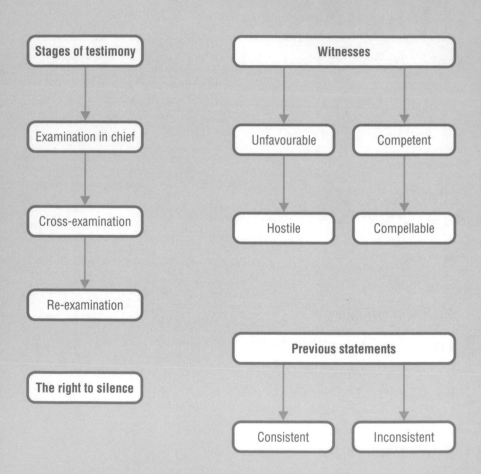

**Stages of testimony**

Examination in chief

Cross-examination

Re-examination

The right to silence

**Witnesses**

Unfavourable

Competent

Hostile

Compellable

**Previous statements**

Consistent

Inconsistent

A printable version of this map is available from **www.pearsoned.co.uk/lawexpress**

# ■ Introduction

## The most obvious form of evidence is a witness.

Of all the various forms of evidence, it is, perhaps, the witness which is the most recognisable, and we are all familiar with the idea of the person in the witness box giving their evidence and being challenged by the other side. In reality, witnesses can provide an invaluable insight into the events at the heart of the trial but, at the same time, it must be remembered that they are subject to all of those weaknesses of memory, bias and dishonesty which make us human. For this reason, the law of evidence imposes a number of restrictions on witness testimony which must be understood.

## ASSESSMENT ADVICE

In examination, you are unlikely to face an essay question on witnesses generally (as this is too wide a subject) but you may be asked to critically evaluate some particular aspect of witness testimony, such as competence and compellability or the use of previous statements. Such questions will rarely ask you to simply recount the relevant provisions – they will also demand some evaluation of the provisions to assess their effectiveness.

Problem questions on witnesses are very common and may either highlight a single rule or principle (if you are very lucky) or feature a number of different problems. Such questions typically involve three or four witnesses, each of whom raises a particular evidential issue. In each case, the examiner will be looking for both a description of the relevant legal principle (with supporting authority) and an application to the facts of the scenario. Do not make the mistake of simply regurgitating the law without offering some assessment of how the evidence of the witness in question will be treated by the court.

# ■ Sample question

Could you answer this question? Below is a typical problem question that could arise on this topic. Guidelines on answering the question are included at the end of this chapter, whilst a sample essay question and guidance on tackling it can be found on the companion website.

## PROBLEM QUESTION

How would you advise the following people?

(a) David is arrested on suspicion of handling stolen goods. He is searched on arrest and a number of the same new sealed DVDs are found in his bag. He is asked by the police to explain why he has them in his possession but he declines to answer.

(b) Karen is arrested following a fight outside a local pub in which another girl is badly beaten. On arrest, Karen is found to have abrasions to her knuckles and a cut on her cheek. When asked to explain these injuries to police she refuses.

(c) Sunil is arrested on suspicion of GBH. In interview, he is asked to explain why he attacked the victim but merely says 'No comment' in response to all questions posed by the police. When the case comes to trial Sunil asserts that he was acting in self-defence as the victim had threatened him that morning.

Would your advice in (c) be different if Sunil had refused to answer on the advice of his solicitor?

# The stages of witness testimony

Before considering some of the detailed rules which govern its presentation, it is first necessary to outline the three stages of witness testimony. Each is designed to fulfil a particular function and each is conducted according to a series of rules and procedures. The result is a process which might appear somewhat elaborate and theatrical but it contains within it a number of fundamental safeguards to ensure that the evidence is presented as objectively as possible and, crucially, that there is adequate opportunity for the other side to challenge the witness and their version of events.

## Examination in chief

The first stage of witness testimony is 'examination in chief', which involves the witness being questioned by the party that has called them to give evidence. In this sense, the witness is being questioned by 'their own side' although, as we will see, this is not always the case. Therefore, the purpose of the questioning is to get them to tell their story, rather than to challenge them – that is left to the other side!

### Refreshing the memory

In giving their evidence, the witness may wish to refresh their memory from a document (usually the statement they made immediately after the events in question). This is unsurprising, given the fact that trials often do not take place until months or years after the incident.

This does, however, raise the question of whether a person giving evidence after reading their statement is later giving evidence of the events themselves or simply what they have read in their statement. Of course a person may read their statement out of court (it would be almost impossible to prevent) but, during their testimony in criminal cases, the matter is now addressed by statute.

**KEY STATUTE**

**Criminal Justice Act 2003, s. 139**

Use of documents to refresh memory

(1) A person giving oral evidence in criminal proceedings about any matter may, at any stage in the course of doing so, refresh his memory of it from a document made or verified by him at an earlier time if –

    (a) he states in his oral evidence that the document records his recollection of the matter at that earlier time, and

    (b) his recollection of the matter is likely to have been significantly better at that time than it is at the time of his oral evidence.

## The rule against leading questions

In conducting the examination in chief, the advocate is prohibited from using **'leading' questions** – that is, a question which either indicates to the witness the desired answer ('Did he steal the watch?') or which assumes the existence of facts which have not yet been established ('What happened after he had stolen the watch?'). Such questions are usually permitted, however, in relation to uncontentious matters such as confirming the person's name and address, etc. The position is somewhat different for witnesses who have been declared 'hostile' (see below).

**KEY DEFINITION: Leading question**

A question which indicates the desired answer or suggests the acceptance of facts as yet unproved.

## Unfavourable and hostile witnesses

Remember that examination in chief is conducted by the party who has called the witness. This raises the question, what happens if the witness refuses to give evidence in support of that party or changes their story? Here, there is a distinction to be made between a witness who is merely 'unfavourable' to the side which called them and one who is 'hostile'.

An **'unfavourable witness'** is one who, although they display no malice, does not provide the information expected of them (e.g. they may be confused or have genuinely changed their mind since their original statement). The absence of malice means that they cannot be attacked or discredited by the side that has called them and so the only remedy available to the party who called the witness is to call additional witnesses who present a contrary version of events. For example, a witness initially states that she saw a blue car parked outside the premises in question but, at trial, she says that she thinks the car was green. This is central to the defence case. If she is not acting with malice, she cannot be attacked by the party which calls her but, if possible, the evidence of a number of other witnesses who will state that the car was, indeed, blue, can be used to lessen the impact of her testimony.

Unlike the unfavourable witness, who is either mistaken or innocently changes their testimony, a **'hostile witness'** is one who not only fails to give evidence in support of the party that called them but also shows no desire to give evidence in support of that party. This is sometimes described in terms of a 'hostile animus' towards the party calling them. This is not uncommon in criminal cases where loyalties and allegiances may change between the commission of the offence and the date of trial, but it also includes, for example, a witness who refuses to give evidence as a result of intimidation. Whatever the cause, a witness who is deemed 'hostile' by the judge may be cross-examined by the party calling them (see the section on cross-examination) in much the same way that a witness for the opposing party would be challenged. In such cases the purpose of the challenge is to demonstrate that they have said something different in an earlier statement. The status of such 'previous inconsistent statements' is considered below.

> ✎ **EXAM TIP**
>
> When discussing hostile witnesses, emphasise that the cross-examination is conducted to highlight the earlier statement which contradicts the evidence the witness is giving at trial. It cannot be used to attack the credibility of the witness generally.

## Previous consistent statements

Traditionally, there was a rule against out of court statements by the witness which were consistent with their evidence at trial (known as the rule against self-corroboration or the rule against narrative). In this way, the testimony of a witness could not be supported by evidence that they had said the same thing to a number of different people prior to the trial. It was argued that to allow such evidence would enable a witness to make their story appear more credible simply by repeating it to as many people as possible before the trial, recognising that the mere fact that the story has been repeated does not necessarily make it any more true. This principle has now been relaxed significantly by the Criminal Justice

Act 2003. For example, section 120(2) allows evidence of a previous consistent statement as evidence to rebut an allegation that the testimony has been fabricated.

**KEY STATUTE**

### Criminal Justice Act 2003, s. 120

**Other previous statements of witnesses**

(1) This section applies where a person (the witness) is called to give evidence in criminal proceedings.

(2) If a previous statement by the witness is admitted as evidence to rebut a suggestion that his oral evidence has been fabricated, that statement is admissible as evidence of any matter stated of which oral evidence by the witness would be admissible.

There is also an exception to cover what has been termed the doctrine of 'recent complaint'. This is frequently raised in sexual offences cases where the prosecution may wish to adduce evidence that the alleged victim reported the offence shortly after the events in question (again to undermine any suggestion that the complaint was a recent fabrication). The 2003 Act extends the admission of such previous consistent statements to all offences.

**KEY STATUTE**

### Criminal Justice Act 2003, s. 120

**Other previous statements of witnesses**

(7) The . . . condition is that –
(a) the witness claims to be a person against whom an offence has been committed,
(b) the offence is one to which the proceedings relate,
(c) the statement consists of a complaint made by the witness (whether to a person in authority or not) about conduct which would, if proved, constitute the offence or part of the offence,
(d) the complaint was made as soon as could reasonably be expected after the alleged conduct,
(e) the complaint was not made as a result of a threat or a promise, and
(f) before the statement is adduced the witness gives oral evidence in connection with its subject matter.

**KEY CASE**

*R* v *Valentine* [1996] 2 Cr App R 213 (CA)

*Concerning: definition of 'recent complaint'*

**Facts**

The complainant alleged that she had been raped by V. The day after the alleged attack she had gone to work and then told a friend about the assault in the evening. It was claimed by the defence that the complaint to the friend was inadmissible due to the passage of time.

**Legal principle**

It was held that what amounted to the first opportunity would depend on the circumstances of the case and the individual in question. The fact that there had been time to make a complaint beforehand did not prevent this being the first reasonable opportunity. Roch LJ: 'A complaint can be recent and admissible, although it may not have been made at the first opportunity which presented itself. What is the first reasonable opportunity will depend on the circumstances.'

**KEY CASE**

*R* v *O* [2006] 2 Cr App R 27 (CA)

*Concerning: definition of 'recent complaint'*

**Facts**

The complainant alleged that she had been sexually abused by her stepfather from the age of 9 until she was 17 years old, at which time she made a complaint to a friend. Some four months later she also complained to her brother.

**Legal principle**

It was held that the passage of time was no bar to the admission of the complaints in evidence. McCombe J: 'In our view, in the context of this case, the timing of the second complaint was, in all the circumstances, made "as soon as could reasonably be expected" after the alleged conduct.'

**Make your answer stand out**

For a more recent discussion of the concept of 'recent complaint' in sexual assault cases, see *R* v *Pritchard (Craig)* [2011] EWCA Crim 2749.

# Cross-examination

The second stage of witness testimony is 'cross-examination', which involves the witness being questioned by the opposing party. Here the objective is to challenge the evidence which they gave in examination in chief or to put to them new matters. Because cross-examination is conducted by the opposing party, it is conducted on the basis that the witness will not be favourable. There is no rule against leading questions or efforts to undermine their credibility as a witness.

📖 **REVISION NOTE**

This section should be revised alongside the section on character evidence covered later **(see Chapter 3)**, as this represents one of the key aspects of evidence relating to issues of credibility.

There are, however, some restrictions on questioning. For example, the questioning must not be designed simply to provoke an argument with the witness. Also, evidence obtained by cross-examination must still satisfy the general rules of admissibility which apply to the evidence that was adduced in examination in chief.

It is important to note that a failure to cross-examine on any particular point amounts to an acceptance of the evidence given by the witness as part of examination in chief. Similarly, there is a duty on the defence, when cross-examining prosecution witnesses, to put the defence case to them in order to confront them with the alternative version of events (and so challenge their evidence).

## Previous inconsistent statements

Remember that the status of 'unfavourable' or 'hostile' witness may arise from testimony which is inconsistent with statements which they had previously given. The issue of previous inconsistent statements may also arise in the cross-examination of witnesses, where it can be put to a witness that the evidence which they gave during examination in chief contradicts a previously made statement. If the witness denies ever making such a statement, then it must be proved against them.

**Criminal Procedure Act 1865, s. 4**

**As to proof of contradictory statements of adverse witness**

If a witness, upon cross-examination as to a former statement made by him relative to the subject matter of the indictment or proceeding, and inconsistent with his present testimony, does not distinctly admit that he has made such statement, proof may be given that he did in fact make it.

The key point to be established is whether the previous statement is 'relative to the subject matter of the indictment or proceeding'.

*R v Funderburk* [1990] 2 All ER 482 (CA)

*Concerning: previous inconsistent statements*

**Facts**

F was charged with sexual intercourse with a 13-year-old girl. The defence wished to cross-examine the girl about a conversation with a potential witness where she had described previous sexual experiences. The trial judge had refused to allow the cross-examination.

**Legal principle**

It was held that cross-examination about the previous statement should have been permitted as this was relevant to both the credibility of the girl's account and also the subject matter of the indictment. Henry J: 'The rules of evidence are to foster the interest of justice and are made for that purpose.'

## Cross-examination and sexual offences

As cross-examination may be used to undermine the credibility of the witness, there are particular issues in allegations of rape or sexual assault where the defence may seek to raise the previous sexual history of the complainant in an attempt to discredit their evidence. This is particularly relevant in cases which turn on the presence or absence of consent where the defence may seek to suggest that a woman who has had a series of sexual partners may be more likely to have consented in this instance. Clearly, such questioning can be extremely distressing for the complainant but, more fundamentally, it may not be relevant to the alleged charge. For example, the fact that a woman has worked for many years as a prostitute does not mean that she cannot be raped. Therefore, her previous sexual history may have little or no bearing on the accuracy of her evidence.

Here a distinction can be made between evidence of previous sexual relations between the complainant and the defendant and between the complainant and previous partners. Clearly, the latter will generally be of minimal relevance, whereas evidence of the relationship between complainant and defendant may be central to issues such as perceived consent. For this reason, the law of evidence first sought to restrict such questioning by requiring leave to question on the complainant's sexual experiences with anyone other than the defendant. The current provisions, however, are considerably broader.

## KEY STATUTE

**Youth Justice and Criminal Evidence Act 1999, s. 41**

**Restriction on evidence or questions about complainant's sexual history**

(1) If at a trial a person is charged with a sexual offence, then, except with the leave of the court –

    (a) no evidence may be adduced, and

    (b) no question may be asked in cross-examination, by or on behalf of any accused at the trial, about any sexual behaviour of the complainant.

(2) This subsection applies if the evidence or question relates to a relevant issue in the case and either –

    (a) that issue is not an issue of consent; or

    (b) it is an issue of consent and the sexual behaviour of the complainant to which the evidence or question relates is alleged to have taken place at or about the same time as the event which is the subject matter of the charge against the accused; or

    (c) it is an issue of consent and the sexual behaviour of the complainant to which the evidence or question relates is alleged to have been, in any respect, so similar –

        (i) to any sexual behaviour of the complainant which (according to evidence adduced or to be adduced by or on behalf of the accused) took place as part of the event which is the subject matter of the charge against the accused, or

        (ii) to any other sexual behaviour of the complainant which (according to such evidence) took place at or about the same time as that event, that the similarity cannot reasonably be explained as a coincidence.

(3) For the purposes of subsection (3) no evidence or question shall be regarded as relating to a relevant issue in the case if it appears to the court to be reasonable to assume that the purpose (or main purpose) for which it would be adduced or asked is to establish or elicit material for impugning the credibility of the complainant as a witness.

Under section 41(2) the court may grant leave for such questioning only if satisfied that the provisions apply and that to refuse may render unsafe a conclusion of the jury or the court on any relevant issue.

It should also be noted that the provisions make a distinction between cases where the issue is one of consent and those where it is not. In cases where consent is not an issue (e.g. where the defendant alleges mistaken identity), the issue for the court is whether to deny the questioning may render unsafe a conclusion of the jury. The Act defines an 'issue of consent' as:

> any issue whether the complainant in fact consented to the conduct constituting the offence with which the accused is charged (and accordingly does not include any issue as to the belief of the accused that the complainant so consented) (s. 42(1)(b)).

Where the issue is one of consent, the criteria in section 41(3)(b) or section 41(3)(c) must be satisfied. See, *R* v *A (I)* [2015] EWCA Crim 118.

---

### ✎ EXAM TIP

In discussing the tests in section 41(3)(b) or section 41(3)(c), remember to point out that section 41(3)(b) is an issue of timing and the fact that the events in question were contemporaneous, whereas section 41(3)(c) looks to the alleged similarity between the events.

---

### KEY CASE

*R* v *Mukadi* [2004] Crim LR 373 (CA)

*Concerning: s. 41(3)(b)*

**Facts**

The complainant entered the supermarket where the defendant worked as a security guard. After conversing, she waited for him to finish work and accompanied him home where sexual intercourse took place. She later alleged rape on the basis that she had not consented. The defence wished to cross-examine the complainant about an incident shortly before the alleged offence where she had climbed into the car of an older male driver and exchanged telephone numbers with him. The trial judge had refused to allow the questioning.

**Legal principle**

It was held that the questioning should have been permitted under section 41(3)(b). The definition of 'sexual behaviour' was a matter of impression and common sense and this was relevant to the case and to the defence. Edwin Jowitt: 'In our judgment, having regard to what the complainant said about her state of mind . . . if the jury had heard evidence about the car incident it could have influenced them . . . in the crucial issue of consent.'

*R* v *Tahed* [2004] EWCA Crim 1220 (CA)

*Concerning: s. 41(3)(c)*

**Facts**

The complainant alleged rape was committed inside a metal playground climbing frame (the issue was one of consent). The defence wished to cross-examine about consensual sexual activity three to four weeks prior to the alleged rape between the complainant and the defendant in the same climbing frame. The trial judge refused leave to cross-examine.

**Legal principle**

It was held that the cross-examination should have been allowed under section 41(3)(c). Waller LJ: 'The effect of that [original] ruling was to exclude evidence in relation to which there was no dispute.'

## Re-examination

The final stage of witness testimony is re-examination, which is conducted by the party who originally called the witness (and who conducted the examination in chief). The purpose is to clarify any matters raised in cross-examination and so questioning is restricted to those matters. This means that no new subjects can be raised at this stage and even topics covered during examination in chief cannot be addressed if they were not part of the cross-examination. In one sense, the purpose of re-examination can be seen as 'damage limitation', to minimise any 'harm' done during cross-examination.

# ■ Competence and compellability of witnesses

For a witness to be called upon to give evidence they must be competent. If they are to be forced to give evidence, with the risk of being held to be in contempt of court if they refuse, they must be *compellable.*

## Competence

**Youth Justice and Criminal Evidence Act 1999, s. 53**

Competence of witnesses to give evidence ▶

(1) At every stage in criminal proceedings all persons are (whatever their age) competent to give evidence.

(2) Subsection (1) has effect subject to subsections (3) and (4).

(3) A person is not competent to give evidence in criminal proceedings if it appears to the court that he is not a person who is able to –

   (a) understand questions put to him as a witness, and

   (b) give answers to them which can be understood.

Questions of competence are decided by the judge but the burden of proof lies with the party who seeks to call the witness. Competence must be proved on the balance of probability.

## Compellability

As a general rule, any witness who is competent to give evidence is also compellable.

# ■ Special categories of witness

Having established the general rules in favour of competence and compellability, there are a number of categories of witness where special rules apply.

## The defendant in criminal cases

It was only with the Criminal Evidence Act 1898 that the defendant in a criminal case gained a general right (i.e. became competent) to give evidence in their own defence. They are not, however, competent as witnesses for the prosecution (Youth Justice and Criminal Evidence Act 1999 s. 53(4)). Similarly, the defendant is not compellable in that they cannot be forced to give evidence in their own defence, although this must be read in light of the changes to the 'right to silence' outlined later in this chapter.

## Spouses or partners of the defendant in criminal cases

Look again at section 53 above. It states that 'all persons' are competent, which includes the spouse or partner of the defendant. Here, the issue is not one of competence but one of compellability – both for the defence and for the prosecution. The complicating factor is the effect on the marriage of requiring one spouse to testify against the other. To preserve domestic harmony the law will require this only in certain circumstances.

**KEY STATUTE**

**Police and Criminal Evidence Act 1984, s. 80**

Compellability of accused's spouse [or civil partner]

(1) In any proceedings the spouse or civil partner of a person charged in the proceedings shall, subject to subsection (4) below, be compellable to give evidence on behalf of that person.

(2) In any proceedings the spouse or civil partner of a person charged in the proceedings shall, subject to subsection (4) below, be compellable –

   (a) to give evidence on behalf of any other person charged in the proceedings but only in respect of any specified offence with which that other person is charged; or

   (b) to give evidence for the prosecution but only in respect of any specified offence with which any person is charged in the proceedings.

(3) In relation to the spouse or civil partner of a person charged in any proceedings, an offence is a specified offence for the purposes of subsection (2A) above if –

   (a) it involves an assault on, or injury or a threat of injury to, the spouse or civil partner or a person who was at the material time under the age of 16;

   (b) it is a sexual offence alleged to have been committed in respect of a person who was at the material time under that age; or

   (c) it consists of attempting or conspiring to commit, or of aiding, abetting, counselling, procuring or inciting the commission of, an offence falling within paragraph (a) or (b) above.

The effects of section 80 may be summarised as follows:

- A spouse/partner is compellable as a witness for the defendant but not if they are both charged in the same proceedings.

- A spouse/partner is only compellable as a witness for the prosecution in relation to the 'specified' offences set out in section 80(3).

**✎ EXAM TIP**

Point out that, if a couple cease to be married, they become competent and compellable in the usual way 'as if that person and the accused had never been married' (s. 80(5)).

# Children

The evidence of child witnesses clearly presents particular difficulties, partly in relation to their understanding of what the effects of their evidence might be and the corresponding need to tell the truth, which goes to the issue of competence.

In assessing the competence of a child to give evidence, it must be recognised that the age of the child can only be a very general indication, as the maturity and understanding of children of similar ages can vary widely. There is also the question of whether the child appreciates that to give evidence on oath implies a duty to tell the truth. For this reason, the competence of children to give evidence, in both civil and criminal cases, is assessed by reference to the following test.

## KEY CASE

*R v Hayes* [1977] 2 All ER 288 (CA)

*Concerning: child witnesses*

**Facts**

H was charged with offences of gross indecency with children. Important prosecution evidence came from the children involved, who were 12, 11 and 9 at the time of trial. The defence challenged the admissibility of the children's evidence, in part because the children gave sworn evidence but there were doubts as to whether they understood the 'sacred' nature of the oath.

**Legal principle**

It was held that the key consideration for a judge deciding whether to permit a child to give evidence on oath is whether the child sufficiently appreciates the solemnity of the occasion and understands that taking an oath involves telling the truth. In doing so, the judge does not have to be satisfied that the child understands the 'divine' sanction of an oath. Bridge LJ: 'The important consideration . . . is whether the child has a sufficient appreciation of the solemnity of the occasion, and the added responsibility to tell the truth . . . over and above the duty to tell truth which is an ordinary duty of normal social conduct.'

## ! Don't be tempted to . . .

Don't assume that the oath has remained unchanged. Over time there have been attempts to broaden the scope of the oath to reflect increasing diversity of faiths within England and Wales and the current version is as follows:

I swear by [substitute Almighty God/Name of God (such as Allah) or the name of the holy scripture] that the evidence I shall give shall be the truth, the whole truth and nothing but the truth.
(Judicial Studies Board)

## KEY CASE

*R* v *Barker* [2010] EWCA Crim 4 (CA)

*Concerning: competence of child witness*

### Facts

The accused was charged with the rape of a child under the age of three. At trial, testimony was allowed from the child who was four and a half at the time but the defence challenged the competence of the child to give evidence.

### Legal principle

It was held that the process was without presumptions or preconceptions and the question of competence was entirely witness or child specific. Lord Judge CJ: 'Dealing with it broadly and fairly, provided the witness could understand the questions put to him and could also provide understandable answers, he or she was competent.'

The competence of children in criminal cases falls under section 53 of the Youth Justice and Criminal Evidence Act (above). The question of whether they give evidence sworn or unsworn is addressed by the following provision.

## KEY STATUTE

### Youth Justice and Criminal Evidence Act 1999, s. 55

Determining whether witness to be sworn

(1)  The witness may not be sworn for that purpose unless –

(a)  he has attained the age of 14, and

(b)  he has a sufficient appreciation of the solemnity of the occasion and of the particular responsibility to tell the truth which is involved in taking an oath.

In civil cases the matter is addressed by the Children Act 1989.

**Children Act 1989, s. 96**

Evidence given by, or with respect to, children

(1) Subsection (2) applies where a child who is called as a witness in any civil proceedings does not, in the opinion of the court, understand the nature of an oath.

(2) The child's evidence may be heard by the court if, in its opinion –

    (a) he understands that it is his duty to speak the truth; and

    (b) he has sufficient understanding to justify his evidence being heard.

## Persons of unsound mind

The situation in relation to persons of unsound mind is not dissimilar to that of child witnesses, with the starting point in criminal cases being the general rule on competence under section 53 of the Youth Justice and Criminal Evidence Act (above).

# ■ Special measures directions for vulnerable witnesses

Having established that certain categories of witness (most notably children and persons of unsound mind) may have difficulty understanding the nature of judicial proceedings, there is also the issue of the inevitable apprehension or distress which they may feel at the prospect of giving evidence. To address this, the Youth Justice and Criminal Evidence Act 1999 provides so-called 'special measures directions' to assist them in giving their evidence.

**Youth Justice and Criminal Evidence Act 1999, s. 16**

Witnesses eligible for assistance on grounds of age or incapacity

(1) For the purposes of this Chapter a witness in criminal proceedings (other than the accused) is eligible for assistance by virtue of this section –

    (a) if under the age of 17 at the time of the hearing; or

    (b) if the court considers that the quality of evidence given by the witness is likely to be diminished by reason of any circumstances falling within subsection (2).

(2)   The circumstances falling within this subsection are –

   (a)   that the witness –
      (i)   suffers from mental disorder within the meaning of the Mental Health Act 1983, or
      (ii)   otherwise has a significant impairment of intelligence and social functioning;
   (b)   that the witness has a physical disability or is suffering from a physical disorder'.

**Youth Justice and Criminal Evidence Act 1999, s. 17**

**Witnesses eligible for assistance on grounds of fear or distress about testifying**

(1)   For the purposes of this Chapter a witness in criminal proceedings (other than the accused) is eligible for assistance by virtue of this subsection if the court is satisfied that the quality of evidence given by the witness is likely to be diminished by reason of fear or distress on the part of the witness in connection with testifying in the proceedings.

(2)   In determining whether a witness falls within subsection (1) the court must take into account, in particular –

   (a)   the nature and alleged circumstances of the offence to which the proceedings relate;
   (b)   the age of the witness;
   (c)   such of the following matters as appear to the court to be relevant, namely –
      (i)   the social and cultural background and ethnic origins of the witness,
      (ii)   the domestic and employment circumstances of the witness, and
      (iii)   any religious beliefs or political opinions of the witness;
   (d)   any behaviour towards the witness on the part of –
      (i)   the accused,
      (ii)   members of the family or associates of the accused, or
      (iii)   any other person who is likely to be an accused or a witness in the proceedings.

(3)   In determining that question the court must in addition consider any views expressed by the witness.

(4)   Where the complainant in respect of a sexual offence is a witness in proceedings relating to that offence (or to that offence and any other offences), the witness is eligible for assistance in relation to those proceedings by virtue of this subsection unless the witness has informed the court of the witness's wish not to be so eligible by virtue of this subsection.

The precise nature of the measures offered will vary depending on the individual witness but may include:

- video-recorded evidence;
- evidence by live video link;
- screening the witness from the accused;
- removal of wigs and gowns;
- removal of the public from the court.

Note also the additional powers available to the court under section 21 in relation to child witnesses in trials for certain specified offences (e.g. sexual offences, assault, kidnapping, etc.).

**KEY STATUTE**

**Youth Justice and Criminal Evidence Act 1999, s. 21**

Special provisions relating to child witnesses

(1) The primary rule in the case of a child witness is that the court must give a special measures direction in relation to the witness which complies with the following requirements –

    (a) it must provide for any relevant recording to be admitted under section 27 (video recorded evidence in chief); and

    (b) it must provide for any evidence given by the witness in the proceedings which is not given by means of a video recording (whether in chief or otherwise) to be given by means of a live link in accordance with section 24.

 Make your answer stand out

The provision of such 'special measures' for witnesses (particularly children) has raised questions over their impact on the Article 6 right to a fair trial of the accused. This was considered by the House of Lords in *R (on the application of D)* v *Camberwell Green Youth Court* [2005] UKHL 4. For a discussion of the subject see, Burton, M., Vulnerable and Intimidated Witnesses and the Adversarial Process in England and Wales (2007) *EvPro* 1(1):11.

# Witness anonymity orders

Under the Coroners and Justice Act 2009 it is also possible to apply for a witness anonymity order.

---

**KEY STATUTE**

**Coroners and Justice Act 2009, s. 86**

Witness anonymity orders

(1) In this Chapter a 'witness anonymity order' is an order made by a court that requires such specified measures to be taken in relation to a witness in criminal proceedings as the court considers appropriate to ensure that the identity of the witness is not disclosed in or in connection with the proceedings.

(2) The kinds of measures that may be required to be taken in relation to a witness include measures for securing one or more of the following –

    (a) that the witness's name and other identifying details may be –
        (i) withheld;
        (ii) removed from materials disclosed to any party to the proceedings;
    (a) that the witness may use a pseudonym;
    (b) that the witness is not asked questions of any specified description that might lead to the identification of the witness;
    (c) that the witness is screened to any specified extent;
    (d) that the witness's voice is subjected to modulation to any specified extent.

---

**KEY STATUTE**

**Coroners and Justice Act 2009, s. 88**

Conditions for making order

(1) This section applies where an application is made for a witness anonymity order to be made in relation to a witness in criminal proceedings.

(2) The court may make such an order only if it is satisfied that Conditions A to C below are met.

(3) Condition A is that the proposed order is necessary –

    (a) in order to protect the safety of the witness or another person or to prevent any serious damage to property, or
    (b) in order to prevent real harm to the public interest (whether affecting the carrying on of any activities in the public interest or the safety of a person involved in carrying on such activities, or otherwise).

▶

(4) Condition B is that, having regard to all the circumstances, the effect of the proposed order would be consistent with the defendant receiving a fair trial.

(5) Condition C is that the importance of the witness's testimony is such that in the interests of justice the witness ought to testify and –

   (a) the witness would not testify if the proposed order were not made, or

   (b) there would be real harm to the public interest if the witness were to testify without the proposed order being made.

(6) In determining whether the proposed order is necessary for the purpose mentioned in subsection (3)(a), the court must have regard (in particular) to any reasonable fear on the part of the witness –

   (a) that the witness or another person would suffer death or injury, or

   (b) that there would be serious damage to property, if the witness were to be identified.

 **Make your answer stand out**

If you are discussing the availability of witness anonymity orders under the 2009 Act you can mention *R* v *Nwankwo (Hugo) and another* [2014] EWCA Crim 1205 as an example of such an order being granted to protect a witness in a murder trial.

# The right to silence

As mentioned previously, the defendant cannot be compelled to give evidence in their defence. Until relatively recently, however, a person accused of a criminal offence retained the right to remain silent and 'put the prosecution to proof'. This meant that the accused could refuse to answer questions at the police station and refuse to give evidence at trial without consequence.

Under the Criminal Justice and Public Order Act 1994 this situation changed and now the defendant who remains silent faces 'adverse inference' – that is, the jury can be directed to draw such inferences 'as appear proper' from the defendant's refusal to answer questions.

The facility for such adverse inference arises where the accused:

■ at any time before being charged with the offence, on being questioned under caution, fails to mention any fact which is later relied on in his defence. This also applies when the accused similarly fails to mention any such fact after being charged with an offence (s. 34);

- chooses at trial not to give evidence in his defence, or, having been sworn, without good cause refuses to answer any question (s. 35);

- fails to account for any object, substance or mark (this might be on his person, clothing, footwear, otherwise in his possession or at the place where he was arrested) where those investigating an offence reasonably believe that the object, substance or mark may be attributable to his participation in the commission of the offence (s. 36);

- fails to account for his presence at a place at or about the time the offence for which he was arrested is alleged to have been committed where those investigating the offence reasonably believe that his presence may be attributable to his participation in the commission of the offence (s. 37).

---

### ✎ EXAM TIP

In any discussion of the effects of CJPOA 1994 in undermining the 'right to silence' it should be noted that this statute was part of the 'law and order' agenda of the Conservative government which had pledged to 'rebalance' the criminal justice system in favour of the prosecution. This agenda can also be seen in the provisions of the Criminal Procedure and Investigations Act 1996 (CPIA) **(discussed in Chapter 9).** You might also mention that the facility for adverse inference under CJPOA 1994 is mirrored by similar provisions under section 11 CPIA.

## Section 34 and police interviews

Of the four possible triggers for adverse inference, it is section 34 which has prompted the most discussion (and generally features most prominently in examination questions). This provision, it will be remembered, applies when the suspect is questioned by the police prior to charge and frequently follows a 'no comment' interview, where the accused refuses to answer any police questions.

When considering the operation of section 34, it is crucial to remember that the central issue is not that the accused fails to answer questions but that he 'failed to mention any fact relied on in his defence'. Therefore, for adverse inference to be drawn, the defendant must raise an issue in his defence at trial which he could reasonably have been expected to mention at interview. This is reflected in the current police caution which states: 'You do not have to say anything. But it may harm your defence if you do not mention when questioned something which you later rely on in court. Anything you do say may be given in evidence.'

**KEY CASE**

*R* v *Essa* [2009] EWCA Crim 43 (CA)

*Concerning: adverse inference and s. 34*

**Facts**

E was accused of a robbery committed on a train and gave a 'no comment' interview to police. At trial he asserted that he had been mistakenly identified as, although he regularly took the train in question, he had not done so on the day of the alleged attack.

**Legal principle**

It was held that the trial judge had been correct to allow section 34 inference to be drawn. Hughes LJ: 'It is important to remember that the significance of section 34 does not lie in silence in interview, it lies in reliance at trial on something that should have been said in interview.'

Of course this requires at least some evidence to be presented at trial. If not, then there is no failure at interview to mention a fact later relied on at trial.

**KEY CASE**

*R* v *Moshaid* [1998] Crim LR 420 (CA)

*Concerning: adverse inference and s. 34*

**Facts**

M was arrested on suspicion of drugs offences and gave a 'no comment' interview. At trial he offered no evidence and called no witnesses.

**Legal principle**

It was held that there was no scope for adverse inference under section 34 for, although the defendant had given a 'no comment' interview, he had not failed to mention anything which was later relied on at trial.

## Section 34 and legal advice

A number of early cases under section 34 centred on whether the defendant could be subject to adverse inference when their failure to answer police questions had been on legal advice. This point is now settled.

*R* v *Condron and Condron* [1997] 1 Cr App R 185 (CA)

*Concerning: s. 34 and legal advice*

Facts

The defendants were arrested on suspicion of possession of heroin with intent to supply. Their solicitor advised them to give a 'no comment' interview as he considered them unfit to be questioned (the police doctor disagreed). At trial, the judge invited the jury to draw adverse inference from their failure to answer police questions. The defendants appealed on the grounds inter alia that adverse inference should not be available where the refusal to answer questions was on legal advice.

Legal principle

It was held that the fact that the defendants' claim that their silence was on legal advice did not prevent the jury from drawing adverse inference. Stuart-Smith LJ: 'That bare assertion is unlikely by itself to be regarded as a sufficient reason for not mentioning matters relevant to the defence.'

This decision led to a challenge under Article 6 ECHR in *Condron* v *United Kingdom* (2001) 31 EHRR 1 where the Strasbourg Court held:

- the right to silence is central to the notion of a fair procedure under Article 6 and particular caution is required before a court can use the accused's silence against him;
- appropriate weight had to be given to the fact that an accused was advised by his lawyer to maintain his silence;
- the defendants had explained their failure to answer police questions on the basis that they had acted on legal advice. Although the trial judge drew the jury's attention to that explanation, he did so in terms which left the jury at liberty to draw an adverse inference, notwithstanding that the jury might have been satisfied as to the plausibility of the explanation;
- as a matter of fairness, the jury should have been directed that, if it was satisfied that the applicants' silence at the police interview could not sensibly be attributed to their having no answer or none that would stand up to cross-examination, it should not draw an adverse inference;
- the Court of Appeal had no means to ascertain whether or not the silence of the defendants played a significant role in the jury's decision to convict. Therefore, any deficiencies in the trial judge's direction were not remedied on appeal;
- as a result, there had been a violation of Article 6(1).

**KEY CASE**

*R* v *Beckles* [2005] 1 All ER 705 (CA)

*Concerning: s. 34 and legal advice*

**Facts**

B was charged with false imprisonment, robbery and attempted murder. On his solicitor's advice he gave a 'no comment' interview. The judge directed the jury that they might draw adverse inference from the silence.

**Legal principle**

Lord Woolf: 'In a case where a solicitor's advice is relied upon by the defendant, the ultimate question for the jury remains under section 34 whether the facts relied on at the trial were facts which the defendant could reasonably have been expected to mention at interview . . . if . . . it is possible to say that the defendant genuinely acted upon the advice, the fact that he did so because it suited his purpose may mean he was not acting reasonably in not mentioning the facts. His reasonableness in not mentioning the facts remains to be determined by the jury. If they conclude he was acting unreasonably they can draw an adverse inference from the failure to mention the facts.'

The position appears to be, therefore, that it is possible for the defendant to remain silent on legal advice and escape adverse inference, but only if the reliance on legal advice is held to be reasonable, that is, not merely a convenient excuse to avoid dealing with questions to which the defendant has no plausible answer. This is reflected in the Judicial Studies Board specimen direction (for judges to deliver to the jury in such cases) which includes the following:

> If, for example, you considered that he had or may have had an answer to give, but genuinely and reasonably relied on the legal advice to remain silent, you should not draw any conclusion against him. But if, for example, you were sure that the defendant remained silent not because of the legal advice but because he had no answer or no satisfactory answer to give, and merely latched onto the legal advice as a convenient shield behind which to hide, you would be entitled to draw a conclusion against him.

# ■ Putting it all together

## Answer guidelines

See the problem question at the start of the chapter.

### Approaching the question

■ This question concerns the 'right to silence' and the changes made by the Criminal Justice and Public Order Act 1994.

■ Your answer should not only state the relevant provisions of the 1994 Act but also apply them to the scenario.

### Important points to include

■ The Act allows for the jury to draw 'adverse inference' from the defendant's failure to answer questions under certain circumstances.

■ In relation to both David and Karen, the appropriate provision is section 36 CJPOA – the failure to explain 'objects, substances or marks'. This would allow the trial judge to direct the jury that they could draw adverse inference from the failure to explain the existence of the DVDs and the injuries.

■ In relation to Sunil, the relevant provision is section 34 – failure to mention when questioned any fact later relied on in the defence (the assertion of self-defence and the alleged earlier confrontation with the victim).

■ The presence of legal advice should be considered in light of the decisions in *R* v *Condron and Condron*, together with *R* v *Beckles.* The central issue is the reasonableness of the reliance on legal advice.

 Make your answer stand out

■ Remember to make clear that, under section 34, it is not the failure to answer questions which triggers adverse inference but the fact that information which is used as part of the defence is not raised at questioning. In this way, a defendant who says nothing at interview and presents no evidence in his defence cannot be subject to adverse inference (*R* v *Moshaid*).

■ In relation to legal advice, mention the Judicial Studies Board specimen direction and the contrast which it makes between the defendant who reasonably refuses to answer questions on legal advice and the defendant who has no credible answer to the question and simply hides behind the legal advice.

## READ TO IMPRESS

Burton, M. (2007) Vulnerable and intimidated witnesses and the adversarial process in England and Wales *EvPro*, 1(1): 11.

Keogh, A. (2003) The right to silence: revisited again. *NLJ*, 153: 1352.

Leng, R. (2001) Silence pre-trial, reasonable expectations and the normative distortion of fact-finding *EvPro*, 5(4): 240.

McEwan, J. (2005) Proving consent in sexual cases: legislative change and cultural evolution, *EvPro* 9(1): 1.

Ormerod, D., Choo, A. and Easter, R. (2010) The 'witness anonymity' and 'investigation anonymity' Provisions. *Crim LR*, 368.

**www.pearsoned.co.uk/lawexpress**

 Go online to access more revision support including quizzes to test your knowledge, sample questions with answer guidelines, podcasts you can download, and more!

# Character evidence

**3**

## Revision checklist

### Essential points you should know:

- [ ] Issues surrounding the presentation of evidence of character
- [ ] Treatment of 'good' character evidence
- [ ] Treatment of 'bad' character evidence
- [ ] The 'character' provisions of the Criminal Justice Act 2003

# ■ Topic map

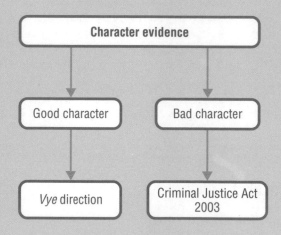

# ■ Introduction

**Does evidence of the defendant's character tell us whether he is guilty? Does evidence of a witness's character tell us whether they are being truthful?**

In considering how the evidence of a witness might be challenged, it is clear that there are two principal lines of attack. Firstly, the evidence itself might be challenged as inaccurate. Secondly, the credibility of the witness themselves might be challenged in order to suggest that they are less likely to be providing accurate evidence. This applies both to witnesses and to the accused and is frequently expressed as 'character evidence'. The rules governing the admissibility of character evidence are not straightforward and this reflects the ambiguities which surround this particular form of evidence. Equally, if the defendant is of previously 'good character' it is understandable that the defence will wish to make the jury aware of the fact, whereas if the defendant is of 'bad character', the prosecution will want to bring this to the attention of the jury (particularly if this takes the form of previous convictions). In both cases, however, it might be wondered how much such evidence is actually relevant to the charge.

## ASSESSMENT ADVICE

Essay questions on character evidence are fairly common, particularly as the introduction of the 'gateways' under CJA 2003 provides an easy framework for examiners. Questions such as, 'Critically assess the admissibility of character evidence under the Criminal Justice Act 2003' require you to set out the previous rules on character evidence, set out the various 'gateways' under the 2003 Act and then offer some evaluation of the new provisions. Do not forget this final element of the answer as it will earn you those valuable marks for analysis.

Problem questions on character evidence are also very common and often follow the example used in relation to the 'right to silence' sample question in the previous chapter (with a number of short scenarios, each of which highlights a different issue). Such questions tend to require a clear statement of the current provisions, rather than the more historical approach of the essay question described above. Such problem questions should only be undertaken if you have a clear grasp of the Act and the various 'gateways'.

# Sample question

Could you answer this question? Below is a typical essay question that could arise on this topic. Guidelines on answering the question are included at the end of this chapter, whilst a sample problem question and guidance on tackling it can be found on the companion website.

---

**ESSAY QUESTION**

'The character "gateways" under the Criminal Justice Act 2003 provide a comprehensive framework of rules to regulate the admission of evidence of character.'

Critically evaluate this statement.

---

# Evidence of character

Although now governed by the Criminal Justice Act 2003, this is merely the latest incarnation of a longstanding series of common law principles which have regulated the admissibility of such evidence. Before considering the provisions, however, it is important to recognise why character evidence is considered so important.

## The function of character evidence

There are two justifications for the parties seeking to adduce evidence of character:

- in relation to the accused, to suggest that the charges are either more likely to be true (based on evidence of 'bad character') or less likely to be true (based on evidence of 'good character');

- in relation to any witness (including the defendant in a criminal case), evidence of 'bad character' may be used in an attempt to undermine the credibility of the witness.

## Character evidence in civil cases

A witness may be asked about aspects of 'bad character', including previous convictions, if this is considered relevant to a fact in issue if the person's character is itself an issue in the case. This is in line with the following principle.

**KEY CASE**

### Hobbs v Tinling & Co. Ltd [1929] 2 KB 1 (CA)

Concerning: questioning of witnesses on matters of character

#### Facts

In an action for libel, the claimant asserted that, apart from a single lapse, he was a man of good character. In cross-examination he was challenged on a number of matters which he had not mentioned and which were suggestive of bad character. He objected to the line of questioning.

#### Legal principle

Scruton LJ: 'When a witness has given evidence material to the issues in the case you can cross-examine him on matters not directly material to the case in order to ask the jury to infer from his answers that he is not worthy of belief, not a credible person, and therefore that they should not accept his answers on questions material to the case as true. This is cross-examination as to his credibility, commonly called cross-examination to credit.'

There are, however, some limitations to this principle. Most importantly, cross-examination that raises evidence of bad character should be restricted to matters that would seriously affect the credibility of the witness on the matter to which he testifies. Also, such matters should not be so remote in time or of such a character that, even if true, they would not impact on the credibility of the witness.

It should also be noted that convictions which are considered 'spent' cannot usually be raised in cross-examination.

**KEY STATUTE**

### Rehabilitation of Offenders Act 1974, s. 4

#### Effect of rehabilitation

(1) Subject to sections 7 and 8 below, a person who has become a rehabilitated person for the purposes of this Act in respect of a conviction shall be treated for all purposes in law as a person who has not committed or been charged with or prosecuted for or convicted of or sentenced for the offence or offences which were the subject of that conviction; and, notwithstanding the provisions of any other enactment or rule of law to the contrary, but subject as aforesaid –

    (a) no evidence shall be admissible in any proceedings before a judicial authority exercising its jurisdiction or functions in Great Britain to prove that any such ▶

> person has committed or been charged with or prosecuted for or convicted of or sentenced for any offence which was the subject of a spent conviction; and
> (b) a person shall not, in any such proceedings, be asked, and, if asked, shall not be required to answer, any question relating to his past which cannot be answered without acknowledging or referring to a spent conviction or spent convictions or any circumstances ancillary thereto.

There is, however, an exception to this general rule under section 7(3) where the court is satisfied 'that justice cannot be done in the case except by admitting or requiring evidence relating to a person's spent convictions'.

# Similar fact evidence

A related concept is that of 'similar fact evidence' which is adduced to suggest a link between some previous misconduct on the part of the witness and the current events. Such evidence is introduced in order to show a propensity towards a certain type of conduct, primarily in criminal cases. Following the Criminal Justice Act 2003, however, such evidence is no longer admissible in criminal trials and so it is only in civil cases that the similar fact doctrine will be raised in future.

**KEY DEFINITION: Similar fact evidence**

Evidence which seeks to highlight a similarity between previous conduct of the accused and the events forming the subject of the present charge.

**KEY CASE**

*R* v *Butler* (1986) 84 Cr App R 12 (CA)

*Concerning: similar fact evidence*

**Facts**

B was charged with the rape of two women. Evidence was adduced from a previous girlfriend of B who gave evidence of (consensual) sexual conduct which they had engaged in during their relationship which was similar to the circumstances of the alleged attacks which formed the basis of the current charges. She also identified the scenes of the attacks as places they had visited for sexual purposes. B was convicted and challenged the admission of the girlfriend's evidence.

**Legal principle**

It was held that such evidence could be admitted if it tended to show that the accused was guilty of the offences charged. The similarity between the girlfriend's account of their sexual encounters and the circumstances of the alleged attacks meant that her evidence should be admitted. Kilner Brown: 'These [details] were not only strikingly similar but in their weight were very substantial indeed.'

**KEY CASE**

*Hales* v *Kerr* [1908] 2 KB 601 (KBD)

*Concerning: similar fact evidence*

**Facts**

In a claim for negligence, the claimant alleged that he had contracted an infection from being shaved at the defendant's barber shop due to the defendant's poor standards of hygiene. In support of this claim, evidence was admitted from two other customers of the shop who had contracted a similar infection.

**Legal principle**

It was held that such evidence could be admitted as it suggested a poor system of hygiene within the shop rather than an isolated incident of infection. Channel JJ: 'Evidence that the act or omission has happened on several occasions is always admissible to show that its happening on a particular occasion is not a mere accident or a mere isolated event.'

**KEY CASE**

*Mood Music Publishing Co. Ltd* v *De Wolfe Publishing Ltd* [1976] Ch 119 (CA)

*Concerning: similar fact evidence*

**Facts**

The defendant publishing company supplied music for a television play. The claimant asserted that the music was subject to their copyright; however, the defendants argued that the similarity between the two works was purely coincidental. In support of their claim the claimants produced evidence of three previous cases where the defendants had reproduced without authority works which were subject to copyright.

▶

**Legal principle**

It was held that, in civil cases, the courts would admit evidence of similar facts if it was logically probative and it was not oppressive or unfair to the other side to admit the evidence. Lord Denning MR: 'The evidence of these three matters is of sufficient probative weight to be relevant to this issue and should be admitted.'

Prior to the replacement of the common law doctrine of similar fact evidence in criminal cases by the statutory gateways of the Criminal Justice Act 2003, the test had been that set out in the following case.

**KEY CASE**

*DPP* v *P* **[1991] 3 All ER 337 (HL)**

*Concerning: similar fact evidence in criminal cases*

**Facts**

P was charged with incest and rape of his two daughters. At trial, the testimony of each girl was admitted as evidence in relation to the alleged offences committed against the other (as 'similar fact' evidence) and P was convicted. The Court of Appeal allowed his appeal on the grounds that there was no 'striking similarity' between the accounts of the daughters which justified their admission under the similar fact rule. The prosecution appealed to the House of Lords.

**Legal principle**

Lord Mackay LC: 'The essential feature of evidence which is to be admitted is that its probative force in support of the allegation that an accused person committed a crime is sufficiently great to make it just to admit the evidence, notwithstanding that it is prejudicial to the accused in tending to show that he was guilty of another crime. Such probative force may be derived from striking similarities in the evidence about the manner in which the crime was committed. . . . But restricting the circumstances in which there is sufficient probative force to overcome prejudice of evidence relating to another crime to cases in which there is some striking similarity between them is to restrict the operation of the principle in a way which gives too much effect to a particular manner of stating it, and is not justified in principle.'

Although this was a criminal case, the test was also considered in the following leading authority on similar fact evidence in civil cases.

**O'Brien v Chief Constable of South Wales Police [2005] UKHL 26 (HL)**

*Concerning: similar fact evidence*

**Facts**

The claimant had served 11 years of a life sentence for murder before his conviction was overturned on appeal. He claimed damages from the Chief Constable for misfeasance in public office and malicious prosecution, alleging that he had been 'framed' by two detectives. As part of his case, the claimant adduced evidence of inappropriate conduct by the officers during two other investigations. On appeal, it was held that the decision to admit the evidence was correct and that the test in *DPP* v *P* should apply.

**Legal principle**

It was held that the evidence was admissible but the test in *DPP* v *P* which had been applied by the Court of Appeal was too strict to be applied in civil cases. The correct approach was to consider whether such evidence was potentially probative of an issue in the action. The test of admissibility in criminal proceedings required an enhanced relevance or probative value because, otherwise, the prejudice that it would cause to the defendant might render the proceedings unfair. Such enhanced protections were not necessary in a civil suit. Lord Carswell: 'In a criminal trial . . . it may be necessary to look for enhanced relevance or substantial probative value, for that may be necessary to offset the degree of prejudice caused.'

# ■ Character evidence in criminal cases

We must now consider the admission of and distinguish between evidence of 'good' character and evidence of 'bad' character. The former remains under the common law but the admission of 'bad' character now falls under the Criminal Justice Act 2003 which introduced a statutory framework which covers not only the defendant but also other witnesses.

## ! Don't be tempted to . . .

It is vital that you are familiar with the various provisions of the CJA 2003 relating to character evidence and, in particular, the various 'gateways'. If you are not, then don't be tempted to attempt a question on this subject.

# Evidence of 'good' character

Clearly the defence may wish to adduce evidence that the accused is a person of 'good' character (e.g. evidence that the person has no previous convictions or that they are otherwise respectable) in order to suggest that it is unlikely that they have committed the alleged offence. Here, the defence is restricted by the rule that only evidence of general reputation is admissible – not evidence of specific 'good deeds' or evidence of the witness's own personal opinion. This is generally justified on the grounds that even the most dishonest or violent individual may perform an isolated act of kindness and, therefore, to present evidence of such an action may present a misleading impression of the general nature of the accused.

---

**KEY CASE**

*R* v *Rowton* (1865) 29 JP 149 (CCR)

*Concerning: character evidence*

**Facts**

R was charged with indecent assault on a 14-year-old boy. During the course of the trial both prosecution and defence sought to adduce evidence of character.

**Legal principle**

Cockburn CJ: 'Evidence is admissible of general reputation of good character, and not of individual opinion. It is clear that if a witness to character is called who knows nothing of the general reputation of the prisoner, but speaks only as to his individual opinion, such evidence, if objected to, is not receivable; he is not allowed to give his individual opinion.'

---

**KEY CASE**

*R* v *Redgrave* (1981) 74 Cr App R 10 (CA)

*Concerning: character evidence*

**Facts**

R was convicted of offences of gross indecency in a public lavatory. At trial, the judge refused to allow evidence of love letters from R's various girlfriends to support his defence that he was not homosexual and so unlikely to have committed the offence.

**Legal principle**

It was held that such evidence was inadmissible as it referred to specific events, rather than general reputation.

---

Having made this point, evidence of the accused's good character is clearly of some relevance to issues of **credibility** and/or **propensity** and so the courts are willing to accept such evidence of character. This is adduced on the basis of the principles set out by the Court of Appeal in the following case.

---

**KEY CASE**

*R* v *Vye* [1993] 3 All ER 241 (CA)

*Concerning: character evidence*

**Facts**

V was convicted of rape and appealed on the grounds that the judge's direction to the jury on the matter of his good character was inadequate.

**Legal principle**

It was held that there were two 'limbs' to a 'good character' direction which the judge should issue to the jury in such cases.

---

## The 'first limb' of the test in *Vye*

The 'first limb' of the test relates to the credibility of the defendant. In this way, the judge must direct the jury that the defendant's good character should be taken into account when considering their evidence providing that the defendant either:

- gives evidence in court; or
- does not give evidence in court, but has made a previous statement to the police or has answered questions during interview.

The precise form of wording varies depending on which of the above applies and is set out in the Judicial Studies Board Specimen Direction No. 23 at www.judiciary.gov.uk/Resources/JCO/Documents/Training/benchbook_criminal_2010.pdf.

---

**KEY DEFINITION: Credibility**

The degree to which a witness or a piece of evidence is likely to be believed.

---

## The 'second limb' of the test in *Vye*

The 'second limb' of the test relates to the propensity of the defendant but, unlike the first limb, this does not require the defendant to give evidence or provide a statement to the police.

Where the defendant is of good character, the judge must direct the jury that the fact that they are of good character may mean that they are less likely to have committed the offence in question.

The likelihood of the accused having engaged in a particular course of conduct based on their history of having engaged in such conduct previously.

## ! Don't be tempted to . . .

If discussing the rule in *Vye*, don't ignore the point that there is no requirement for the judge to issue a good character direction unless the issue is raised by the defence. See *Barrow* v *R* [1998] AC 846 (PC). Note also that a defendant of good character is entitled to the *Vye* direction even where they are jointly tried with a co-defendant of bad character.

## The effect of previous convictions

The most obvious blemish on a defendant's good character is the existence of previous convictions and so it might be thought that a good character direction would never be given where the accused has a criminal record. There are, however, instances where such a person may still benefit from a judge's direction in much the same way as a person with no previous convictions, providing that this does not amount to misleading the jury. In this way, if the accused has convictions which are either old or of limited relevance to the current charge then they may be described as 'of good character with no relevant convictions'.

**KEY CASE**

*R* v *Gray* [2004] EWCA Crim 1074 (CA)

*Concerning: character direction*

Facts

G was charged with murder. He had a previous conviction for driving a car with excess alcohol, without a licence or insurance. Consequently, the judge gave no direction about character.

**Legal principle**

It was held that, where previous convictions were minor and of no relevance to the offence charged, the defendant was entitled to a *Vye* direction modified to the extent that reference was made to the defendant's admitted wrongdoing. Rix LJ: 'Where the previous conviction can only be regarded as irrelevant or of no significance in relation to the offence charged, that discretion ought to be exercised in favour of treating the defendant as of good character.'

This means that the defendant is entitled to the 'first limb' of the *Vye* direction (credibility) and a modified 'second limb' (propensity). Equally, a person with no previous convictions may still not be entitled to a good character direction if they have admitted other misconduct.

**KEY CASE**

*R* v *Zoppola-Barraza* [1994] Crim LR 833 (CA)

*Concerning: character direction*

**Facts**

The accused was charged with unlawful importation of cannabis. He had no previous convictions but admitted smuggling jewels and gold into the country on previous occasions.

**Legal principle**

Alliott J: 'It is an affront to common sense to hold that such a person is entitled to the same direction that is intended to benefit those who can truly be considered to be of good character.'

# Evidence of 'bad' character

Evidence of 'bad' character in criminal cases is now governed by the Criminal Justice Act 2003.

**KEY STATUTE**

**Criminal Justice Act 2003, s. 98**

**Bad character**

References in this Chapter to evidence of a person's 'bad character' are to evidence of, or of a disposition towards, misconduct on his part.

# 'Bad' character and witnesses

**KEY STATUTE**

## Criminal Justice Act 2003, s. 100

### Non-defendant's bad character

(1) In criminal proceedings evidence of the bad character of a person other than the defendant is admissible if and only if –

    (a) it is important explanatory evidence,

    (b) it has substantial probative value in relation to a matter which –

        (i) is a matter in issue in the proceedings, and

        (ii) is of substantial importance in the context of the case as a whole,

or

    (c) all parties to the proceedings agree to the evidence being admissible.

# 'Bad' character and the defendant

Unfortunately, the provisions regulating the admissibility of evidence relating to the 'bad' character of the defendant are slightly more complex. Under the 2003 Act there are seven grounds, known as 'gateways', under which such evidence may be admitted. These are found in section 101.

**KEY STATUTE**

## Criminal Justice Act 2003, s. 101

### Defendant's bad character

(1) In criminal proceedings evidence of the defendant's bad character is admissible if, but only if –

    (a) all parties to the proceedings agree to the evidence being admissible,

    (b) the evidence is adduced by the defendant himself or is given in answer to a question asked by him in cross-examination and intended to elicit it,

    (c) it is important explanatory evidence,

    (d) it is relevant to an important matter in issue between the defendant and the prosecution,

    (e) it has substantial probative value in relation to an important matter in issue between the defendant and a co-defendant,

    (f) it is evidence to correct a false impression given by the defendant, or

    (g) the defendant has made an attack on another person's character.

**EXAM TIP**

In discussing the gateways, do not fall into the trap of assuming that they can only be used singly. It is quite possible to argue that more than one of the gateways could apply at the same time.

## Section 101(1)(a) – all parties to the proceedings agree to the evidence being admissible

This is the simplest gateway to understand. If the defence do not object, then the evidence can be admitted.

## Section 101(1)(b) – the evidence is adduced by the defendant himself or is given in answer to a question asked by him in cross-examination and intended to elicit it

The meaning of this provision may not be immediately clear but the principle is relatively straightforward. For example, the defendant may suspect that their 'undesirable' conduct may be revealed anyway and so decide to raise the matter themselves, in the hope of appearing slightly more honest to the jury. Alternatively, the accused may decide to disclose their previous convictions to demonstrate their propensity to commit one sort of crime rather than another.

**KEY CASE**

*R* v *Speed* [2013] EWCA Crim 1650 (CA)

*Concerning: s. 101(1)(b)*

**Facts**

The accused was charged with indecently exposing himself to small children. He had no previous convictions for offences of indecency but had convictions for robbery and drugs offences.

**Legal principle**

Sir Bernard Rix: 'It was in his interests for the jury to be made aware that he had no previous convictions for sexual offending, but to achieve that end he would have to disclose his significant past criminal history.' That disclosure was therefore adduced pursuant to section 101(1)(b) of the 2003 Act.

## Section 101(1)(c) – it is important explanatory evidence

This is defined as follows:

**KEY STATUTE**

**Criminal Justice Act 2003, s. 102**

**Important explanatory evidence**

For the purposes of section 101(1)(c) evidence is important explanatory evidence if –

(a) without it, the court or jury would find it impossible or difficult properly to understand other evidence in the case, and

(b) its value for understanding the case as a whole is substantial.

**KEY CASE**

*R* v *Edwards* [2005] EWCA Crim 1813 (CA)

*Concerning: s. 101(1)(c)*

**Facts**

D was charged with robbery. A witness identified him as the attacker and claimed to recognise him as she had bought heroin from him for some months before the alleged attack.

**Legal principle**

It was held that it was necessary to allow evidence of the circumstances of the previous meetings. Rose LJ: 'Only if that was done . . . would it be possible for her sensibly to explain . . . the basis of her ability to identify him in the circumstances which she did.'

Note also the following decision on the same point but before the implementation of section 101(1)(c).

**KEY CASE**

*R* v *Phillips* [2003] 2 Cr App R 528 (CA)

*Concerning: s. 101(1)(c)*

**Facts**

P was charged with the murder of his wife in their house. His defence was that the crime had been committed by an intruder.

> **Legal principle**
>
> It was held that evidence of their stormy relationship was admissible. Dyson LJ: 'The evidence was part of the continuing background of the relationship and without the totality of the evidence before the jury the evidence would have been incomprehensible.'

**KEY CASE**

*R* v *MP* [2015] EWCA Crim 924 (CA)

*Concerning: s. 101(1)(c)*

**Facts**

The appellant was convicted of four counts of rape committed against his sister when she was a teenager. The alleged offences took place in the 1970s but a formal complaint was not made to police until 2013. The complainant testified that, although she had not consented to the intercourse, she had not resisted at the time because she feared that her brother would become violent. At trial, the judge refused a prosecution application to allow evidence of previous convictions for sexual offences (as evidence of propensity) but did allow evidence of previous convictions for violent offences under s 101(1)(c) to support the complainant's explanation for not resisting for fear of violence.

**Legal principle**

It was held that the judge had been justified in admitting evidence of the previous convictions. Pitchford LJ: 'What the convictions did, in our view, was to provide specific relevant background to the assertion . . . that he was indeed a frightening man, in particular, to women. In our judgment, the judge was not arguably wrong to admit the bad character evidence in order to explain this background that had taken place so many years before.'

## Section 101(1)(d) – it is relevant to an important matter in issue between the defendant and the prosecution

**KEY STATUTE**

**Criminal Justice Act 2003, s. 103**

**Matter in issue between the defendant and the prosecution**

(1)  For the purposes of section 101(1)(d) the matters in issue between the defendant and the prosecution include –    ▶

(a) the question whether the defendant has a propensity to commit offences of the kind with which he is charged, except where his having such a propensity makes it no more likely that he is guilty of the offence;

(b) the question whether the defendant has a propensity to be untruthful, except where it is not suggested that the defendant's case is untruthful in any respect.

(2) Where subsection (1)(a) applies, a defendant's propensity to commit offences of the kind with which he is charged may (without prejudice to any other way of doing so) be established by evidence that he has been convicted of –

(a) an offence of the same description as the one with which he is charged, or

(b) an offence of the same category as the one with which he is charged.

(3) Subsection (2) does not apply in the case of a particular defendant if the court is satisfied, by reason of the length of time since the conviction or for any other reason, that it would be unjust for it to apply in his case.

As you can see, this gateway addresses both issues of propensity and credibility (expressed in terms of a 'propensity to be untruthful') under a simple test of relevance. In this way, such evidence may be admitted if relevant to any of the substantive 'matters in issue' between prosecution and defence. This clearly has the potential to be an extremely wide category and so may well allow the prosecution to succeed in presenting character evidence which would have been ruled inadmissible under the old common law provisions.

## Propensity

**KEY CASE**

*R* v *Chopra* [2007] 1 Cr App R 225 (CA)

*Concerning: character evidence (propensity) and CJA 2003, s. 101(1)(d)*

**Facts**

C (a dentist) was charged with the indecent assault of three female patients, the first of whom alleged an assault ten years previously, the second, one year ago and the third, recently. At trial, the evidence of each of the complainants was allowed in support of the others (as evidence of propensity) and C was convicted. On appeal, he challenged the admissibility of the evidence.

**Legal principle**

It was held that, whereas previously, evidence of the defendant's propensity to offend in the manner now charged was prima facie inadmissible, following the 2003 Act it is prima facie admissible. As such, the evidence of the complainants was admissible under section 101(1)(d). Hughes LJ: 'There must in each case be an examination of whether the evidence really does tend to establish the relevant propensity. There will have to be sufficient similarity to make it more likely that each allegation is true.'

**KEY CASE**

*R v Hanson* [2005] 2 Cr App R 299 (CA)

*Concerning: character evidence (propensity) and CJA 2003, s. 103*

Facts

H was one of three applicants whose convictions had been based on character evidence. In considering the appeals, the court was required to set out the requirements for evidence of propensity under section 103.

Legal principle

It was held that, where the Crown sought to adduce evidence of a defendant's bad character, in the form of previous convictions, to establish his propensity to commit offences of the kind with which he was charged, there were three questions to be considered:

■ Did the history of his convictions establish a propensity to commit offences of the kind charged?

■ Did that propensity make it more likely that the defendant had committed the offence charged?

■ Was it unjust to rely on the convictions of the same description or category; and, in any event, would the proceedings be unfair if they were admitted?

Rose LJ: 'Evidence of bad character cannot be used simply to bolster a weak case, or to prejudice the minds of a jury against a defendant.'

**KEY CASE**

*R v Brima* [2007] 1 Cr App R 316 (CA)

*Concerning: character evidence (propensity) and CJA 2003, s. 101(1)(d)*

Facts

B was charged with murder by stabbing. At trial, evidence was adduced of his previous convictions which included a stabbing and a robbery where he had held a knife to the throat of the victim. On appeal, B challenged the admissibility of the evidence. ▶

**Legal principle**

It was held that the trial judge had correctly concluded that the bad character evidence in question had the potential to establish propensity on the part of the defendant to commit this sort of offence.

---

**KEY CASE**

*R* v *Conway (Patrick Peter)* [2015] EWCA Crim 1063 (CA)

*Concerning: character evidence (propensity) and CJA 2003, s. 101(1)(d)*

**Facts**

The appellant was convicted of the manslaughter of his friend whom he had struck during a drunken night out. The defence argued that the fatal blow was struck in self-defence. The trial judge allowed the prosecution to present footage taken some two years previously of the appellant fighting on the underground, losing his temper and striking another of his friends. This was adduced under s 101(1)(d) as evidence of behaviour which demonstrated the propensity of the appellant to commit assaults, including towards his friends, when intoxicated. The defence challenged the decision to admit this evidence.

**Legal principle**

The appeal would be dismissed. Sharp LJ: 'The admission of this evidence was carefully considered by the judge . . . and his decision to admit was neither wrong nor unreasonable.'

## Credibility/'propensity to be untruthful'

This is a little more difficult as, in most cases, the fact that the defendant is 'untruthful' will be a matter in issue between prosecution and defence. This might suggest that character evidence will almost always be admissible under section 103(1)(b), but this is not the case. In *R* v *Hanson* (above) Rose LJ stated:

> As to propensity to untruthfulness, this . . . is not the same as propensity to dishonesty . . . Parliament deliberately chose the word 'untruthful' to convey a different meaning, reflecting a defendant's account of his behaviour, or lies told when committing an offence. Previous convictions, whether for offences of dishonesty or otherwise, are therefore only likely to be capable of showing a propensity to be untruthful where, in the present case, truthfulness is an issue and, in the earlier case, either there was a plea of not guilty and the defendant gave an account, on arrest, in interview, or in evidence, which the jury must have disbelieved, or the way in which the offence was committed shows a propensity for untruthfulness, for example, by the making of false representations.

**KEY CASE**

*R v Campbell* [2007] EWCA Crim 1472 (CA)

*Concerning: character evidence (propensity to be untruthful) and CJA 2003, s. 101(1)(d)*

**Facts**

C was convicted of false imprisonment and actual bodily harm. At trial, evidence was adduced of his violent conduct towards two previous partners.

**Legal principle**

Lord Philips CJ: 'The question of whether a Defendant has a propensity for being untruthful will not normally be capable of being described as an important matter in issue between the Defendant and the prosecution. A propensity for untruthfulness will not, of itself, go very far to establishing the committal of criminal offence . . . the only circumstance in which there is likely to be an important issue as to whether a Defendant has a propensity to tell lies is where telling lies is an element of the offence charged.'

In this way it would appear that this section will be restricted to convictions for offences such as perjury or deception.

**✎ EXAM TIP**

It should be noted that sections 103(1)(a) and 103(2)(a) come close to the old common law doctrine of 'similar fact' evidence by allowing evidence of previous convictions to be admitted as evidence of propensity. This has allowed details of previous convictions (which were traditionally kept from a jury) to be more readily admitted in evidence.

## Section 101(1)(e) – it has substantial probative value in relation to an important matter in issue between the defendant and a co-defendant

As you can see, there are similarities between this gateway and that under section 101(1)(d) but here the issue is not between the defendant and the prosecution, but rather between the defendant and a co-defendant. As with section 101(1)(d), this allows for evidence of both propensity and credibility but note that such evidence must be of 'substantial probative value', rather than merely 'relevant' as required for section 101(1)(d). Note also that this gateway cannot be relied upon by the prosecution – only by a co-defendant and, even then, only when the evidence in question has 'substantial probative value in relation to an important matter in issue' between them.

The most obvious example of where the accused might wish to adduce evidence of the bad character of their co-defendant is in the case of a 'cut-throat defence' (where each denies responsibility and blames the other).

## KEY CASE

### R v *Musone* [2007] EWCA Crim 1237 (CA)

*Concerning: character evidence and CJA 2003, s. 101(1)(e)*

**Facts**

M (together with a co-defendant) was accused of murdering another inmate in their prison cell. At trial M sought to adduce evidence of an earlier murder committed by the co-defendant in order to suggest that the other was more likely to have committed the offence with which they were both charged.

**Legal principle**

It was held that the evidence was admissible and that admissibility under section 101(1)(e) depends solely on the court's assessment of the quality of the evidence. Moses LJ: 'Once evidence of a defendant's bad character is admissible under section 101(1)(e) the section confers no express power on a court to exclude such evidence on grounds of unfairness.'

## KEY CASE

### R v *Johnson* [2007] EWCA Crim 1651 (CA)

*Concerning: character evidence and CJA 2003, s. 101(1)(e)*

**Facts**

J and a co-defendant were accused of importing cocaine. Each blamed the other and, as part of this defence, evidence of a single earlier drugs conviction against one of the defendants was adduced by the other.

**Legal principle**

It was held that the evidence was admissible. Pill LJ: 'The evidence had substantial probative value in relation to an important matter in issue between the Defendants.'

## KEY CASE

### R v *Hesse and another* [2015] EWCA Crim 884 (CA)

*Concerning: character evidence and CJA 2003, s. 101(1)(e)*

**Facts**

Two men, Hesse and Lewis, were convicted of a drug-related murder, the victim being stabbed to death. At trial, both of the accused denied any responsibility for the death, each blaming the other for the stabbing. These contradictory accounts raised issues of credibility between the men and the question of which of the two, on the basis of the conflicting defences advanced, was more likely to have committed the offence. At trial, the judge allowed Lewis to admit evidence of a number of violent attacks which Hesse had committed on former girlfriends. The judge admitted the evidence under section 101(1)(e) on the basis that it demonstrated that Hesse had a tendency to 'fly off the handle' and that this was relevant to the issue of whether it was he rather than Lewis who had stabbed the deceased to death. Hesse appealed against conviction.

**Legal principle**

The appeal would be dismissed. Treacy LJ: 'The language used in [the trial judge's] ruling shows he was satisfied that matters went beyond a mere propensity and that they had an enhanced capability of proving a matter in issue between the two appellants.'

## Section 101(1)(f) – it is evidence to correct a false impression given by the defendant

This gateway represents the modern incarnation of the old common law principle that, where a defendant presents themselves as of 'good character', the prosecution is entitled to adduce evidence to challenge this impression.

CJA 2003 articulates this principle in the following terms:

**KEY STATUTE**

**Criminal Justice Act 2003, s. 105**

Evidence to correct a false impression

(1) For the purposes of section 101(1)(f) –

   (a) the defendant gives a false impression if he is responsible for the making of an express or implied assertion which is apt to give the court or jury a false or misleading impression about the defendant;

   (b) evidence to correct such an impression is evidence which has probative value in correcting it.

Note that section 105 covers both 'express or implied' assertions and so addresses situations where the defendant does not actually state that they are of good character but, instead, adduces some other evidence which gives that impression.

---

**KEY CASE**

*R* v *Sutton* [2007] EWCA Crim 1387 (CA)

*Concerning: character evidence and CJA 2003, s. 101(1)(f)*

**Facts**

S was charged with sexual offences against a seven-year-old girl. His defence was that any touching had been entirely innocent and that he had no sexual interest in children. As a result, the prosecution was permitted to adduce evidence in the form of a statement from a former girlfriend that S had previously formed inappropriate relationships with children which could be construed as grooming, and that he had had thousands of indecent computer images of children.

**Legal principle**

It was held that, although the judge's direction in relation to the evidence had not been entirely consistent, the evidence was admissible. Latham LJ: 'although the direction was not complete . . . it properly identified for the jury the purpose of the evidence and pointed the jury in the right direction.'

---

**KEY CASE**

*R* v *Garrett* [2015] EWCA Crim 757 (CA)

*Concerning: character evidence and CJA 2003, s. 101(1)(f)*

**Facts**

The appellant was convicted of possessing criminal property contrary to section 329(1)(c) of the Proceeds of Crime Act 2002 following the defrauding of an elderly doctor into transferring large sums of money into an account held by the appellant. He had a number of previous juvenile convictions, but also more recent convictions for violence, taking vehicles without consent and theft, although the prosecution made no application to admit evidence of these at trial. When giving evidence, however, the appellant testified that he had been 'in trouble' as a child but that, after leaving the army, he had led a responsible life. During cross-examination he also stated that he had been in a few cases with the police 'where I've been a victim and they have not helped me'. This, the prosecution argued, created a misleading impression and so justified adducing evidence of the adult convictions under s 101(1)(f). The trial judge agreed.

> **Legal principle**
>
> The appeal would be dismissed. Davis LJ: 'the initial answers given by the applicant were apt to convey the impression that in effect the applicant had been a bit of a tearaway in terms of violence whilst a minor . . . but thereafter he had in effect led a responsible life. Furthermore, the impression was also given that he had in the past been a victim of crime and stitched up by the police, which again did not sit at all well with the actuality of the totality of his antecedent history.'

It should be noted that a simple denial of the charge is not sufficient to justify the admission of character evidence under section 101(1)(f) and that it is not necessary for the defendant to give evidence on their own behalf. The 'misleading impression' can equally be conveyed by counsel on the defendant's behalf. Also, the evidence presented by the prosecution must go no further than is necessary to correct the impression presented by the defendant. In this way, if the accused asserts that he is a peaceful person, evidence of his previous convictions for violent offences may be admitted but evidence of, for example, a driving offence would not.

## Section 101(1)(g) – the defendant has made an attack on another person's character

This final gateway addresses the situation where the defendant attacks the character of another person. This is defined by section 106.

**KEY STATUTE**

**Criminal Justice Act 2003, s. 106**

Attack on another person's character

(1) For the purposes of section 101(1)(g) a defendant makes an attack on another person's character if –

    (a) he adduces evidence attacking the other person's character,

    (b) he (or any legal representative appointed under section 38(4) of the Youth Justice and Criminal Evidence Act 1999 (c 23) to cross-examine a witness in his interests) asks questions in cross-examination that are intended to elicit such evidence, or are likely to do so, or

    (c) evidence is given of an imputation about the other person made by the defendant –

        (i) on being questioned under caution, before charge, about the offence with which he is charged, or

        (ii) on being charged with the offence or officially informed that he might be prosecuted for it.

(2) In subsection (1) 'evidence attacking the other person's character' means evidence to the effect that the other person –

    (a) has committed an offence (whether a different offence from the one with which the defendant is charged or the same one), or

    (b) has behaved, or is disposed to behave, in a reprehensible way; and 'imputation about the other person' means an assertion to that effect.

(3) Only prosecution evidence is admissible under section 101(1)(g).

It is clear that there is a thin line between a defendant who strongly denies the charge and one who alleges some wrongdoing on the part of others (e.g. the police). It should be noted that, unlike section 105, there is no mention of implied assertions in section 106 but that still does not mean that a defendant might not fall foul of the section by presenting evidence which suggests misconduct on the part of others.

The gateway may also be opened even when the attack on the character of another person is an essential element of the defence case.

## KEY CASE

**R v *Singh (James Paul)* [2007] EWCA Crim 2140 (CA)**

*Concerning: character evidence and CJA 2003, s. 101(1)(g)*

### Facts

S was accused of robbery. As part of his defence, he asserted that he and the complainant had smoked crack cocaine together before the alleged attack. It was held that the evidence of the crack smoking constituted an attack on the character of the complainant and so left the defendant open to his own previous convictions being presented in evidence.

### Legal principle

It was held that the trial judge had been correct in admitting the evidence. Hughes LJ: 'It seems to us that the Recorder in this instance sufficiently in common sense terms demonstrated to the jury the reason why the character of the defendant was in issue and the purpose for which it could be used.'

Note that there is a discretionary power to exclude such evidence.

KEY STATUTE

**Criminal Justice Act 2003, s. 101(3)**

The court must not admit evidence under subsection (1)(d) or (g) if, on an application by the defendant to exclude it, it appears to the court that the admission of the evidence would have such an adverse effect on the fairness of the proceedings that the court ought not to admit it.

 Make your answer stand out

For a more recent discussion of the possible consequences of an application under section 101(1)(f) see *R* v *Butler* [2015] EWCA Crim 854.

# Putting it all together

## Answer guidelines

See the essay question at the start of the chapter.

### Approaching the question

As with other legal essays, the key to this question is to provide both the factual overview of the key provisions and also a degree of analysis or evaluation. This second element is crucial if you wish to obtain the highest mark possible. In this regard, always make sure to fully exploit the opportunity provided by your conclusion, which should be a substantial paragraph!

### Important points to include

■ Begin by outlining what is meant by 'good' character evidence and 'bad' character evidence, highlighting the problems with both (i.e. in the case of 'good' character evidence that testimony of an isolated good deed does not mean that the accused is not guilty and with 'bad' character evidence that this may prejudice the jury against the accused on the basis of past misdeeds rather than the current evidence).

▶

- Emphasise the distinction between the rules governing the presentation of evidence of the character of the accused and that of witnesses generally.
- Identify the statutory framework of 'gateways' under the Criminal Justice Act 2003.
- Outline each of the gateways as discussed in this chapter.
- Emphasise the considerable scope for overlap between many of the gateways.
- Conclude that the imposition of a statutory framework produces a degree of clarity but that there is still ample scope for the accused to be challenged on their previous convictions.

 Make your answer stand out

- Mention the replacement of the previous common law rules on 'similar fact' evidence by the CJA 2003 provisions.
- Indicate that the 2003 Act made similar changes to the law relating to hearsay evidence (discussed in the next chapter).

## READ TO IMPRESS

Crinion, C. (2010) Adducing the good character of prosecution witnesses. *Crim LR*, 570.

Durston, G. (2004a) Bad character evidence and non-party witnesses under the Criminal Justice Act 2003, *EvPro*, 8(4): 233.

Durston, G. (2004b) Comment: impact of the Criminal Justice Act 2003 on similar fact evidence. 68 *JoCL* 307.

Forster, S. (2006) Revealing background evidence to the jury: a question of a need to know? *JPN*, 170: 484.

Fortson, R. and Ormerod, D. (2009) Bad character evidence and cross-admissibility. *Crim LR*, 313.

Mirfield, P. (2009) Character and credibility *Crim LR*, 3: 135–51.

Mullarkey, I. (2006) Putting it to them: adducing evidence of non-defendant's bad character under the Criminal Justice Act 2003, *JPN*, 170: 729.

Munday, R. (2006) Case management, similar fact evidence in civil cases, and a divided law of evidence, *EvPro* 81: 102.

Plowden, P. (2005) Making sense of character evidence. *NLJ*, 155: 47.

Redmayne, M. (2011) Recognising propensity. *Crim LR*, 177.

Tandy, R. (2009) The admissibility of a defendant's previous criminal record: a critical analysis of the Criminal Justice Act 2003. *Statute Law Review*, 30: 203.

**www.pearsoned.co.uk/lawexpress**

Go online to access more revision support including quizzes to test your knowledge, sample questions with answer guidelines, podcasts you can download, and more!

# Hearsay

**4**

## Revision checklist

### Essential points you should know:

- [ ] What is meant by 'hearsay evidence'
- [ ] The historical prohibition on such evidence under the common law
- [ ] The statutory regime for the admission of hearsay evidence under the Criminal Justice Act 2003
- [ ] The remaining common law rules preserved by the 2003 Act

# ■ Topic map

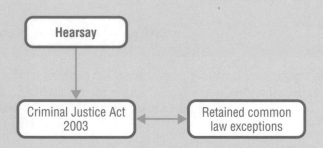

# ■ Introduction

## We have all heard of hearsay evidence, but what does it mean?

The term 'hearsay' is frequently heard but less frequently understood – particularly by students of the law of evidence! Perhaps more than any other topic, hearsay causes confusion and anxiety and this is made worse by the fact that it remains one of the most popular topics for examination questions. The good news, however, is that hearsay is not as difficult as you might think and, as with the rules on character evidence covered earlier **(see Chapter 3)**, the Criminal Justice Act 2003 has done much to simplify the situation. As long as you adopt a methodical approach to revising the topic it should present few problems and it is possible to achieve high marks in examination.

## ASSESSMENT ADVICE

### Essay questions

Questions on hearsay are likely to resemble those on character evidence, requiring you to consider the historical common law rules and the changes made by CJA 2003. Remember that a good answer will not just list the provisions but will also address the analytical component of the question by offering some evaluation of the concept and the regulatory framework.

### Problem questions

These are very common and usually consist of a number of examples of evidence which may or may not be hearsay and which raise different provisions of the 2003 Act. Such questions require a thorough understanding of the provisions, as the inability to answer *all* parts of the question will drastically reduce the mark awarded.

## □□ REVISION NOTE

As both character evidence and hearsay evidence are now governed by the Criminal Justice Act 2003 and in a largely similar manner, it is useful to revise these topics together; the ability to make reference to this similarity in an examination question will earn extra marks for analysis.

# Sample question

Could you answer this question? Below is a typical problem question that could arise on this topic. Guidelines on answering the question are included at the end of this chapter, whilst a sample essay question and guidance on tackling it can be found on the companion website.

---

**PROBLEM QUESTION**

Simon and John are drinking in town one night when they witness an incident outside a city centre bar. Alan is attacked by Dan, a well-known local criminal, who stabs him in the chest and runs off before the police arrive. When PC Bright reaches the scene, he administers first aid to Alan who tells him, 'It were that Dan what did it.' Alan then slips into unconsciousness and dies in the ambulance on the way to hospital.

The next morning, both Simon and John give statements to the police identifying Dan as the attacker. Six weeks later John is killed in a car accident.

It is many months before the case comes to trial but finally Simon is informed that he is due to give evidence on Friday. On Monday he receives a telephone call. He does not recognise the voice but hears, 'Stay at home on Friday or else.' He is very frightened by this and refuses to attend court, believing that his life will be in danger if he gives evidence.

Discuss.

---

# What is 'hearsay'?

**KEY DEFINITION: Hearsay**

A statement originally made out of court, repeated in court for the purpose of proving the truth of the statement.

---

**KEY STATUTE**

**Civil Evidence Act 1995, s. 1**

**Admissibility of hearsay evidence**

(1)  In civil proceedings evidence shall not be excluded on the ground that it is hearsay.

(2) In this Act –

    (a) 'hearsay' means a statement made otherwise than by a person while giving oral evidence in the proceedings which is tendered as evidence of the matters stated.

In criminal cases the Criminal Justice Act 2003 provides a broad definition of the term 'statement'.

### KEY STATUTE

**Criminal Justice Act 2003, s. 115(2)**

A statement is any representation of fact or opinion made by a person by whatever means; and it includes a representation made in a sketch, photofit or other pictorial form.

### KEY CASE

*R* v *Sharp* [1988] 1 All ER 65 (HL)

*Concerning: definition of hearsay evidence*

**Facts**

The facts of this case are lengthy and complicated and to summarise them here would add little to an understanding of the legal principle outlined below. Remember that examiners are usually looking for an understanding of the ratio and legal principle and that reciting the facts in an exam will not improve your grade.

**Legal principle**

Lord Havers: 'I accept the definition of the hearsay rule [as] "an assertion other than one made by a person while giving oral evidence in the proceedings is inadmissible" as evidence of any fact asserted.'

In this way, the key elements of hearsay evidence are:

- a statement originally made by a person not in the court which is repeated in court;
- for the purpose of proving that the statement is true.

Traditionally, hearsay evidence has been held to be inadmissible. This situation, however, has been subject to radical change in both the civil and the criminal courts.

It is important to realise that *both* key elements must be present for the evidence to be considered as hearsay (thereby raising the possibility that it will be excluded). The first element, that the statement was originally made by a person not in the court and is later repeated in court, does not generally cause too much difficulty, although it is important to remember that this can also take the form of a written document (e.g. the piece of paper on which a person has noted the registration number of a car). By contrast, the second element, that the statement is adduced for the purpose of proving that the statement is true, often causes considerable difficulty.

In order to understand what is meant by 'adduced for the purpose of proving that the statement is true', consider the following cases.

**KEY CASE**

*Sparks* v *R* [1964] AC 964 (PC)

*Concerning: definition of hearsay evidence*

Facts

S was charged with the indecent assault of a four-year-old girl. As part of his defence, he wished to adduce a statement given to police by the girl's mother, recounting a conversation with her daughter, during which the girl had described her attacker as 'a coloured boy' (S was white).

Legal principle

It was held that the statement was inadmissible as hearsay evidence. The purpose of adducing the statement in evidence was to prove that it was true (i.e. that the attacker was not white).

**KEY CASE**

*Subramaniam* v *Public Prosecutor* [1956] 1 WLR 965 (PC)

*Concerning: definition of hearsay evidence*

Facts

S was arrested in possession of ammunition in Malaya and sentenced to death. He argued that he had been acting under duress, having been threatened by terrorists that he would be killed if he did not assist them. He sought to adduce evidence of the threats but this was ruled inadmissible as hearsay.

> **Legal principle**
>
> On appeal, evidence of the threats was allowed. It was not hearsay as the purpose of adducing the statement was not to prove that it was true but, rather, that it had been made and that it had caused S to act out of fear. De Silva: 'It is not hearsay and is admissible when it is proposed to establish by the evidence, not the truth of the statement, but the fact that it was made.'

The contrast between the two cases is clear. In *Sparks,* the whole purpose of adducing the statement was to say that what the girl had said was true (i.e. that the attacker was not white) whereas, in *Subramaniam,* the important point was not whether the threats to kill were actually true (how could anyone know whether they would have been carried out) but, instead, whether the statement had been made because this supported the defence that S had acted under duress.

In this way, the question of whether a particular statement constitutes hearsay evidence often turns on the purpose for which it is adduced.

**!  Don't be tempted to . . .**

This is the most difficult aspect of hearsay and the one which requires the greatest care. In considering any statement which may be considered hearsay, always think carefully about precisely *why* the statement is being adduced and don't make the mistake of declaring a statement hearsay simply because it was originally made out of court.

**KEY CASE**

*Ratten* v *R* [1972] AC 378 (PC)

*Concerning: definition of hearsay evidence*

Facts

R was accused of murdering his wife by shooting her in the kitchen of their home. His defence was that the weapon had discharged accidentally whilst being cleaned. The prosecution wished to adduce evidence of a 999 call made from the house shortly before the shooting where the deceased had been hysterical and said, 'Get me the police please'. This was challenged as hearsay evidence by the defence.  ▶

**Legal principle**

It was held that the statement was not hearsay as the purpose of adducing it into evidence was not to prove that it was true but rather to indicate events which undermined the defendant's account of a tragic accident. Lord Wilberforce: 'Even on the assumption that there was an element of hearsay in the words used, they were safely admitted.'

## Justification for the rule against hearsay

The reasons why such evidence has traditionally been excluded include:

- the original statement was not made on oath and so the party had no appreciation that they were required to tell the truth;
- because the statement was originally made by someone other than the witness, they cannot be cross-examined on the content and meaning of the statement;
- the original content, tone or emphasis of the statement may become distorted or exaggerated in the retelling, thereby conveying a misleading impression;
- it would be relatively easy to make up a statement, supposedly made by another person, and present it as evidence.

## Hearsay and implied assertions

An additional factor in considering hearsay cases is the overlap between hearsay and what have been termed 'implied assertions'.

**KEY CASE**

*R* v *Kearley* [1992] 2 AC 228 (HL)

*Concerning: definition of hearsay evidence*

**Facts**

Whilst conducting a search of K's house on suspicion of possession with intent to supply drugs, police received a number of calls to the house by people asking to buy drugs. The prosecution sought to adduce evidence from the officers involved to suggest that K was, in fact, dealing from the house. The defence objected on the basis that such statements were hearsay.

> **Legal principle**
>
> It was held that such statements were implied assertions as they merely indicated the state of mind or belief of those calling at the house. As such, the statements were irrelevant to the prosecution case. Lord Griffiths: 'The sole possible relevance of the words spoken is that by manifesting the speaker's belief that the defendant is a supplier they impliedly assert that fact.'

## Hearsay in civil cases

As stated above, section 1 of the Civil Evidence Act 1995 states that, 'in civil proceedings evidence shall not be excluded on the ground that it is hearsay'. As a result, there is no rule against the presentation of hearsay evidence in civil cases. This can largely be justified on the grounds that such cases are decided by a judge who is more than capable of assessing the weight to be attached to such evidence. It should be noted, however, that a party wishing to adduce hearsay evidence must give notice of this fact to the other party.

## Hearsay in criminal cases

The position in criminal cases is somewhat more complex, mainly due to the presence of the jury who, unlike a judge, may be swayed by potentially unreliable hearsay evidence. Traditionally this has meant that such evidence was inadmissible in criminal cases, but there has been a considerable relaxation of this principle with the implementation of the Criminal Justice Act 2003. As with character evidence **(discussed in Chapter 3)** the Act achieves this by means of a number of statutory exceptions to the general rule against hearsay evidence.

---

**📖 REVISION NOTE**

Note that, even where hearsay evidence is adduced under the provisions of CJA 2003, the court retains the power to exclude such evidence under section 78 PACE **(which is discussed in Chapter 8).**

---

**KEY STATUTE**

**Criminal Justice Act 2003, s. 114**

**Admissibility of hearsay evidence**

(1)  In criminal proceedings a statement not made in oral evidence in the proceedings is admissible as evidence of any matter stated if, but only if – ▶

> (a) any provision of this Chapter or any other statutory provision makes it admissible,
> (b) any rule of law preserved by section 118 makes it admissible,
> (c) all parties to the proceedings agree to it being admissible, or
> (d) the court is satisfied that it is in the interests of justice for it to be admissible.

Of these grounds, section 114(1)(c) is the most straightforward – that the parties have agreed to the statement being admitted in evidence. This arises where a witness statement is presented in evidence under the Criminal Justice Act 1967, section 9.

## KEY STATUTE

### Criminal Justice Act 1967, s. 9

**Proof by written statement**

(1) In any criminal proceedings, *other than committal proceedings,* a written statement by any person shall, if such of the conditions mentioned in the next following subsection as are applicable are satisfied, be admissible as evidence to the like extent as oral evidence to the like effect by that person.

(2) The said conditions are –

    (a) the statement purports to be signed by the person who made it;

    (b) the statement contains a declaration by that person to the effect that it is true to the best of his knowledge and belief and that he made the statement knowing that, if it were tendered in evidence, he would be liable to prosecution if he wilfully stated in it anything which he knew to be false or did not believe to be true;

    (c) before the hearing at which the statement is tendered in evidence, a copy of the statement is served, by or on behalf of the party proposing to tender it, on each of the other parties to the proceedings; and

    (d) none of the other parties or their solicitors, within seven days from the service of the copy of the statement, serves a notice on the party so proposing objecting to the statement being tendered in evidence under this section.

## ! Don't be tempted to . . .

Don't assume that the grounds under section 114(1) CJA 2003 are mutually exclusive. For example, a statement mutually agreed by the parties under section 9 CJA 1967 also satisfies both section 114(1)(a) and section 114(1)(c).

# Section 114(1)(a) – any provision of this Chapter or any other statutory provision makes it admissible

The main exceptions under this provision are to be found in section 116 and section 117.

---

**KEY STATUTE**

**Criminal Justice Act 2003, s. 116**

Cases where a witness is unavailable

(1) In criminal proceedings a statement not made in oral evidence in the proceedings is admissible as evidence of any matter stated if –

    (a) oral evidence given in the proceedings by the person who made the statement would be admissible as evidence of that matter,

    (b) the person who made the statement (the relevant person) is identified to the court's satisfaction, and

    (c) any of the five conditions mentioned in subsection (2) is satisfied.

(2) The conditions are –

    (a) that the relevant person is dead;

    (b) that the relevant person is unfit to be a witness because of his bodily or mental condition;

    (c) that the relevant person is outside the United Kingdom and it is not reasonably practicable to secure his attendance;

    (d) that the relevant person cannot be found although such steps as it is reasonably practicable to take to find him have been taken;

    (e) that through fear the relevant person does not give (or does not continue to give) oral evidence in the proceedings, either at all or in connection with the subject matter of the statement, and the court gives leave for the statement to be given in evidence.

---

In relation to the criteria imposed by section 116(2) some, such as where the person is dead or unfit to be a witness, present little difficulty. Under subsections (c) and (d), however, the question of what is 'reasonably practicable' will largely turn on the facts of the individual case.

---

**KEY CASE**

*R v Castillo and others* [1996] 1 Cr App R 438

*Concerning: definition of 'reasonably practicable' under CJA 2003, s. 116(2)*

**Facts**

In a trial for drugs offences the prosecution sought to adduce a written statement from a witness in Venezuela on the grounds that it was not reasonably practicable for him to attend. The prosecution also sought to adduce a statement from a Venezuelan police officer confirming that the witness was unable to attend.

**Legal principle**

It was held that the court had to consider a number of factors in admitting such statements, including the importance of the witness's evidence and how prejudicial it was to the defendant if the witness did not attend, the reasons for non-attendance and the expense and inconvenience of bringing the witness to court. Stuart Smith LJ: 'It must be construed in the light of the normal steps which would be taken to arrange the attendance of a witness at trial . . . having regard to the means and resources available to the parties.'

---

**KEY CASE**

*R v Marshall (Stewart)* [2014] EWCA Crim 2957 (CA)

*Concerning: definition of 'that the relevant person is unfit to be a witness because of his bodily or mental condition' under CJA 2003, s. 116(2)(b)*

**Facts**

The appellant was convicted of conspiracy to burgle and of an associated count of money laundering. The prosecution alleged that, with others, the appellant had targeted a number of elderly and vulnerable people offering building work which was often unnecessary and overpriced. They had also used access to the victims' properties to steal valuables such as jewellery. Many of the victims were over 80 and some over 90. Due to their age and various medical ailments, including dementia, the trial judge allowed an application under section 116(2)(b) to admit statements each of them had made to family members and police officers about the incidents in question. The defence appealed against conviction.

**Legal principle**

The Appeal would be dismissed. Sharp LJ: 'this evidence spoke for itself and entitled the judge to draw the conclusion he could be sure to the requisite standard that the statutory grounds for the admission of all this evidence had been met.'

---

Similarly, the grounds on which a witness will be unable to give evidence through fear under section 116(2)(e) are to be broadly defined and cover both a person who refuses to testify at all and one who begins to give evidence but is unable to continue through fear.

**✎ EXAM TIP**

When discussing the provisions of section 116(2) remember to point out that, whereas hearsay evidence is automatically admissible under section 116(2)(a)–(d), leave of the court is required to admit evidence under section 116(2)(e).

**KEY CASE**

*R* v *Martin* [1996] Crim LR 589 (CA)

*Concerning: definition of 'fear' under CJA 2003, s. 116(2)(e)*

**Facts**

In relation to a witness in an arson trial the court was required to consider the grounds on which a statement could be admitted in evidence from a witness in fear.

**Legal principle**

It was held that the grounds on which such a statement could be admitted were sufficiently wide to cover even a witness who was in fear as a result of a mistaken belief in a threat. Schiemann LJ: 'The words are expressed in extremely wide form, and they are designed to combat an evil.'

**KEY CASE**

*R* v *Docherty* [2006] EWCA Crim 2716 (CA)

*Concerning: definition of 'fear' under CJA 2003, s. 116(2)(e)*

**Facts**

In relation to a witness in an assault trial the court was required to consider the grounds on which a statement could be admitted in evidence from a witness in fear.

**Legal principle**

It was held that 'fear' under section 116(2)(e) was to be broadly construed. Tuckey LJ: 'The exercise which the judge was required to perform was a balancing exercise: broadly the risk of unfairness to the defence because the evidence could not be challenged, as against risk of unfairness to the prosecution because it could not put before the jury all the available evidence.'

*R* v *Harvey and others* [2014] EWCA Crim 54 (CA)

*Concerning: definition of 'fear' under CJA 2003, s. 116(2)(e)*

Facts

The appellants were convicted of a number of offences including burglary, firearms offences, witness intimidation and perverting the course of justice. The men appealed against conviction, arguing that the trial judge had erred in admitting into evidence the signed witness statements from two critical prosecution witnesses as hearsay evidence under section 116(2)(e).

Legal principle

The Appeal would be dismissed. Fulford LJ: 'the evidence that the two witnesses were in fear was of significant strength, and there was abundant material on which the judge could conclude that [the accused] were all involved in, or connected with, violent gangs.'

The next category to be considered relates to 'business and other documents'.

**Criminal Justice Act 2003, s. 117**

**Business and other documents**

(1)  In criminal proceedings a statement contained in a document is admissible as evidence of any matter stated if –

   (a)  oral evidence given in the proceedings would be admissible as evidence of that matter,
   (b)  the requirements of subsection (2) are satisfied, and
   (c)  the requirements of subsection (5) are satisfied, in a case where subsection (4) requires them to be.

(2)  The requirements of this subsection are satisfied if –

   (a)  the document or the part containing the statement was created or received by a person in the course of a trade, business, profession or other occupation, or as the holder of a paid or unpaid office,
   (b)  the person who supplied the information contained in the statement (the relevant person) had or may reasonably be supposed to have had personal knowledge of the matters dealt with, and
   (c)  each person (if any) through whom the information was supplied from the relevant person to the person mentioned in paragraph (a) received the information in the course of a trade, business, profession or other occupation, or as the holder of a paid or unpaid office.

Here, the requirements of section 117(2) require particular consideration. First, under section 117(2)(b), the person supplying the information contained in the original statement must have 'had or may reasonably be supposed to have had personal knowledge of the matters dealt with'. Secondly, under section 117(2)(a) the original statement must have been created or received by a person 'in the course of a trade, business, profession or other occupation, or as the holder of a paid or unpaid office' and, furthermore, section 117(2)(c) makes clear that this applies to each person who receives the document in the course of its transmission from the maker of the original document to court.

---

**KEY STATUTE**

**Criminal Justice Act 2003, s. 117**

(4)  The additional requirements of subsection (5) must be satisfied if the statement –

  (a)  was prepared for the purposes of pending or contemplated criminal proceedings, or for a criminal investigation, but

  (b)  was not obtained pursuant to a request under section 7 of the Crime (International Co-operation) Act 2003 (c. 32) or an order under paragraph 6 of Schedule 13 to the Criminal Justice Act 1988 (c. 33) (which relate to overseas evidence).

(5)  The requirements of this subsection are satisfied if –

  (a)  any of the five conditions mentioned in section 116(2) is satisfied (absence of relevant person etc), or

  (b)  the relevant person cannot reasonably be expected to have any recollection of the matters dealt with in the statement (having regard to the length of time since he supplied the information and all other circumstances).

---

This category of statements 'prepared for the purposes of pending or contemplated criminal proceedings, or for a criminal investigation' is wide enough to include witness statements taken by police officers or police station custody records. Here, one of the requirements of section 116(2) must be satisfied and the maker of the original statement cannot reasonably be expected to have recollection of the matters recorded in the statement.

## Section 114(1)(b) – any rule of law preserved by section 118

The effect of CJA 2003 was to abolish the existing common law rules on the admissibility of hearsay evidence, though section 114 provides that some such rules are preserved and these are listed in section 118. These include:

■  published works dealing with matters of a public nature (such as histories, scientific works, dictionaries and maps) which are admissible as evidence of facts of a public nature stated in them;

- public documents (such as public registers, and returns made under public authority with respect to matters of public interest) are admissible as evidence of facts stated in them;
- records (such as the records of certain courts, treaties, Crown grants, pardons and commissions) which are admissible as evidence of facts stated in them;
- evidence relating to a person's age or date or place of birth which may be given by a person without personal knowledge of the matter;
- evidence of a family tradition such as a marriage;
- character evidence;
- confession evidence;
- expert evidence;
- evidence of common enterprise.

## Res gestae

The other major exception preserved by section 118 is the rule known as *res gestae*.

---

**KEY STATUTE**

**Criminal Justice Act 2003, s. 118(1)**

**Res gestae**

(4) Any rule of law under which in criminal proceedings a statement is admissible as evidence of any matter stated if –

    (a) the statement was made by a person so emotionally overpowered by an event that the possibility of concoction or distortion can be disregarded,

    (b) the statement accompanied an act which can be properly evaluated as evidence only if considered in conjunction with the statement, or

    (c) the statement relates to a physical sensation or a mental state (such as intention or emotion).

---

In relation to the first category of statement, by a person 'emotionally overpowered', this rule is often described in terms of 'excited utterances'.

---

**KEY CASE**

*R v Andrews* [1987] AC 281 (HL)

*Concerning: res gestae*

---

**Facts**

A few minutes after being stabbed, whilst receiving first aid from a police officer, the victim named the defendant as his attacker. He died some weeks later and so, at trial, the prosecution was permitted to adduce evidence of the statement. A appealed, arguing that the statement should not have been admitted.

**Legal principle**

It was held that the statement had been properly admitted in evidence. It had been an instinctive and spontaneous response to a startling or dramatic occurrence in which the victim had been deeply involved. Lord Ackner: 'The judge must be satisfied that the circumstances were such that, having regard to the special feature of malice, there was no possibility of any concoction or distortion to the advantage of the maker or the disadvantage of the accused.'

In such cases, the statement must usually be made in the immediate aftermath of the events in question, so as still to dominate the mind of the person making the statement. The greater the time which has passed before the statement is made, the greater the possibility of reflection and concoction.

**KEY CASE**

*Tobi* v *Nicholas* (1988) 86 Cr App R 323 (DC)

*Concerning: res gestae*

**Facts**

Some 20 minutes after a relatively minor traffic accident, one of the parties made a statement identifying the defendant. The prosecution sought to admit the statement under the res gestae exception.

**Legal principle**

It was held that the statement should not be admitted. Twenty minutes was too long. Furthermore, the accident was not such an unusual, startling or dramatic event as to dominate the thoughts of the victim. Glidewell LJ: 'The event in this case was not so unusual or dramatic as in the ordinary way to dominate the thoughts of the victim.'

However, the passage of time should be balanced against the seriousness of the event, and so wholly exceptional circumstances may be held to have dominated the mind of the person making the statement for a longer period.

*R v Carnall* [1995] Crim LR 944 (CA)

*Concerning: res gestae*

Facts

A murder victim identified C as his attacker after crawling for almost an hour to reach assistance. The defence argued that the passage of time prevented the admission of the statement under the res gestae exception.

Legal principle

Lord Taylor CJ: 'It is not necessary that the evidence claimed to be part of the res gestae should have occurred at, or within minutes of, the event which precipitated it. It must be a matter for the trial judge in any given case to look at all the circumstances. The crucial question is whether there is any real possibility of concoction or distortion, or whether the judge feels confident that the maker of the statements was at the time dominated in his thoughts by the event which had occurred so that what he said could be regarded as unaffected by *ex post facto* reasoning or fabrication.'

*Barnaby* v *DPP* [2015] EWHC 232 (Admin) (DC)

*Concerning: res gestae*

Facts

The appellant was convicted of assaulting his girlfriend who made three 999 calls to the emergency services. In the first two calls she stated that she had just been attacked and that the assailant, her boyfriend, was still in the house. In the third call she told the operator again that she had been attacked and that her boyfriend had just left the house. She subsequently refused to make a statement to police and so the prosecution sought to rely on the transcripts of the calls. The defence challenged the admission of the transcripts, arguing that they were not admissible under the *res gestae* provisions of the 2003 Act.

Legal principle

The trial judge had been correct in admitting the transcripts. Fulford LJ: 'this would have been a startling and dramatic event that would have dominated the thoughts of [the complainant] and her utterances would have been instinctive and spontaneous.'

The category of statements which accompany 'an act which can be properly evaluated as evidence only if considered in conjunction with the statement' is illustrated by the following example.

**KEY CASE**

*R* v *McCay* [1991] 1 All ER 232 (CA)

*Concerning: res gestae*

**Facts**

A witness at an identification parade identified 'Number 8' (the defendant) but, at trial, could not remember what number he had said at the parade. The prosecution was permitted to adduce a statement from a police officer supervising the parade who had heard the witness identify 'Number 8'. The defence challenged this statement as inadmissible hearsay.

**Legal principle**

It was held that the statement had been properly admitted in evidence. Russell LJ: 'the contemporary statement accompanied a relevant act and was necessary to explain that relevant act. The statement was not relevant as to the identity of the assailant, but it was relevant as to the identification of the suspect by the witness.'

The final category concerns statements which relate to 'a physical sensation or a mental state' and this recognises that, in many instances, the only way of gaining any indication of a person's intentions is to consider things which they might have said at the time.

**KEY CASE**

*R* v *Moghal* (1977) 65 Cr App R 56 (CA)

*Concerning: res gestae and evidence of state of mind*

**Facts**

M was charged with murder but claimed that the crime had been committed by his mistress, S. There was evidence that S had predicted the man's death and declared her wish to kill him at a family conference some six months before the murder.

**Legal principle**

It was held that the statement could be admitted as evidence of the state of mind of S. Lord Scarman: 'Evidence of her state of mind and feeling at these times was, therefore, admissible.'

### *R* v *Gilfoyle* [1996] 3 All ER 883 (CA)

*Concerning: res gestae and evidence of state of mind*

**Facts**

G was accused of the murder of his wife, who had been found hanged in an apparent suicide. G produced a suicide note written by his wife stating an intention to take her own life. Three friends of the deceased made statements recounting conversations where she had described assisting her husband (an auxiliary nurse) with a project on suicide by writing 'specimen suicide notes'.

**Legal principle**

Beldam LJ: 'Accordingly, we were satisfied that, if we considered it necessary in the interests of justice, the fact that the statements were made could be proved to show that when she wrote the notes [she] was not of a suicidal frame of mind, and that she wrote them in the belief that she was assisting the appellant in a course at work.'

## Section 114(1)(d) – the court is satisfied that it is in the interests of justice for it to be admissible

This provides a residual power of the courts (sometimes described in terms of a 'safety valve') to admit hearsay evidence when it is considered to be 'in the interests of justice' to do so and represents a significant extension of the power to admit such evidence.

In exercising the discretion to admit hearsay evidence under section 114(1)(d) the court is required to consider the following criteria:

### Criminal Justice Act 2003, s. 114

**Admissibility of hearsay evidence**

(1) In deciding whether a statement not made in oral evidence should be admitted under subsection (1)(d), the court must have regard to the following factors (and to any others it considers relevant) –

    (a) how much probative value the statement has (assuming it to be true) in relation to a matter in issue in the proceedings, or how valuable it is for the understanding of other evidence in the case;

    (b) what other evidence has been, or can be, given on the matter or evidence mentioned in paragraph (a);

(c) how important the matter or evidence mentioned in paragraph (a) is in the context of the case as a whole;
(d) the circumstances in which the statement was made;
(e) how reliable the maker of the statement appears to be;
(f) how reliable the evidence of the making of the statement appears to be;
(g) whether oral evidence of the matter stated can be given and, if not, why it cannot;
(h) the amount of difficulty involved in challenging the statement;
(i) the extent to which that difficulty would be likely to prejudice the party facing it.

**KEY CASE**

*R* v *L* **[2008] EWCA Crim 973 (CA)**

*Concerning: the 'interests of justice' under CJA 2003, s. 114(1)(d)*

**Facts**

The appellant was convicted of the rape of his daughter. His wife had provided a statement which undermined his version of events, unaware that she could not be compelled to give evidence against him. When she subsequently refused to give evidence, the prosecution applied to admit her statement under section 114(1)(d).

**Legal principle**

Lord Phillips CJ: 'There is an obvious paradox in excusing the wife from giving evidence, but then placing before the jury in the form of a hearsay statement the very evidence that she does not wish to give . . . but . . . the judge was entitled to rule that the admission of the wife's statement was fair and in the interests of justice.'

## Previous inconsistent statements

The 2003 Act provides that previous inconsistent statements may be admitted in order to discredit their testimony and also as evidence of any matter contained in the statement.

**KEY STATUTE**

**Criminal Justice Act 2003, s. 119**

**Inconsistent statements**

(1) If in criminal proceedings a person gives oral evidence and –

    (a) he admits making a previous inconsistent statement, or

    (b) a previous inconsistent statement made by him is proved by virtue of section 3, 4 or 5 of the Criminal Procedure Act 1865 (c. 18),

(2)  the statement is admissible as evidence of any matter stated of which oral evidence by him would be admissible.

(3)  If in criminal proceedings evidence of an inconsistent statement by any person is given under section 124(2)(c), the statement is admissible as evidence of any matter stated in it of which oral evidence by that person would be admissible.

## Previous consistent statements

The Act also provides for the admission of previous consistent statements.

### KEY STATUTE

**Criminal Justice Act 2003, s. 120**

**Other previous statements of witnesses**

(4)  A previous statement by the witness is admissible as evidence of any matter stated of which oral evidence by him would be admissible, if –

 (a)  any of the following three conditions is satisfied, and

 (b)  while giving evidence the witness indicates that to the best of his belief he made the statement, and that to the best of his belief it states the truth.

(5)  The first condition is that the statement identifies or describes a person, object or place.

(6)  The second condition is that the statement was made by the witness when the matters stated were fresh in his memory but he does not remember them, and cannot reasonably be expected to remember them, well enough to give oral evidence of them in the proceedings.

(7)  The third condition is that –

 (a)  the witness claims to be a person against whom an offence has been committed,

 (b)  the offence is one to which the proceedings relate,

 (c)  the statement consists of a complaint made by the witness (whether to a person in authority or not) about conduct which would, if proved, constitute the offence or part of the offence,

 (d)  the complaint was made as soon as could reasonably be expected after the alleged conduct,

 (e)  the complaint was not made as a result of a threat or a promise, and

 (f)  before the statement is adduced the witness gives oral evidence in connection with its subject matter.

# Multiple hearsay statements

The term 'multiple hearsay' refers to statements which are relayed through more than one person before being repeated in court. For example, instead of A telling B something which B later states in evidence, A tells B who tells C who then tells D before D repeats the statement in court. Although such statements can be adduced in evidence, there is clearly a greater capacity for error which is recognised by the 2003 Act.

**KEY STATUTE**

**Criminal Justice Act 2003, s. 121**

**Additional requirement for admissibility of multiple hearsay**

(1) A hearsay statement is not admissible to prove the fact that an earlier hearsay statement was made unless –

    (a)  either of the statements is admissible under section 117, 119 or 120,

    (b)  all parties to the proceedings so agree, or

    (c)  the court is satisfied that the value of the evidence in question, taking into account how reliable the statements appear to be, is so high that the interests of justice require the later statement to be admissible for that purpose.

## Attacking the credibility of hearsay statements

One of the disadvantages of hearsay evidence is that there is no opportunity for the jury to observe the witness giving their evidence and so assess their credibility.

**KEY STATUTE**

**Criminal Justice Act 2003, s. 124**

**Credibility**

(1) This section applies if in criminal proceedings –

    (a)  a statement not made in oral evidence in the proceedings is admitted as evidence of a matter stated, and

    (b)  the maker of the statement does not give oral evidence in connection with the subject matter of the statement.

(2) In such a case –

    (a)  any evidence which (if he had given such evidence) would have been admissible as relevant to his credibility as a witness is so admissible in the proceedings; ▶

(b) evidence may with the court's leave be given of any matter which (if he had given such evidence) could have been put to him in cross-examination as relevant to his credibility as a witness but of which evidence could not have been adduced by the cross-examining party;
(c) evidence tending to prove that he made (at whatever time) any other statement inconsistent with the statement admitted as evidence is admissible for the purpose of showing that he contradicted himself.

It should also be noted that the Act allows for a case to be halted completely where it is based on unconvincing hearsay evidence.

## KEY STATUTE

**Criminal Justice Act 2003, s. 125**

**Stopping the case where evidence is unconvincing**

(1) If on a defendant's trial before a judge and jury for an offence the court is satisfied at any time after the close of the case for the prosecution that —
  (a) the case against the defendant is based wholly or partly on a statement not made in oral evidence in the proceedings, and
  (b) the evidence provided by the statement is so unconvincing that, considering its importance to the case against the defendant, his conviction of the offence would be unsafe,

(2) the court must either direct the jury to acquit the defendant of the offence or, if it considers that there ought to be a retrial, discharge the jury.

## KEY CASE

*R* v *Ibrahim* [2012] 4 All ER 225 (CA)

*Concerning: CJA 2003 s. 125*

**Facts**

The appellant was convicted of rape. The victim W had made a number of statements to police but had died before the case came to trial. There were serious discrepancies in her account and the defence argued that the statements were so unconvincing that, given their importance to the case, the jury should be directed to acquit.

> **Legal principle**
>
> Aikens LJ: 'If an untested hearsay statement is not shown to be reliable and it is a statement that is part of the central corpus of evidence without which the case on the relevant count cannot proceed, then . . . the statement is almost bound to be "unconvincing" such that a conviction based on it will be unsafe.'

## Hearsay and human rights

It has been recognised that the admission of hearsay evidence may conflict with Article 6 of the European Convention on Human Rights and in particular Article 6(3)(d).

> **KEY STATUTE**
>
> **European Convention on Human Rights, Art. 6(3)**
>
> Everyone charged with a criminal offence has the following minimum rights:
>
> (a) to examine or have examined witnesses against him and to obtain the attendance and examination of witnesses on his behalf under the same conditions as witnesses against him.

The relationship between Article 6 and the hearsay provisions of the 2003 Act were considered by the Grand Chamber of the ECtHR in *Al-Khawaja and Tahery* v *UK* (2012) 54 EHRR 23 which set out a series of principles applicable to such cases. In particular, the case addressed the key question of whether a conviction based solely or decisively on hearsay evidence could be viewed as compatible with Article 6. In an earlier decision (*Al-Khawaja and Tahery* v *UK* (2009) 49 EHRR 1) the ECtHR had held that this was highly unlikely but the UK courts declined to follow this interpretation in *R* v *Horncastle* [2010] 2 AC 373 (SC), viewing the matter as one for the national courts. The decision of the Grand Chamber in *Al-Khawaja and Tahery* is consistent with this approach. Providing there are sufficient counterbalancing factors and procedural safeguards in place, a conviction based solely or decisively on hearsay evidence may be Article 6 compliant. It was later held by the Court of Appeal in *R* v *Riat* [2012] EWCA Crim 1509 that the courts should resolve any differences between *Horncastle* and *Al-Khawaja and Tahery* in favour of the former.

# ■ Putting it all together

## Answer guidelines

See the problem question at the start of the chapter.

### Approaching the question

As with all legal problem questions, there may be a temptation to launch straight into the application of the provisions to the facts of the scenario. Always take the time to establish the relevant legal principles and definitions first, making good use of supporting authorities to emphasise your general grasp of the topic – then move on to the detailed application.

### Important points to include

Begin by outlining what is meant by hearsay and the reasons why such evidence was traditionally deemed inadmissible.

- Set out the main changes contained in the Criminal Justice Act 2003 in relation to hearsay evidence.
- In relation to Alan, there is a possible application of the res gestae exception retained by section 118 CJA 2003 (the facts presented resemble those in *R* v *Andrews*).
- As John has died, his statement may be adduced under section 116(2)(a).
- It is possible that Simon's statement may be adduced under section 116(2)(e).
- Conclude that all three statements can be used.

 Make your answer stand out

- Point out that the fear suffered by Simon can be broadly construed, even including a mistaken belief in the threat.
- Remember to state that there remains the judicial discretion to admit such evidence under section 114(1)(d) where the court considers that it is 'in the interests of justice' to do so.

## READ TO IMPRESS

Allan, T. (1990) A parade of problems: hearsay in the Court of Appeal. *NLJ*, 140(7 December): 1723.

Birch, D. and Hirst, M. (2010) Interpreting the new concept of hearsay. *The Cambridge Law Journal*, 69: 72–97.

Cooper, J. (2010) The limits of hearsay evidence. *JPN*, 174: 610.

Durston, G. (2004) Hearsay evidence and the new inclusionary discretion. *JPN*, 168: 788.

Jones, I. (2011) A political judgment? Reconciling hearsay and the right to challenge, *EvPro* 14(3): 232.

Munday, R. (2007) The judicial discretion to admit hearsay evidence. *JPN*, 171: 276.

Stockdale, M. and Piasecki, E. (2012) The safety-valve: discretion to admit hearsay evidence in criminal proceedings *Journal of Criminal Law*, 76: 314.

Turner, A.J. (2008) Developments in hearsay. *JPN*, 172: 196.

Wilcock, P. and Bennathan, J. (2004) The new rules of hearsay evidence. *NLJ*, 154(30 July): 1174.

Worthen, T. (2008) The hearsay provisions of the Criminal Justice Act 2003: so far, not so good?. *Crim LR*, 431.

**www.pearsoned.co.uk/lawexpress**

 Go online to access more revision support including quizzes to test your knowledge, sample questions with answer guidelines, podcasts you can download, and more!

# Opinion and expert evidence

5

## Revision checklist

**Essential points you should know:**

- [ ] The distinction between evidence of fact and evidence of opinion
- [ ] The rule prohibiting evidence of opinion and the exceptions to this general prohibition
- [ ] The role and status of expert evidence
- [ ] Issues surrounding the presentation of expert evidence
- [ ] Debates surrounding the use of expert evidence

# ◼ Topic map

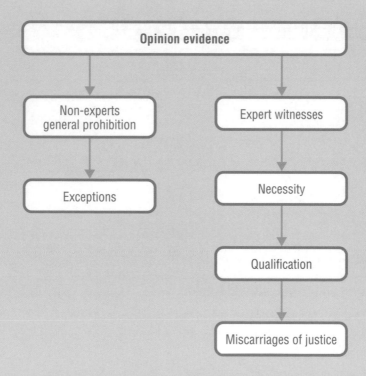

# ■ Introduction

## Everyone is entitled to their opinion, except in court!

Earlier (see Chapter 2) we considered the role of witnesses within the trial process but left unanswered the question, 'What do witnesses give evidence of?' The answer, as far as the law of evidence is concerned, is that they give evidence of *fact* and not of *opinion* but, as we shall see, this is not quite as simple as it first appears, particularly when the witness is an 'expert' witness. The treatment of expert evidence is assuming increasing importance within the law of evidence and so is a regular feature in evidence examinations. For this reason, it is advisable to have a thorough knowledge of the topic.

## ASSESSMENT ADVICE

### Essay questions

These usually focus on expert testimony and may ask you to consider the rules governing the appointment of expert witnesses and the treatment of expert testimony or, alternatively, to consider the aftermath of recent successful appeals resulting from flawed expert evidence. In each case a detailed knowledge of the provisions and background debate is required. Such discussions will also involve consideration of the expense involved in using expert witnesses, and it is this desire to reduce costs which lies behind many of the suggested reforms.

### Problem questions

These usually take the form of a scenario involving a number of witnesses, each designed to test your knowledge on a particular facet of opinion evidence. As with essay questions, the focus tends to be on expert testimony and problem questions may address issues such as the recognition of 'expert' status, the consultation of previous data existing within the discipline and the disclosure of expert reports.

# ■ Sample question

Could you answer this question? Below is a typical problem question that could arise on this topic. Guidelines on answering the question are included at the end of this chapter, whilst a sample essay question and guidance on tackling it can be found on the companion website.

---

### PROBLEM QUESTION

As part of the trial of Barry for murder, the prosecution wishes to call the following expert witnesses:

■ Professor Smart, a consultant psychiatrist, who will give evidence that Barry, who had just lost his job and whose mother had just died at the time of the alleged offence, was likely to be suffering from depression at the time (his defence is one of diminished responsibility).

■ Ian, a youth worker who trains the local youth club football team, who will give evidence of Barry's knee injury and the extent to which it would have caused sufficient pain to disrupt his sleep, thereby increasing his anxiety levels.

Discuss.

---

# ■ Witnesses and evidence of opinion

The starting point for any discussion of opinion evidence is the general principle that such evidence is inadmissible. Witnesses are called upon to give evidence not of what they think, but of the relevant facts which are within their knowledge. It is for the judge or the jury (depending on the nature of the case) to interpret the evidence – not the individual witness who is there simply to offer their part of the factual account of events.

## Fact or opinion?

Although the basic principle is relatively simple, the distinction between fact and opinion is not always so straightforward. For example, it might be argued that almost all identification evidence is based on opinion – 'That is the person I saw' might also be expressed as, 'I *think* that is the person I saw'. Similarly, evidence that a person was walking quickly, that they were elderly or that they were shabbily dressed might all be seen as evidence of opinion, rather than of fact. Clearly, a rigid application of this rule would be impractical and impede the giving of evidence by witnesses and, for this reason, the courts take a pragmatic approach to the distinction between fact and opinion evidence.

# ■ Expert evidence

The main exception to the general rule against evidence of opinion relates to expert evidence.

# When is expert evidence required?

*Folkes* v *Chadd* (1783) 3 Doug KB 157

*Concerning: admissibility of expert evidence*

**Facts**

It was alleged that earthworks which had been erected to prevent the sea from flooding farmlands had contributed to damage to a local harbour. As part of the case, expert evidence was presented as to the cause and extent of the damage.

**Legal principle**

Lord Mansfield: 'On certain matters . . . upon which the court itself cannot form an opinion, special study, skill or experience being required for the purpose, "expert" witnesses may give evidence of their opinion.'

The need for expert evidence arises where there is specialised evidence which requires some form of interpretation in order for its significance to be fully appreciated by the court (such interpretation representing the 'opinion' of the expert). This can range from common forms of evidence, such as fingerprints, bloodstains or DNA, to areas such as ear prints, voice identification or handwriting analysis. It is also important to recognise that 'expert' does not necessarily mean 'scientific', as the court may require testimony on anything from the value of a particular antique to the authenticity of a painting and, in each case, an expert witness may be required.

This leaves the court with two questions to address:

- Is an expert required at all?
- Is the person put forward by the parties as an 'expert' suitably qualified to offer such evidence.

## Is an expert required?

Remember that expert evidence will only be admitted where the matter concerned is one which is outside the knowledge or understanding of the court or jury.

*R* v *Turner* [1975] QB 834 (CA)

*Concerning: admissibility of expert evidence*                    ▶

## Facts

T was charged with murdering his girlfriend. His defence was one of provocation, following her admission that she had engaged in affairs with other men and that he was not the father of her unborn child. At trial, the defence applied to adduce expert evidence from a psychiatrist to show that T was likely to have been provoked by learning of these facts. The application was denied by the trial judge and T was convicted. He appealed on this point.

## Legal principle

It was held that the likelihood of T having been provoked in the circumstances were matters within the competence and experience of the jury. As such, the trial judge had been correct to exclude the psychiatric evidence. Lawton LJ: 'Jurors do not need psychiatrists to tell them how ordinary folk who are not suffering from any mental illness are likely to react to the stresses and strains of life.'

---

**KEY CASE**

### *R* v *Smith* [1979] 3 All ER 605 (CA)

*Concerning: admissibility of expert evidence*

## Facts

S was accused of murder and raised the defence of automatism, alleging that he had attacked the victim whilst he was asleep. The prosecution adduced expert evidence to undermine this claim and this evidence was challenged by the defence.

## Legal principle

It was held that automatism was a medical condition which was not within the experience of an ordinary person. Lane LJ: 'The fundamental question, it seems to us, is really that of automatism, a mental condition on which the jury is entitled to have expert help.'

---

**KEY CASE**

### *R* v *Land* [1998] 1 All ER 403 (CA)

*Concerning: admissibility of expert evidence*

## Facts

L was convicted of possessing indecent photographs of a child. On appeal it was argued that, whereas the trial judge had left it to the jury to decide for themselves whether the images were of children, expert evidence from a doctor or child development expert should have been adduced to assess the ages of the individuals pictured in order to establish that they were indeed children.

**Legal principle**

It was held that the jury was as well placed as any expert to assess whether those depicted in the photographs were under 16 years. Therefore, evidence from an expert was not required. Judge LJ: 'the jury is as well placed as an expert to assess any argument addressed to the question . . . whether the person depicted in the photograph is under 16 years.'

✎ **EXAM TIP**

Make clear that you also appreciate the financial aspects of expert evidence – experts cost money and the court will be reluctant to sanction such expense from public funds (legal aid) without clear justification.

# Is the person an expert?

Having established that expert evidence is required, the court must then consider whether the person put forward by the party in question is suitably qualified to be considered an 'expert'. In a profession or discipline where there is a formal training or qualification process, this may be relatively simple to establish but, where there is no such process, the court must look elsewhere for an indication of the person's expertise.

**KEY CASE**

*R* v *Silverlock* [1894] 2 QB 766 (CCR)

*Concerning: the status of an 'expert'*

**Facts**

As part of a trial for obtaining money by false pretences, evidence was required to establish the authenticity of samples of handwriting.

**Legal principle**

It was held that the person offering expert evidence need not have any professional qualification, providing that the court was satisfied with their skill and expertise. Lord Russell CJ: 'There is no decision which requires that the evidence of a man who is skilled in comparing handwriting, and who has formed a reliable opinion from past experience, should be excluded because his experience has not been gained in the way of his business.'

**KEY CASE**

*R* v *Murphy* [1980] QB 434 (CA)

*Concerning: the status of an 'expert'*

**Facts**

M was charged with causing death by driving recklessly. The trial judge allowed expert evidence on the probable cause of the collision from a police officer with extensive experience in road traffic accidents. M appealed against his conviction on the grounds that the evidence of the police officer was wrongly admitted as he was not an 'expert'.

**Legal principle**

It was held that the police officer was entitled to give evidence in the capacity of an 'expert'. Eveleigeh LJ (citing Lord Widgery): 'as long as he keeps within his reasonable expertise, which is a matter for the judge, he is entitled to be heard on every aspect as an expert, to that extent, if no further.'

**KEY CASE**

*R* v *Clare and Peach* [1995] Crim LR 947 (CA)

*Concerning: the status of an 'expert'*

**Facts**

The defendants were charged with violent disorder following an incident between rival football supporters after a match. The incident had been captured by poor quality CCTV. As part of the prosecution case, a police officer who had been responsible for filming the crowd at the match was permitted to compare his high quality colour recording with that of the incident captured on CCTV to confirm the identity of the defendants. The defendants appealed against their convictions on the grounds that the officer should not have been afforded the status of 'expert'.

**Legal principle**

Lord Taylor of Gosforth CJ: '. . . [the officer] had special knowledge that the Court did not possess . . . acquired . . . by lengthy and studious application to material which was itself admissible evidence. To afford the jury the time and facilities to conduct the same research would be utterly impracticable. Accordingly, it was in our judgment legitimate to allow the officer to assist the jury by pointing to what he asserted was happening in the crowded scenes on the film.'

**R v Edwards [2001] EWCA Crim 2185 (CA)**

*Concerning: the status of an 'expert'*

**Facts**

E was arrested with a large quantity of ecstasy tablets and charged with possession with intent to supply. He argued that the drugs were for his personal use and claimed to consume a large number of tablets daily. He called a drugs charity worker to provide expert evidence that this was possible. The prosecution called a police officer to provide expert testimony that this was unlikely. The evidence of both experts was held to be inadmissible by the trial judge.

**Legal principle**

It was held that the trial judge had been correct to exclude the evidence. Neither individual possessed sufficient expertise to qualify as an 'expert' and so avoid the general rule against opinion evidence. Henry LJ: 'the anecdotal evidence was not supported by any forensic evidence . . . and the judge was right to exclude it. It was valueless, and the judge was right to so treat it.'

# The duty imposed on the expert witness

**Civil Procedure Rules 1998, r. 35.3**

Experts – overriding duty to the court

(1) It is the duty of an expert to help the court on the matters within his expertise.

(2) This duty overrides any obligation to the person from whom he has received instructions or by whom he is paid.

**Criminal Procedure Rules 2005, r. 33.2**

Expert's duty to the court

(1) An expert must help the court to achieve the overriding objective by giving objective, unbiased opinion on matters within his expertise.

(2) This duty overrides any obligation to the person from whom he receives instructions or by whom he is paid.

# What is the basis for the expert's opinion?

Remember the definition of hearsay from the previous chapter?

A statement made otherwise than by a person while giving oral evidence in the proceedings which is tendered as evidence of the matters stated.

This can potentially cause problems for expert witnesses. For example, an expert may wish to refer to important research conducted within their field to support their interpretation of the evidence. Similarly, they may wish to use calculations based on official data. If the rule against hearsay were to be strictly applied, however, the expert would be confined to giving evidence of their own work only, which would cause major difficulty. It would be illogical to prevent experts from making use of the accumulated knowledge within their discipline and so the courts need to arrive at a pragmatic solution.

---

**KEY CASE**

*R* v *Abadom* [1983] 1 All ER 364 (CA)

*Concerning: references to other published works*

**Facts**

A was charged with robbery. The prosecution wished to adduce expert evidence that glass fragments found in A's shoes shared the same refractive index as a window broken during the robbery. The expert based his conclusion on the appropriate Home Office Research Establishment statistics, which the defence argued were inadmissible as hearsay evidence.

**Legal principle**

It was held that an expert was entitled to draw on the work of others in his field of expertise as part of the process of arriving at his conclusion without infringing the hearsay rule, providing that the expert referred to that material in his evidence, so that the cogency and probative value of his conclusion could be tested by reference to that material. Kerr LJ: 'the statistical tables of analyses made by the Home Office forensic laboratories had appeared in a textbook or other publication, it could not be doubted that [the witness] would have been entitled to rely on them for the purposes of his evidence.'

---

# The 'ultimate issue' rule

It has long been argued that an expert witness should not be permitted to give their opinion on the 'ultimate issue' between the parties. This was justified on the grounds that it usurped the function of the judge (in a civil case) or jury (in a criminal case) by answering the question at the heart of the case. It should be noted, however, that this rule has been abolished in civil cases by the Civil Evidence Act 1995, section 3, which allows an expert to give evidence on 'any relevant matter' and, although the rule still technically exists in criminal cases, it is widely ignored.

A rule which has, traditionally, prevented an expert witness from giving an opinion on the central question of guilt in the case.

*DPP* v *A and BC Chewing Gum Ltd* [1967] 2 All ER 504 (QB)

*Concerning: admissibility of expert evidence*

Facts

The respondent company sold cards with chewing gum which were aimed at children of all ages with the intention that children would swop the cards among themselves. The content of some of the cards resulted in charges under the Obscene Publications Act 1959 but, at trial, the magistrates refused to hear expert evidence of child psychiatrists, as to the likely effect of the cards on children of various ages. This was because an opinion on whether the cards had a tendency to deprave and corrupt was the very issue that the court had to decide. The DPP appealed against the decision not to admit the expert evidence.

Legal principle

Lord Parker CJ: 'I can quite see that, when considering the effect of something on an adult, an adult jury may be able to judge just as well as an adult witness called on the point . . . but certainly when dealing with children of different age groups and children from five upwards, any jury and any justices need all the help that they can get, information which they may not have, as to the effect on different children. For those reasons, I think that certainly in so far as this objection is based on common law it fails.'

He also commented:

'I myself would go a little further, in that I cannot help feeling that, with the advance of science, more and more inroads have been made into the old common law principles. Those who practise in the criminal courts see every day cases of experts being called on the question of diminished responsibility, and, although technically the final question "Do you think he was suffering from diminished responsibility?" is strictly inadmissible, it is allowed time and time again without any objection.'

# Format of the expert's report

The format of the expert's report is dictated in civil cases by Practice Direction 35.

**KEY STATUTE**

**Practice Direction 35, 3.2**

**An expert's report must:**

(1) give details of the expert's qualifications;

(2) give details of any literature or other material which the expert has relied on in making the report;

(3) contain a statement setting out the substance of all facts and instructions given to the expert which are material to the opinions expressed in the report or upon which those opinions are based;

(4) make clear which of the facts stated in the report are within the expert's own knowledge;

(5) say who carried out any examination, measurement, test or experiment which the expert has used for the report, give the qualifications of that person, and say whether or not the test or experiment has been carried out under the expert's supervision;

(6) where there is a range of opinion on the matters dealt with in the report –

    (a) summarise the range of opinion; and

    (b) give reasons for his own opinion;

(7) contain a summary of the conclusions reached;

(8) if the expert is not able to give his opinion without qualification, state the qualification; and

(9) contain a statement that the expert –

    (a) understands his duty to the court; and

    (b) has complied with that duty.

Virtually identical provisions dictate the contents of expert reports in criminal cases and are detailed in r. 33.3 of the Criminal Procedure Rules.

# Reform of expert evidence

Recent years have witnessed a number of reforms aimed at streamlining the effectiveness (and cost) of expert evidence. In relation to civil proceedings, this process began with the Woolf reforms which led to the introduction of the Civil Procedure Rules. In criminal cases, a series of successful appeals based on discredited expert evidence has raised concerns over the use of such testimony.

The Law Commission conducted research into the area and a report 'Expert Evidence in Criminal Proceedings in England and Wales' was published in 2011, together with a draft Bill designed to address some of the perceived weaknesses in the current system. The main recommendation was for a new reliability-based admissibility test for expert evidence in criminal proceedings which would be applied in appropriate cases and result in the exclusion of unreliable expert opinion evidence. The report can be found at http://www.lawcom.gov.uk/wp-content/uploads/2015/03/lc325_Expert_Evidence_Report.pdf

## Procedure

In civil cases, rather than each side appointing their own expert witness, the court may order a single expert to be appointed. Also, in cases where the parties have their own experts, the court may order the respective experts to enter into a dialogue with a view to reaching agreement on the issues (which, in turn, may encourage the parties to settle the case). Similar provisions apply in criminal cases under the Criminal Procedure Rules.

---

**□ REVISION NOTE**

Another key aspect of expert evidence relates to the disclosure of expert reports. The subject of disclosure is considered later in the text (see Chapter 9) and should be revised in conjunction with this chapter.

---

# ■ Expert evidence and miscarriages of justice

The role of expert evidence in a number of notorious miscarriages of justice has raised concerns over the extent to which a jury may be swayed by the evidence of apparently eminent experts which ultimately proves to be defective. In particular, a series of cases surrounding infant deaths highlighted the dangers of expert testimony.

---

**KEY CASE**

*R v Cannings* [2004] EWCA Crim 1 (CA)

*Concerning: expert evidence*

**Facts**

C was the mother of four children, three of whom had died suddenly when only a few weeks old. She was charged with their murder but asserted that the children were all the victim of sudden infant death syndrome (cot death). There was nothing to suggest either mental illness on C's part or any abuse within the family. Expert evidence adduced by the prosecution suggested that it was highly improbable for three children within one family ▶

to die naturally in this way. C was convicted but appealed when fresh medical evidence came to light of similar child deaths within her extended family.

**Legal principle**

The appeal was upheld. New research and the family medical history cast doubt on the medical evidence which was the central pillar of the prosecution case. Consequently the conviction was unsafe. Judge LJ: 'In cases like the present, if the outcome of the trial depends exclusively or almost exclusively on a serious disagreement between distinguished and reputable experts, it will often be unwise, and therefore unsafe, to proceed.'

---

**KEY CASE**

*R* v *Clark* [2003] EWCA Crim 1020 (CA)

*Concerning: expert evidence*

**Facts**

C was charged with the murder of her two children who died at 8 and 11 weeks. A forensic pathologist who conducted post-mortem examinations on the children concluded that the deaths were unnatural, but the defence contended that both infants had been the victim of cot death. After an unsuccessful appeal, the case was referred back to the Court of Appeal by the Criminal Cases Review Commission when evidence emerged that the pathologist had omitted from his findings the traces of a potentially fatal bacteria which he had found in one of the children. This provided an alternative cause of death which he had ignored.

**Legal principle**

The failure to mention the possibility of an alternative cause of death had rendered the conviction unsafe and so the appeal would be allowed. Kay LJ: 'We are quite satisfied that if the evidence in its entirety, as it is now known, had been known to the Court it would never have concluded that the evidence pointed overwhelmingly to guilt.'

---

As a result, the Court of Appeal suggested the following approach in relation to expert evidence in family cases in *Re U (Serious Injury: Standard of Proof)* [2004] EWCA Civ 567:

1. The cause of an injury or an episode that cannot be explained scientifically remains equivocal.

2. Recurrence is not in itself probative.

3. Particular caution is necessary in any case where the medical experts disagree, one opinion declining to exclude a reasonable possibility of natural cause.

4. The court must always be on guard against the over-dogmatic expert, the expert whose reputation or *amour propre* is at stake, or the expert who has developed a scientific prejudice.

5. The judge in care proceedings must never forget that today's medical certainty may be discarded by the next generation of experts or that scientific research will throw light into corners that are at present dark.

 **Make your answer stand out**

Following these cases, attention focused on the evidence of the senior paediatricians Sir Roy Meadow and David Southall, which was seen as instrumental in some of the cases. For a discussion of the cases and issues raised see, Williams, L. H. P. (2008) In practice: paediatricians in child protection: the risks, *Fam Law* 573.

# ■ Putting it all together

## Answer guidelines

See the problem question at the start of the chapter.

### Approaching the question

Remember to begin with clear definitions of both opinion evidence and expert evidence. A solid background to the consideration of the scenario will enhance your answer. Similarly, a brief conclusion, drawing together your findings, will emphasise the analytical component of your answer.

### Important points to include

■ In relation to Professor Smart, it is unlikely that the court would allow evidence of a matter which is likely to be within the experience of the jury. This mirrors the decisions in *R* v *Turner* and *R* v *Land.*

■ In relation to Ian, it is unlikely that he would be considered to possess sufficient expertise to qualify as an 'expert witness'. A voluntary role as a youth club football coach would not equip him to offer expert opinion on the consequences of a knee injury. This would more usually be addressed by a doctor or possibly physiotherapist specialising in such injuries.

▶

Make your answer stand out

- Point out that, in relation to both issues, the court may seek to appoint a single expert, rather than each side appointing their own.
- Emphasise the two questions that the court will pose when considering an application to present expert evidence: is this a matter on which the court requires expert testimony? And, if so, is this person qualified to offer such expert testimony?

## READ TO IMPRESS

Botsford, P. (2008) Expert witnesses: knowledge is power. 20 *LS Gaz*, 19 June.

Durston, G. (2005) The admissibility of novel 'Fields' of expert evidence. *JPN*,169: 968.

Dwyer, D. (2008) Legal remedies for the negligent expert. *EvPro* 12(2): 93.

Law Commission, (2011) *Expert evidence in criminal proceedings in England and Wales,* London: HMSO.

Pamplin. C. (2013) Switching experts. *NLJ*, 163: 22.

Shaw, K. (2011) Expert evidence reliability; time to grasp the nettle. *JOCL*, 75: 368.

Solon, M. (2008) Professional experts (Expert witness supplement). *NLJ*. 158: 138.

Solon, M. (2011a) End of the amateur expert?, *NLJ*, 161: 601.

Solon, M. (2011b) The end of expert frolics, *NLJ*, 161: 1607.

Williams, L. H. P. (2008) In practice: paediatricians in child protection: the risks. *Fam Law*, 573.

Wilson, A. (2005) Expert testimony in the dock. *JoCL*, 69: 330.

**www.pearsoned.co.uk/lawexpress**

 Go online to access more revision support including quizzes to test your knowledge, sample questions with answer guidelines, podcasts you can download, and more!

# Confession evidence

**6**

## Revision checklist

**Essential points you should know:**

- [ ] How the law of evidence defines a 'confession'
- [ ] The difficulties associated with confession evidence
- [ ] The grounds on which the admissibility of confession evidence may be challenged
- [ ] The operation of section 76 PACE
- [ ] The operation of section 78 PACE

# ■ Topic map

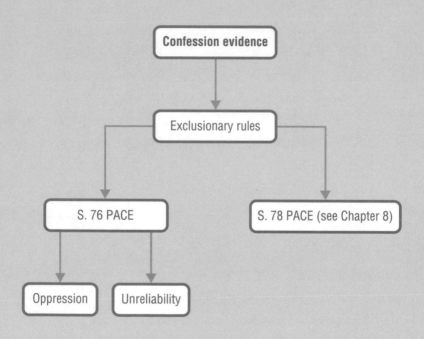

Confession evidence

Exclusionary rules

S. 76 PACE

S. 78 PACE (see Chapter 8)

Oppression

Unreliability

# ■ Introduction

## What better evidence is there than a confession?

Of all the forms of evidence which might be adduced in a criminal trial, a confession is perhaps the most powerful. The fact that the accused has admitted the offence appears to render any other evidence largely irrelevant, but at the same time it is well recognised that many people confess to crimes which they did not commit and so the law of evidence makes special provision for the treatment of confession evidence. This topic is extremely common in evidence examinations and has the benefit of being a relatively straightforward area. This means that, with a little preparation, it is possible to achieve very high marks.

## ASSESSMENT ADVICE

### Essay questions

Questions on confession evidence may ask you to consider the effectiveness of the current exclusionary rules in protecting those who have made false confessions. Such questions require a clear grasp of the relevant provisions (including section 78 PACE which is covered in Chapter 8).

### Problem questions

These are perhaps more common and will usually centre on a police interrogation, which raises the possibility of exclusion under PACE. Once again, a good answer will require a firm grasp of the provisions and supporting common law authorities.

# ■ Sample question

Could you answer this question? Below is a typical problem question that could arise on this topic. Guidelines on answering the question are included at the end of this chapter, whilst a sample essay question and guidance on tackling it can be found on the companion website.

# ■ Confessions

At the same time, a confession is both the best and the worst form of evidence. Most members of a jury will be highly influenced by the fact that the defendant has admitted the offence and may be inclined to convict on that evidence alone. At the same time, however, the history of criminal justice is filled with examples of confessions which later emerged to be untrue and there are numerous factors (including pressure from police interviewers and mental illness) which may lead an individual to make a false admission of guilt. Once a jury has learned that the accused has made a confession, it is very difficult to undo the damage which this causes and so, if at all possible, the defence will seek to challenge the admissibility of any confession in the hope of preventing it ever reaching the jury. As will be seen, there are a small number of mechanisms by which this might be achieved.

## The Police and Criminal Evidence Act 1984 (PACE)

The provisions relating to the exclusion of confession evidence (and other forms of evidence) are found under the Police and Criminal Evidence Act 1984 (PACE). It should be remembered that PACE was introduced as a response to widespread concerns over the abuse of police powers in the late 1970s and early 1980s, and so the exclusionary rules within the Act were largely (but not exclusively) designed to prevent evidence which has been obtained as a result of police misconduct from reaching the jury.

Make your answer stand out

Make clear to the examiner that you understand the function of the exclusionary rules by emphasising that, despite the origins of PACE 1984, deliberate police misconduct is not always required for evidence to be excluded.

## PACE Codes of Practice

When considering the application of PACE you must also be aware of the Codes of Practice which set out the detailed procedures in relation to key areas of the statute. The current Codes are as follows:

| Code of Practice | Subject |
|---|---|
| A | Powers of stop search and public encounters |
| B | Search of premises and seizure of property |
| C | Detention, treatment and questioning of suspects (except terrorism offences) |
| D | Identification procedures |
| E | Audio recording of police interviews |
| F | Visual recording of police interviews |
| G | Powers of arrest |
| H | Detention, treatment and questioning of suspects (terrorism offences) |

 Make your answer stand out

Although not directly relevant to confessions, impress the examiner with your up-to-date knowledge by mentioning that the Codes of Practice are subject to regular revision, such as the recent (January 2015) changes to Code A, clarifying 'reasonable grounds for suspicion' in the context of stop search.

Clearly Code C, which regulates detention and questioning, is central to many challenges to confession evidence and, as will be seen, the fact that the police have breached the Code may impact on the decision of the court to allow or exclude the confession. The Code covers issues such as access to legal advice, medical treatment and meal and sleep breaks.

---

### ✎ EXAM TIP

Although you are unlikely to face an examination question on the Codes of Practice, the examiner will be impressed by some knowledge of Code of Practice C as it relates to confession evidence. The current Code can be found at www.gov.uk/government/publications/pace-code-c-2014

---

### ✎ EXAM TIP

When discussing the exclusionary rules under PACE remember to point out that, whereas most of the provisions in the 1984 Act concern the treatment of suspects before charge, the exclusionary rules extend into the trial process itself by regulating the admissibility of certain forms of evidence. This is in keeping with the origins of PACE as a mechanism for preventing the abuse of police powers and miscarriages of justice.

---

# ■ What is a confession?

Although you may think you know what a confession is, the definition provided by PACE is probably slightly more complex.

---

### KEY STATUTE

**Police and Criminal Evidence Act 1984, s. 82(1)**

In this Part of this Act –

'confession' includes any statement wholly or partly adverse to the person who made it, whether made to a person in authority or not and whether made in words or otherwise

---

As you can see, there are a number of additional elements here which require some explanation.

## 'Wholly or partly adverse to the person who made it'

Typically, we might think of a confession as: 'I did it', but section 82 clearly also includes statements which are only *partly* adverse to the person making them. This reflects the fact that people tend not to say 'I did it' but rather 'I did it but . . .' or I did it because . . .'

This raises the distinction between 'inculpatory statements' (those which incriminate the maker of the statement) and 'exculpatory statements' (those which favour the maker of the statement – also known as 'self-serving statements'). Obviously there is also the possibility of a statement which admits some things and denies others and these are known as 'mixed statements'.

**KEY DEFINITION: A 'mixed statement'**

A statement which is partly in favour of the person making it and partly against them.

**KEY CASE**

*R* v *Garrod* [1997] Crim LR 445 (CA)

*Concerning: 'mixed statements'*

**Facts**

G was charged with conspiring to obtain by deception. In relation to a possible 'good character' direction, the court was required to establish when a statement could be considered 'mixed'.

**Legal principle**

Evans LJ: 'Where the statement contains an admission of facts which are significant to any issue in the case, meaning those which are capable of adding some degree of weight to the prosecution case on an issue which is relevant to guilt, then the statement must be regarded as "mixed".'

In this way, the section 82 definition of confessions includes both mixed statements and those which are wholly inculpatory. It does not include purely exculpatory statements and this extends to statements which are initially exculpatory but later cease to be so.

**KEY CASE**

*R* v *Hasan* [2005] UKHL 22 (HL)

*Concerning: mixed statements*

**Facts**

H was charged with aggravated burglary. H alleged that he had acted under threats from 'S' who, in making the threats, had claimed involvement in a number of murders. As part of an entirely separate inquiry, H had given an 'off the record' interview to ▶

police, during which he indicated that he had not been threatened by 'S' until after the burglary. At the time, this 'off the record' interview statement by H was viewed as exculpatory. At trial, the prosecution sought to adduce the earlier statement as evidence undermining H's defence of duress.

### Legal principle

It was held that such a statement, which was exculpatory at the time it was made but which later assumed a character more negative to the maker, is not covered by section 82. Lord Steyn: 'it is wholly implausible that the draftsman would have made express reference only to wholly or partly adverse statements if he also had in mind covering under the definition of "confession" wholly exculpatory statements.'

---

## KEY CASE

### *R* v *Sliogeris* [2015] EWCA Crim 22 (CA)

*Concerning: definition of a 'confession'*

### Facts

The appellant was one of four men accused of murder. At trial, Sliogeris and Staponka ran a 'cut throat' defence, with each blaming the other for the attack. The appeal centred on a statement allegedly made by another of the co-accused, Pocius, to his landlord in which Pocius had said that he had seen Sliogeris beat the man to death. At trial, Pocius elected not to give evidence and, as a co-defendant, he was not compellable. On learning of Pocius' refusal to give evidence, Staponka, applied to have the alleged hearsay statement admitted as it assisted his defence by supporting his assertion that it was not him, but Sliogeris, who had been the attacker. It was held that the statement was a confession under section 76 PACE 1984 and so could be admitted under the exception to the hearsay rule which applied to confession evidence.

### Legal principle

Held – although the conviction was upheld, the alleged statement was held not to be a confession. The trial judge had accepted that it was a 'mixed statement' as Pocius had admitted being present (which was inculpatory) but had blamed Sliogeris (which was exculpatory). The Court of Appeal, however, saw this as two separate statements, one inculpatory and one exculpatory. As Staponka sought to rely on the exculpatory statement, this could not be a confession. Elias LJ: '[Staponka] is relying upon another comment made by Pocius, which is logically quite distinct from his admission of his presence, namely that the appellant had committed the offence. That is an exculpatory statement and does not itself amount to a confession.'

## Confessions and co-defendants

A related question is whether, if A makes a confession implicating both himself and his co-defendant B, that confession can be used in evidence against both defendants or, alternatively, only against A who made the statement.

As a general rule, a confession by A cannot be used as evidence against B subject to the following exception.

---

**KEY CASE**

*R* v *Hayter* [2005] UKHL 6 (HL)

*Concerning: confessions of co-defendants*

**Facts**

H was the alleged intermediary between B (who wanted her husband killed) and R (the hitman). The case against R turned largely on his confession but the evidence against H was purely circumstantial. The trial judge directed the jury that, only if they could convict B and R, would it be open to them to also convict H. All three were convicted and H appealed that he had, effectively, been convicted as a result of the confession by R.

**Legal principle**

The appeal failed. The jury was entitled to decide the guilt of R, based on his confession, and then use the finding of R's guilt as evidence against H. Lord Brown: 'there is no good reason why A's guilt should not ordinarily be regarded by the jury as a fact capable of being used evidentially against B.'

---

**!** Don't be tempted to . . .

Don't forget to make a distinction between a confession by A, which is made out of court and which cannot be used in evidence against B, and the situation where A gives evidence in court. Where the accused gives evidence, he is, as part of his testimony, able to implicate a co-defendant. Don't confuse the two scenarios.

## 'Whether made in words or otherwise'

Note that section 82 also extends to statements which are not made in words (verbal or written) and so includes conduct (most obviously, a nod of the head).

## *Li Shu-Ling* v *R* [1988] 3 All ER 138 (PC)

*Concerning: 'in words or otherwise'*

### Facts

L was charged with murdering a woman by strangling her in her apartment. Having admitted involvement to police (and whilst still under caution), he agreed to take part in a re-enactment of events, showing how he had killed the victim. At trial he put forward a different defence and sought to have the re-enactment excluded.

### Legal principle

It was held that the re-enactment constituted a confession and so could be admitted in evidence. Lord Griffiths: 'if an accused can say what he did there is no reason why he should not show what he did.'

Note that, under very limited circumstances, a confession may also be inferred from the silence of the accused.

## *Parkes* v *R* [1976] 3 All ER 380 (PC)

*Concerning: silence as confession*

### Facts

P and the victim lived in separate rooms of a house owned by the victim's mother. Having found her daughter bleeding from stab wounds, the mother then found P in the yard of the house holding a knife. She twice asked him if he had committed the crime but he refused to answer and, when she threatened to detain him until the police arrived, he tried to stab her.

### Legal principle

It was held that, as the parties were speaking on equal terms, rather than in a police interview, the failure to respond to the mother's accusation amounted to a confession (compounded by the attempt to stab the mother). Lord Diplock: '[the trial judge] was perfectly entitled to instruct the jury that the appellant's reaction to the accusation including his silence were matters which they could take into account along with other evidence in deciding whether the appellant in fact committed the act with which he was charged.'

> ! **Don't be tempted to . . .**
>
> Despite the decision in *Parkes,* be wary of stating that as a general rule silence can be taken as a confession. Remember that, in *Parkes,* the parties were on equal terms and so the principle could *not* be applied to a police interview. Also, the question of a suspect's failure to answer questions is now addressed by the 'right to silence' provisions of the Criminal Justice and Public Order Act 1994 **(discussed in Chapter 2).**

# ■ Admissibility of confession evidence

The provisions governing both the admissibility of confession evidence and the power to exclude confession evidence are found in section 76 PACE 1984.

> ! **Don't be tempted to . . .**
>
> When discussing the power of the court to exclude confession evidence, be careful not to confuse the powers under section 76 PACE, which apply to confession evidence *only,* and those under section 78 and section 82(3) PACE **(discussed in Chapter 8)** which extend to *all* forms of evidence (including confessions).

### KEY STATUTE

**Police and Criminal Evidence Act 1984, s. 76**

Confessions

(1) In any proceedings a confession made by an accused person may be given in evidence against him in so far as it is relevant to any matter in issue in the proceedings and is not excluded by the court in pursuance of this section.

(2) If, in any proceedings where the prosecution proposes to give in evidence a confession made by an accused person, it is represented to the court that the confession was or may have been obtained –

    (a) by oppression of the person who made it; or

    (b) in consequence of anything said or done which was likely, in the circumstances existing at the time, to render unreliable any confession which might be made by him in consequence thereof, ▶

> the court shall not allow the confession to be given in evidence against him except in so far as the prosecution proves to the court beyond reasonable doubt that the confession (notwithstanding that it may be true) was not obtained as aforesaid.

Therefore, under section 76(1) a confession will be admissible unless it is excluded. In addition, the following should also be noted:

- the section only applies where 'the prosecution *proposes* to give in evidence a confession made by an accused person'. It can be deduced from this that the power to exclude will only apply *before* the confession is admitted into evidence;
- in relation to the requirement that the confession must be adduced by 'the prosecution' for section 76 to apply, this must be read subject to the changes relating to confessions of co-accused (see below);
- the confession must be made by the 'accused person'. Therefore, if there is any doubt whether the confession was actually made by the accused, then it may be held inadmissible;
- note that if the prosecution is unable to prove that the confession was correctly obtained, then 'the court *shall  not* allow the confession to be given in evidence'. This suggests little discretion on the part of the court.

## KEY CASE

*R* v *Ward and others* [2001] Crim LR 316 (CA)

*Concerning: confession 'by an accused person'*

### Facts

W was charged with conspiracy to steal from motor vehicles. As part of the prosecution case, evidence was adduced of three separate occasions on which a car had been stopped by police and the passenger had identified himself as W, providing accurate name, address and date of birth. The officers concerned, however, were unable to verify that the passenger was, indeed, W. The court was required to consider whether statements from the passenger could be treated as a confession by W.

### Legal principle

It was held that in such cases a clear direction should be given to the jury that only if the jury were sure from the contents of the statement and any surrounding evidence that it was the appellant giving an accurate identification should they rely on this as an admission by the appellant.

Under section 76(2), when the defence allege that the confession should be excluded under section 76(2)(a) or section 76(2)(b), it falls to the prosecution to prove that the confession was not obtained in breach of those provisions and this applies 'notwithstanding that it might be true'. In other words, the confession may be excluded even if it is known to be true, where the prosecution cannot prove that section 76(2)(a) or section 76(2)(b) do not apply.

---

**KEY CASE**

*R* v *Cox* [1991] Crim LR 276 (CA)

*Concerning: exclusion of confessions known to be true*

**Facts**

C was accused of a number of burglaries. He was interviewed by police in breach of the relevant PACE Codes of Practice in that, as a person of very low IQ, he should have only been interviewed in the presence of an 'appropriate adult'. During the interview he confessed to some of the offences. At trial, the defence applied to have the confession excluded under section 76(2) but, during the hearing on this point, C admitted that he had indeed committed the offences. C was convicted and appealed.

**Legal principle**

The conviction was quashed. Lord Lane CJ: 'The true question was not whether the confession was unreliable or untrue, so much as whether the confession, true or not, was obtained in consequence of anything done which was likely to render any confession unreliable . . . namely was it likely that the failure to have the appropriate adult present would result in any confession being unreliable; not whether the confession actually made was true.'

---

It now remains to consider the two grounds under which a confession may be excluded, section 76(2)(a) and section 76(2)(b).

# Section 76(2)(a) – [*a confession obtained*] 'by oppression of the person who made it'

This is the most serious ground for exclusion of a confession, requiring conduct constituting 'oppression' which is directly linked to the making of the confession – that is the confession must have been made as a result of the oppression.

**Police and Criminal Evidence Act 1984, s. 76(8)**

In this section 'oppression' includes torture, inhuman or degrading treatment, and the use or threat of violence (whether or not amounting to torture).

It might be argued that being in police custody and facing interrogation is inherently 'oppressive', but it is evident that the definition employed by the Act requires far more than this.

KEY CASE

*R* v *Fulling* [1987] 1 WLR 1196 (HL)

*Concerning: 'oppression'*

**Facts**

F was charged with obtaining property by deception. She gave a series of 'no comment' interviews before being told by a police officer that her lover had been having an affair with another woman who was being held in the next cell. F became so distressed on hearing this that she made a statement admitting the offences in order to be moved from the cell. She appealed against her conviction, arguing that the confession had been obtained by oppression.

**Legal principle**

The appeal was dismissed. The conduct of the officer did not constitute 'oppression'. Lord Lane CJ: 'oppression in section 76(2)(a) should be given its ordinary dictionary meaning . . . "Exercise of authority or power in a burdensome, harsh, or wrongful manner; unjust or cruel treatment of subjects, inferiors, etc.; the imposition of unreasonable or unjust burdens".'

KEY CASE

*R* v *Emmerson* (1991) 92 Cr App R 284 (CA)

*Concerning: 'oppression'*

**Facts**

E was arrested and interviewed regarding a number of thefts. During one interview a police officer had spoken in a raised voice and sworn at him. This, it was argued, justified the exclusion of the subsequent confession on grounds of oppression.

**Legal principle**

It was held that the conduct of the officer displayed 'impatience and irritation' but fell short of what was required for 'oppression'. Lloyd LJ: 'We have each come to the conclusion independently that the conduct of the police officer was not in any sense oppressive.'

KEY CASE

*R* v *Paris* (1992) 97 Cr App R 99 (CA)

*Concerning: 'oppression'*

**Facts**

Three men were arrested for murder. One of them, Miller, was on the borderline of mental handicap but was subjected to prolonged questioning during which he denied the offence over 300 times.

**Legal principle**

The conduct was oppressive under section 76(2)(a). Lord Taylor CJ: 'On hearing [the] tape, each member of this Court was horrified. Miller was bullied and hectored. The officers . . . were not questioning him so much as shouting at him what they wanted him to say. Short of physical violence, it is hard to conceive of a more hostile and intimidating approach by officers to a suspect. It is impossible to convey on the printed page the pace, force and menace of the officers' delivery.'

Note that what will be considered 'oppressive' for one person will not necessarily be so for another, depending on their characteristics. In this way, a person of greater confidence and intelligence may be expected to have greater tolerance levels.

KEY CASE

*R* v *Seelig* [1991] 4 All ER 429 (CA)

*Concerning: 'oppression'*

**Facts**

S was a merchant banker investigated by the Department of Trade in relation to alleged fraud. He made a series of admissions but sought to have these excluded under section 76(2)(a).

> **Legal principle**
>
> Watkins LJ: 'The present case is, as we have said, concerned with extremely astute, professional men who have been advised at one time or another by very experienced City solicitors. There was, in our judgment, sound reason for admitting the so-called confessions.'

It was also noted in *Seelig* that, although deliberate misconduct was not absolutely essential to a claim for the exclusion of a confession under section 76(2)(a), it would be highly unusual for there not to be some such behaviour.

# Section 76(2)(b) – [*a confession obtained*] 'in consequence of anything said or done which was likely, in the circumstances existing at the time, to render unreliable any confession'

The second ground for exclusion is considerably broader than section 76(2)(a), looking to 'anything said or done' which is likely to render the confession unreliable. This is often described simply in terms of 'unreliability'.

## KEY CASE

*R* v *Kenny* [1994] Crim LR 284 (CA)

*Concerning: 'unreliability'*

**Facts**

K was interviewed by police and made a confession, in breach of PACE Code of Practice C (governing the detention and questioning of suspects) in that, as a person suffering from learning difficulties, he should only have been interviewed in the presence of an 'appropriate adult'. After the trial judge had admitted the confession, K changed his plea to guilty but later appealed against his conviction.

**Legal principle**

It was held that the confession should not have been admitted in evidence. The court followed the dicta from *R* v *Cox* (above): 'The true question was not whether the confession was unreliable or untrue, so much as whether the confession, true or not, was obtained in consequence of anything done which was likely to render any confession unreliable . . . namely was it likely that the failure to have the appropriate adult present would result in any confession being unreliable; not whether the confession actually made was true.'

Note that section 76(2)(b) is considerably wider in its scope than section 76(2)(a) and so can include confessions made as a result of some inducement by the police.

**KEY CASE**

*R v Northam* (1968) 52 Cr App R 97 (CA)

*Concerning: 'unreliability' and inducements*

**Facts**

N was awaiting trial on charges of burglary. When questioned by a police officer about another outstanding burglary, he asked whether, if he admitted to this offence, it could be 'taken into consideration', rather than forming the basis of a separate charge. The officer indicated that this would be done and so N confessed to the offence. Ultimately, however, the offence was tried separately and the confession adduced in evidence.

**Legal principle**

It was held that the confession had been obtained as a result of an inducement and that this rendered it potentially unreliable. It should, therefore, not have been admitted in evidence. Winn LJ: 'It is not the magnitude, it is not the cogency to the reasonable man or to persons with such knowledge as is possessed by lawyers and others which is the proper criterion. It is what the average, normal, probably quite unreasonable person in the position of the appellant at the time might have thought was likely to result to his advantage from the suggestion agreed to by the police officer.'

**KEY CASE**

*R v McGovern* (1990) 92 Cr App R 228 (CA)

*Concerning: 'unreliability'*

**Facts**

M was arrested in connection with a killing. She was six months pregnant and of low IQ. She was questioned, having been denied a solicitor (in breach of PACE). She became extremely upset and made a confession. Later, in a second interview, she was allowed access to a solicitor and made a second confession. She was convicted of manslaughter on grounds of diminished responsibility and appealed against conviction.

**Legal principle**

It was held that the first confession was rendered unreliable by the denial of legal advice and that this extended to the second confession (where a solicitor had been present) as this was a direct consequence of the first interview. Therefore neither confession ▶

should have been admitted and so the conviction would be quashed. Farquharson LJ: 'If, accordingly, it be held, as it is held here, that the first interview was in breach of the rules and in breach of section 58, it seems to us that the subsequent interview must be similarly tainted.'

 **Make your answer stand out**

To impress the examiner, cite the recent example of *R* v *W (L)* [2015] EWCA Crim 1021 where the complainant in an alleged rape instigated an SMS conversation with the accused in order to obtain a confession. As part of this exchange the accused texted '[you] can't prove I raped you'. Defence applications to have this excluded under both section 76 and section 78 were rejected.

## 'Anything said or done'

One important aspect of section 76(2)(b) is that it requires the confession to be rendered unreliable by 'anything said or done', which suggests that some external action is required. As the following decision indicates, this requirement can present some difficulty.

**KEY CASE**

*R* v *Goldenberg* (1988) 88 Cr App R 285 (CA)

*Concerning: 'anything said or done'*

**Facts**

G was arrested on suspicion of possession of drugs with intent to supply. Suffering from drug withdrawal and desperate to be released from custody, he asked to be interviewed and made an admission. Following conviction, G appealed, arguing that the confession should be excluded as unreliable under section 76(2)(b).

**Legal principle**

It was held that the wording of section 76(2)(b) required the confession to be the consequence of something 'said or done'. In this instance, the thing which had been 'said or done' was G's own request for the interview. This wording of section 76(2)(b) is restricted to something or someone external to the person making the confession and, therefore, the confession could not be excluded under this section. Neill LJ: 'In our judgment, the words "said or done" in section 76(2)(b) of the 1984 Act do not extend so as to include anything said or done by the person making the confession.'

This decision appeared to suggest that a confession obtained from a suspect suffering from drug withdrawal would not qualify for exclusion under section 76(2)(b) as it was not 'anything said or done', with the implication that this must be an event which is external to the person making the confession. That said, once it is established that there has been an *external* event, the personal characteristics of the accused can be considered in order to determine whether it was likely to have rendered the subsequent confession unreliable.

**KEY CASE**

*R* v *Walker* [1998] Crim LR 211 (CA)

*Concerning: 'unreliability'*

**Facts**

W was arrested for assault and, during questioning by police, made a confession. She was known to be a drug addict but she also suffered from a personality disorder which was not known to the questioning officers. Evidence of this disorder was presented at trial in an attempt to have the confession excluded, but the trial judge declined to exclude under section 76(2)(b).

**Legal principle**

It was held on appeal that the confession should have been excluded. Potter LJ (quoting the earlier unreported decision in *R* v *Watkinson* (1996)): 'Any mental or personality abnormalities may be of relevance when deciding the likely effect of things said or done upon a person being interviewed, whether or not they amount to mental handicap. They form part of the relevant circumstances to which the Court must have regard when considering challenge to admissibility under section 76.'

## Section 76(2)(b) and breaches of PACE

A related question is whether police misconduct (such as breaches of PACE and the related Codes of Practice) is required to justify exclusion under section 76(2)(b). The judgment in *Walker* would suggest not.

**KEY CASE**

*R* v *Harvey* [1988] Crim LR 241 (CA)

*Concerning: 'unreliability'*

**Facts**

H and her lover were arrested in connection with the murder of another person. H and her lover had been the only people present when the person had died, but neither had ▶

admitted to committing the crime. On learning that her lover had confessed to the killing, H made a confession that it was she, rather than her lover, who had committed the murder. The lover, however, later retracted her confession and died before the trial. H was convicted.

**Legal principle**

It was held that H was a woman of low intelligence and suffered from a psychiatric disorder. It was possible that she had admitted to the crime on hearing of her lover's confession simply in an attempt to take the blame. As a consequence, although there had been no wrongdoing on the part of the police, the confession should have been excluded as potentially unreliable.

Similarly, a confession might still be adduced even where there *have* been such breaches.

**KEY CASE**

*R* v *Alladice* (1988) 87 Cr App R 380 (CA)

*Concerning: 'unreliability'*

**Facts**

A was arrested and questioned on suspicion of robbery and made certain admissions which led to his conviction. During questioning he had been refused access to a solicitor, contrary to section 58 PACE. A appealed against conviction on the grounds that the confession should have been excluded under section 76(2)(b).

**Legal principle**

It was held that, although there had been a breach of section 58, the confession had been rightly admitted in evidence. A had been fully aware of his rights and had shown himself more than capable of coping with the interviews. The presence of the solicitor would have provided little additional protection to him, and so his confession was not likely to be unreliable as a consequence of the refusal to grant access to the solicitor. Rose J: 'the solicitor's presence would not have improved the appellant's case.'

That said, breaches of PACE and the Codes of Practice are potentially serious and have been used to justify exclusion of confession evidence.

KEY CASE

**R v Barry (1991) 95 Cr App R 384 (CA)**

*Concerning: 'unreliability' and breaches of PACE*

**Facts**

B was arrested in connection with a large-scale fraud and offered to make a confession in exchange for assistance in gaining bail as he wished to retain custody of his young son. As a result, there were a series of unrecorded interviews without a solicitor, which contravened PACE and the Codes of Practice. H was convicted and appealed on the grounds that the confession evidence should not have been admitted.

**Legal principle**

It was held that the trial judge had given insufficient weight to the numerous breaches of PACE and that this rendered the confession potentially unreliable.

# Confessions of co-accused

As mentioned above, the wording of section 76 indicates that the provision will apply only to a confession which 'the prosecution proposes to give in evidence', which suggests that section 76 would not apply where a defendant seeks to adduce a confession by a co-accused. This apparent anomaly is addressed by section 76A, which was inserted into PACE by the Criminal Justice Act 2003.

KEY STATUTE

**Police and Criminal Evidence Act 1984, s. 76A**

**Confessions may be given in evidence for co-accused**

(1) In any proceedings a confession made by an accused person may be given in evidence for another person charged in the same proceedings (a co-accused) in so far as it is relevant to any matter in issue in the proceedings and is not excluded by the court in pursuance of this section.

(2) If, in any proceedings where a co-accused proposes to give in evidence a confession made by an accused person, it is represented to the court that the confession was or may have been obtained –

    (a) by oppression of the person who made it; or

    (b) in consequence of anything said or done which was likely, in the circumstances existing at the time, to render unreliable any confession which might be made by him in consequence thereof,

▶

(3) the court shall not allow the confession to be given in evidence for the co-accused except in so far as it is proved to the court on the balance of probabilities that the confession (notwithstanding that it may be true) was not so obtained.

Note that, although section 76A largely resembles section 76, the burden of proof on the co-accused under section 76A(2) is only to the civil standard of the 'balance of probabilities', unlike the duty on the prosecution under section 76(2) which is to the higher criminal standard of 'beyond reasonable doubt'.

 Make your answer stand out

Impress the examiner by making a link between this aspect of confession evidence and the possibility of a statement by a co-accused being admitted as hearsay evidence under CJA 2003, section 114 in the 'interests of justice' even where it does not constitute a 'confession' for the purposes of PACE section 82. See *R* v *Sliogeris* [2015] EWCA Crim 22.

# Confessions by mentally handicapped persons

As might be expected, PACE provides additional protection in relation to confessions made by mentally handicapped persons. Such safeguards are intended to address the increased vulnerability of such individuals when subjected to police questioning.

**KEY STATUTE**

**Police and Criminal Evidence Act 1984, s. 77**

**Confessions by mentally handicapped persons**

(1) Without prejudice to the general duty of the court at a trial on indictment [with a jury] to direct the jury on any matter on which it appears to the court appropriate to do so, where at such a trial –

    (a) the case against the accused depends wholly or substantially on a confession by him; and

    (b) the court is satisfied –

(2)   that he is mentally handicapped; and

(3)   that the confession was not made in the presence of an independent person.

---

**KEY CASE**

*R* v *J* [2003] EWCA Crim 3309 (CA)

*Concerning: confessions and PACE s. 77*

**Facts**

J, who was mentally subnormal and extremely suggestible, was questioned in relation to the murder of a woman. He was interviewed by officers without an appropriate adult and on some occasions without a solicitor. During the course of the interviews he made certain admissions but, in a final interview with a solicitor present, he denied the offence and alleged that he had been told to confess by the interviewing officers. The officers asserted that they were unaware of J's mental vulnerability but a document later came to light which suggested that they had, in fact, been aware of his condition.

**Legal principle**

The appeal was allowed. The fact that the officers knew of J's mental health and chose to interview him in contravention of section 77 rendered the resulting confession unsafe. Keene LJ: 'a prudent officer would have taken steps to have had a responsible adult present.'

---

# ◼ Facts discovered as a result of inadmissible confessions

A final point relates to information discovered as a result of a confession which is later held to be inadmissible. Can this additional information be adduced in evidence or is it also inadmissible?

---

**KEY STATUTE**

**Police and Criminal Evidence Act 1984, s. 76**

(1)   The fact that a confession is wholly or partly excluded in pursuance of this section shall not affect the admissibility in evidence –

(a)   of any facts discovered as a result of the confession.

This means that the prosecution may use the additional material but cannot reveal that it was found as a result of the confession which was subsequently held to be inadmissible. It is, however, open to the accused to give evidence that the additional information was discovered as a result of their earlier statement under section 76(5).

# ■ Putting it all together

## Answer guidelines

See the problem question at the start of the chapter.

### Approaching the question

Questions on confessions are always popular with examiners, not least because there are so many facets of the topic which enable the better student to excel. This is one topic where a grasp of the subtleties pays dividends.

### Important points to include

■ Begin with a definition of a 'confession' under PACE 1984 and some indication of the particular difficulties surrounding confession evidence.

■ Part (a) requires some discussion of what may constitute 'oppression' under section 76(2)(a). Clearly, mere shouting is insufficient unless it reaches the level of *R* v *Paris* – there is little here to indicate that this is the case.

■ Part (b) raises the concept of 'unreliability' under section 76(2)(b). There may be breaches of Code of Practice C in the conduct of such a lengthy interview when Paragraph 12.8 of the Code suggests a break after each two hours of questioning. The statement of the officer relating to Jim's son echoes that in *R* v *Fulling* which was not held to be oppression. It may, however, be possible to argue unreliability and your answer should also address the other exclusionary rules **(discussed in Chapter 8)**.

 Make your answer stand out

Note that any discussion of section 76 would have to recognise that Jim has an extensive criminal record and is well acquainted with police procedure. In this way, echoing *R* v *Seelig,* the court may conclude that, even if there are breaches of procedure, Jim is more than capable of dealing with the situation.

## READ TO IMPRESS

Durston, G. (2004) The admissibility of co-defendants' confessions under the Criminal Justice Act 2003. *JPN*, 168: 488.

Hartshorne, J. (2004) Defensive use of a co-accuseds' confession and the Criminal Justice Act 2003. *EvPro*, 8 (3): 165.

Lowenstein, J. (2006) The psychological and procedural issues in the occurrence of false confessions by vulnerable individuals. *JPN*, 170: 207.

Munday, R. (2005) The Court, the dictionary, and the true meaning of 'oppression': a neo-Socratic dialogue on English legal method. *Stat Law* 26: 103.

Stockdale. M. (2013) Confessions and the Criminal Justice Act 2003. *Journal of Criminal Law*, 77: 231.

**www.pearsoned.co.uk/lawexpress**

 Go online to access more revision support including quizzes to test your knowledge, sample questions with answer guidelines, podcasts you can download, and more!

# Hazardous evidence

**7**

## Revision checklist

### Essential points you should know:

☐ The role of corroboration and care warnings
☐ Lies by the defendant
☐ Difficulties associated with identification evidence
☐ Identification evidence and PACE Code D
☐ The *Turnbull* direction

# ■ Topic map

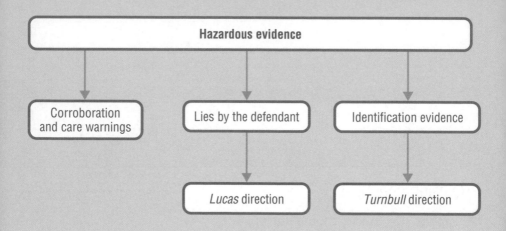

# ■ Introduction

**All forms of evidence are hazardous, but some more than others.**

As we have seen earlier **(in Chapter 6)**, confession evidence can be highly persuasive but is also often found to be unreliable. In the same way, a number of other forms of evidence are regarded as 'hazardous' and so require some degree of caution. Historically, this found expression in the law of corroboration – the requirement that there be some other supporting evidence on the point in question. As will be seen, however, this has largely been abolished in favour of a number of discretionary 'care warnings' which apply in certain specific circumstances.

## ASSESSMENT ADVICE

**Essay questions**

These may ask you to discuss the demise of corroboration generally or, alternatively, to consider a specific area (for example, identification evidence) which raises particular issues of safety/integrity and so requires a care warning.

**Problem questions**

These may also address an area such as identification evidence or may be split into three or four parts, each asking you to consider a different aspect of the topic.

# ■ Sample question

Could you answer this question? Below is a typical essay question that could arise on this topic. Guidelines on answering the question are included at the end of this chapter, whilst a sample problem question and guidance on tackling it can be found on the companion website.

## ESSAY QUESTION

Evidence of identification is both compelling and dangerous. How does the law of evidence seek to minimise the risks of such evidence?

# ■ Corroboration

The principle of **corroboration** is, essentially, straightforward: that the possibility of an unjust outcome to a case (whether civil or criminal) is reduced if the decision is based on more than one piece of evidence. In this way, a party may seek to adduce evidence from a number of witnesses to make the same point or support the evidence of a witness with other forms of evidence (such as scientific or documentary evidence). The intention of this process is that the cumulative effect of the various pieces of evidence will increase the weight of the argument being advanced. That is quite different, however, to a party being *compelled* by the court to adduce such supporting evidence. This used to be the case in relation to the evidence of children (abolished by the Criminal Justice Act 1988), complainants in sexual offences cases and accomplices of the accused giving evidence for the prosecution (abolished by the Criminal Justice and Public Order Act 1994).

As a general rule there is no requirement for corroborating evidence although, as with most general rules, there are exceptions and these form the basis of part of this chapter. We must also consider the related categories of evidence which require the judge to issue a care warning (i.e. a warning to the jury to treat the evidence with care).

---

**KEY DEFINITION: Corroboration**

A requirement for supporting evidence from another source on the same point.

---

## Corroboration required by statute

There are a small number of statutory provisions which impose a requirement for corroborating evidence.

### Speeding

**KEY STATUTE**

**Road Traffic Regulation Act 1984, s. 89**

**Speeding offences generally**

(1) A person who drives a motor vehicle on a road at a speed exceeding a limit imposed by or under any enactment to which this section applies shall be guilty of an offence.

(2) A person prosecuted for such an offence shall not be liable to be convicted solely on the evidence of one witness to the effect that, in the opinion of the witness, the person prosecuted was driving the vehicle at a speed exceeding a specified limit.

This provision also represents something of an exception to the general prohibition on opinion evidence discussed earlier (see Chapter 5).

It should be noted, however, that this only applies to evidence of opinion. Evidence of fact requires no such corroboration.

### KEY CASE

*Nicholas* v *Penny* [1950] 2 All ER 89 (DC)

*Concerning: corroboration and speeding*

Facts

A police officer drove behind the accused for some distance and gave evidence that his speedometer indicated a speed of 40 mph (the speed limit on the road was 30 mph).

Legal principle

It was held that a person could be convicted of exceeding the speed limit on the evidence of one police officer if this was supported by evidence of a speedometer or other mechanical means which meant that the officer's evidence became evidence of fact (the speedometer reading) and not of mere opinion (what he *thought* the speed was).

## Perjury

### KEY STATUTE

Perjury Act 1911, s. 13

Corroboration

A person shall not be liable to be convicted of any offence against this Act, or of any offence declared by any other Act to be perjury or subornation of perjury, or to be punishable as perjury or subornation of perjury, solely upon the evidence of one witness as to the falsity of any statement alleged to be false.

Note that, in relation to perjury, the corroboration is only required to prove that the statement in question was untrue. In this way, if the falsity of the statement is admitted by the accused, then there is no requirement to call other witnesses to support this (*R* v *O'Connor* [1980] Crim LR 43 (CA)).

# ■ Discretionary care warnings

As already indicated, the requirement for mandatory care warnings in relation to corroboration and certain categories of evidence was abolished by the following provision.

---

**KEY STATUTE**

**Criminal Justice and Public Order Act 1994, s. 32**

**Abolition of corroboration rules**

(1) Any requirement whereby at a trial on indictment it is obligatory for the court to give the jury a warning about convicting the accused on the uncorroborated evidence of a person merely because that person is –

    (a) an alleged accomplice of the accused, or

    (b) where the offence charged is a sexual offence, the person in respect of whom it is alleged to have been committed, is hereby abrogated.

---

Note, however, that section 32 merely states that the requirement for an 'obligatory' warning is abrogated. This leaves the possibility of a discretionary warning which may be required in relation to the evidence of *any* witness. The elements of such a warning and the circumstances where such a warning might be required were outlined in the following case.

---

**KEY CASE**

*R* v *Makanjuola* **[1995] 3 All ER 730 (CA)**

*Concerning: corroboration and s. 32*

**Facts**

M was convicted of the indecent assault of a young girl. He appealed, in part, on the grounds that, notwithstanding the removal of the requirement for a mandatory warning by section 32, the trial judge had erred in not issuing a discretionary warning.

**Legal principle**

It was held that it was for the trial judge to decide whether or not to give a warning to the jury and, if so, the terms in which the warning was to be given. The decision whether to give such a warning depended on the content and manner of the witness's evidence, the circumstances of the case and the issues raised. Lord Taylor: 'We see no reason why the absence of a corroboration direction renders the admission of recent complaint to show consistency unfair or inappropriate.'

---

Subsequent decisions have provided some indication of when such a discretionary warning might be warranted.

## KEY CASE

**R v Jones and Jenkins [2003] EWCA Crim 1966 (CA)**

*Concerning: discretionary care warning*

**Facts**

The defendants had been part of a group which had followed a man out of a pub where they had been drinking. The man was later attacked and died from his injuries. Each of the defendants blamed the other for the murder.

**Legal principle**

It was held that, in such cases of 'cut-throat defence', where the defendants blame each other, the jury should be directed to treat evidence of one defendant which was adverse to a co-defendant with caution because of the co-defendant's own interest in the outcome of the case. Auld LJ: 'a judge, in exercising his discretion as to what to say to the jury should at least warn them, where one defendant has given evidence adverse to another, to examine the evidence of each with care because each has or may have an interest of his own to serve.'

## KEY CASE

**Benedetto and Labrador v R [2003] 1 WLR 1545 (PC)**

*Concerning: discretionary care warning*

**Facts**

Both appellants were charged with the murder of a woman. Their convictions were largely based on the evidence of P who had been imprisoned with the men and who claimed to have overheard them admitting to the offence. The men appealed on the grounds that the trial judge had failed to warn the jury of P's extensive criminal record and the impact which this might have on his credibility as a witness.

**Legal principle**

The appeals were allowed. In such cases of 'cell confession', the witness would usually have a motive to gain favour with the authorities and so their evidence had to be treated with caution, and thus a warning would usually be required. Lord Hope: 'It would be hard to imagine a witness who was less deserving of belief . . . even those facts about his background which he was prepared to admit to while he was giving his evidence were more than enough to show that he was not to be trusted.'

Having set out the general rules on corroboration and care warnings, two forms of evidence require particular attention: evidence of lies by the defendant and identification evidence.

# Evidence of lies by the defendant

There may be circumstances where the prosecution wishes to adduce evidence that the defendant has told lies on a previous occasion, either to demonstrate an inconsistency with their later account of events or to undermine their general credibility. There is a danger, however, that a jury will hear or learn of the prior untruth and assume that this automatically indicates the guilt of the defendant. For this reason, evidence of previous lies by the defendant usually requires the judge to issue a warning to the jury. Such a warning takes the form of a '*Lucas* direction' which, as with other types of judge's direction, is named after the leading decision on the matter.

---

**KEY CASE**

*R* v *Lucas* [1981] QB 720 (CA)

*Concerning: lies by the defendant*

**Facts**

The accused was convicted partly on the evidence of an alleged accomplice. The jury were directed by the judge that the accused's lies in the witness box could be viewed as circumstantial evidence which served to corroborate the evidence of the accomplice.

**Legal principle**

On appeal, it was held that a lie was capable of amounting to corroboration if it was deliberate, related to a material issue, the motive was realisation of guilt and a fear of the truth and the statement had been clearly shown to be a lie by evidence other than that of the accomplice. The statement made by the defendant was not shown to be a lie other than by evidence of the accomplice and so the judge's direction was in error. Lord Lane CJ: 'when a defendant tells lies there may be reasons for those lies which are not connected with guilt of the offences charged and that one [task] would be to decide, if the defendant had told lies, what was their purpose.'

---

The circumstances in which a *Lucas* direction will be required were summarised in *R* v *Burge*; *R* v *Pegg* [1996] 1 Cr App R 163 (CA) where it was held that such a direction would be needed:

- where the defendant relies on an alibi;
- where evidence to corroborate the defendant was sought and that evidence contained lies by the defendant;

- where the Crown asserts that the defendant lied in relation to a separate issue, and seeks to rely on that lie as evidence of guilt in relation to the current charge;

- where, even though the prosecution does not seek to rely on the defendant's lies relating to a separate issue, the judge reasonably foresees a real danger that the jury might still rely on the previous lie as evidence of guilt in relation to the current charge.

In such cases, the judge is required to issue a direction to the jury stating:

- that the lie must be admitted or proved beyond reasonable doubt; and

- that the mere fact that the defendant lied is not in itself evidence of guilt since defendants may lie for innocent reasons; so only if the jury is sure that the defendant did not lie for an innocent reason can a lie support the prosecution case.

---

**KEY CASE**

*R* v *Barnett* [2002] EWCA Crim 454 (CA)

*Concerning: lies by the defendant*

**Facts**

B was found to have a stolen painting worth £40,000 under his bed and gave a number of conflicting accounts of how it had come into his possession. The prosecution highlighted the lies but the trial judge failed to issue a *Lucas* direction to the jury.

**Legal principle**

It was held that this did not fall within any of the categories set out in *Burge* and *Pegg*. The purpose of adducing evidence of the earlier lies had been to draw attention to the inconsistency in B's account. Jackson J: 'In so far as the appellant offered any explanations for his changes of story, the judge placed those explanations before the jury . . . accordingly, a *Lucas* direction was not required.'

---

**KEY CASE**

*R* v *Sunalla (Adel Abdulwaheb)* [2014] EWCA Crim 1870 (CA)

*Concerning: lies by the defendant*

**Facts**

The appellant was convicted of an offence under section 111A of the Social Security Administration Act 1992. The prosecution alleged that he had concealed savings in a number of bank accounts which took him above the threshold for Income Support. The appellant claimed that the money in the accounts was not his but, instead, belonged to a Lybian friend who was unable to open UK accounts himself. At trial, the prosecution ▶

adduced evidence of interviews in which he had asserted that he only had one bank account when, in fact, there were a number of accounts and stated that some of the accounts had been closed when they had not. The prosecution argued that these lies were deliberate attempts to conceal the money. No *Lucas* direction had been given.

**Legal principle**

Held – in upholding the appeal. Haddon-Cave J: 'This was a paradigm case for a Lucas direction . . . the prosecution were very clearly relying on lies in interview as a central part of the prosecution case.'

# Identification evidence

The second category of evidence which requires particular attention is identification evidence, which resembles confession evidence in being, at the same time, both extremely compelling and potentially unreliable. Witnesses are frequently required to identify persons whom they have only seen fleetingly and often in confused or stressful circumstances. Mistaken identity may often occur in good faith, but the effects can be extremely serious for the defendant and, for this reason, there is an obvious need for caution in relation to such evidence.

As with evidence of lies by the defendant, the hazards associated with identification evidence are addressed by means of a judge's direction, but there are additional safeguards which apply where the identification has been made by means of a formal procedure conducted under police supervision, such as an identification parade.

## Identification and Code D

Earlier **(see Chapter 6)** we considered the impact of PACE Code of Practice C (on the detention and questioning of suspects) in relation to confession evidence. When considering identification evidence, we must also consider Code of Practice D which regulates the identification of persons by police officers. Remember that this is designed to allow a witness to confirm the person that they saw, but there are two additional points to consider:

■ The police may seek identification evidence where the suspect's identity is known and when it is not known. Where the suspect *is* known, the witness should be presented with a series of people (including the suspect) and asked to pick out the person, rather than have a 'one-to-one' confrontation with the suspect. This is based on the theory that the witness who identifies the suspect from a group is more likely to actually recognise the person whereas, in a 'one-to-one' confrontation, the witness may feel under pressure to identify the suspect, either out of sympathy with the victim of the alleged offence or simply because the police have arrested the person. Where the suspect's identity is not known, the police may present the witness with 'mugshots' of known offenders or take the witness back to the location of the offence, in the hope that the witness will be able to recognise the person they saw.

■ The suspect will usually wish to participate in an identification procedure such as the traditional 'identification parade', which confronts the witness with a series of similar looking people, in the hope that the witness will either be unable to make a positive identification or will pick someone other than the suspect.

Code D provides a hierarchy of identification procedures. Traditionally, the 'identification parade' was viewed as the preferable option, but this can cause practical difficulties centred on the requirement that the other people in the parade are sufficiently similar to the suspect to actively challenge the recollection of the witness. For example, if the suspect is a very short man with one leg and ginger hair, the police would need to find another eight people who match the general appearance of the suspect, which may not be easy to achieve at short notice. The cost and inconvenience this can cause led to a revision of Code D which now provides for the following methods of identification.

## Video identification

The vast majority of identification procedures are now conducted by video identification which resembles the traditional identification parade in that the witness is confronted with a series of individuals, including the suspect. The key difference (and advantage from the perspective of the police) is that the process takes place by the witness viewing a series of videotapes, which removes the necessity to physically assemble the group for a parade. Instead, images of people who resemble the suspect are selected from a central database and compiled for viewing by the witness.

 **Make your answer stand out**

Although video identification is easier for the police to arrange, it has not entirely removed the difficulties of finding images of people who are similar in appearance to the suspect. See Taylor, C. W. (2005) 'Video Identification under PACE Code D: R v Marcus', International Journal of Evidence and Proof, 9(3) 204–10.

## Identification parade

This is the traditional method which is familiar from television and film, where the witness is presented with a series of individuals, including the suspect.

## Group identification

This method may be used as an alternative to the identification parade (whether video or physical) and involves the witness being placed in a public place where there are a number of people, including the suspect.

---

**KEY CASE**

### *R* v *Stott* [2004] EWCA Crim 615 (CA)

*Concerning: group identification*

**Facts**

Having arrested S for robbery, the police sought to hold a video identification, but the defendant's solicitor objected to some of the other images selected and so the identification procedure could not be held. As an alternative, the police arranged a group identification, which placed the defendant in a group of people in a bar. The witness surveyed the group and asked the defendant to stand before positively identifying him. S was convicted and appealed, arguing that the police should have conducted a traditional identification parade rather than a group identification and that he should not have been asked to stand before the witness had made a positive identification.

**Legal principle**

The appeal was dismissed. Code D did not require the police to hold an identification parade rather than a group identification and there was no impropriety in asking S to stand simply to allow the witness to confirm her suspicion that S was the person she had seen. Brown J: 'There was here no breach of the code, and nothing in the way in which the exercise was carried out to indicate any unsafe procedure.'

---

## Confrontation

Where the suspect refuses to participate in another form of identification procedure, it may be necessary to stage a confrontation between the suspect and the witness. In such cases, the two are brought together (usually at the police station) and the witness is asked if this is the person they saw. Obviously, the circumstances of the meeting will suggest to the witness that this is indeed the person they saw and so this is regarded as a less satisfactory procedure. It should be noted, however, that this apparent unfairness to the suspect is largely countered by the fact that it is their refusal to participate in another (fairer) procedure which has necessitated the confrontation in the first place.

*R* v *Kelly* [2003] EWCA Crim 596 (CA)

*Concerning: confrontation*

**Facts**

K was accused of the robbery of a travel agent, during which a member of staff had been held at knifepoint. She identified K as her attacker following a confrontation staged by the police. K appealed against his conviction, arguing that the police should not have used the confrontation as this was an unsatisfactory means of identification.

**Legal principle**

The appeal was dismissed. K had refused to participate in any of the preferable forms of identification procedure and so the police had been justified in using the confrontation. May LJ: 'even if that was a technical breach of the Code, we are completely unconvinced that that fact, taken in the circumstances of this case, should have led the judge to either exclude the evidence or withdraw the case from the jury at the close of the prosecution case.'

In many respects, confrontation resembles 'dock identification' (asking the witness to point to the person in court). Again, this is not favoured as an identification procedure, as the fact that the accused is on trial and there are no other people to choose from may encourage the witness to confirm the identification even if they are not entirely certain.

**📖 REVISION NOTE**

Note that breaches of Code D may lead to the exclusion of the identification evidence under section 78 PACE, which is discussed further later on (see **Chapter 8**).

# ◼ The *Turnbull* direction

The other key issue which must be addressed in any discussion of the treatment of identification evidence is the direction which the judge must issue to the jury. This seeks to emphasise the particular hazards associated with identification evidence and so cause the jury to treat the evidence with particular care. As with the *Lucas* direction discussed above, the direction relating to identification takes its name from a leading decision on the subject, in this case *R* v *Turnbull* [1977] QB 244 (CA). This requires the judge to:

- ◼ warn the jury of the need for particular caution before convicting on the basis of the identification evidence;
- ◼ require the jury to consider closely the circumstances and conditions in which the identification was made; and

■ explain to the jury the need for the direction, highlighting the danger of mistaken witnesses and the miscarriages of justice which have occurred as a consequence.

It is possible for an appeal to succeed if the judge's direction is later found to have been inadequate.

---

**KEY CASE**

*R* v *Pattinson* [1996] 1 Cr App R 51 (CA)

*Concerning: identification and the* Turnbull *direction*

**Facts**

The appellants were convicted of the robbery of a jeweller's shop. Security camera pictures were too poor to enable identification so a number of witnesses were produced to identify the robbers. The judge issued a *Turnbull* direction.

**Legal principle**

The appeals would be allowed. Although the judge had issued the *Turnbull* direction, she had not sufficiently emphasised the history of miscarriages of justice arising from mistaken identification evidence. Similarly, she had not summarised the weaknesses of the identification evidence in this case. Henry LJ: 'the summing-up might have been better focused on the question of identification had all the evidence as to identification been dealt with as a discrete part of the evidence.'

---

# When is the direction required?

Not all cases involving identification evidence require a *Turnbull* direction to be given. Only in those cases where the prosecution relies 'wholly or substantially' on the evidence of identity is the judge obliged to issue a direction to the jury.

---

**✎ EXAM TIP**

In discussing this point, you might emphasise that a judge, wary of leaving themselves open to a successful appeal based on their failure to issue a direction, may well make such a direction even where the identification evidence is only a small part of the prosecution case and so is not strictly necessary.

---

It should also be noted that the fact that the evidence is of *recognition* (of someone whom the witness has known previously) does not mean that a *Turnbull* direction will not be required. The necessity for a direction will depend on the individual circumstances of the case. For example, where the defendant admits being present at the scene but denies committing the offence, there may be no need for a direction (*R* v *Slater* [1995] 1 Cr App R 584 (CA)), but where, for example, there is a public disorder involving a number of people, one of whom was the accused, a *Turnbull* direction may be required (*R* v *Thornton* [1995] 1 Cr App R 578 (CA)).

---

### ✎ MAKE YOUR ANSWER STAND OUT

For a useful discussion of the *Turnbull* direction by the Court of Appeal see *R* v *S (P) and another* [2015] EWCA Crim 783.

---

# ■ Putting it all together

## Answer guidelines

See the essay question at the start of the chapter.

### Approaching the question

Remember to adopt a clear structure, making good use of your introduction and conclusion. Take each step incrementally, making sure to focus on developing a fluent narrative.

### Important points to include

- Outline the dangers of mistaken identification, based on the fallibility of human memory, and comment on the disproportionate impact which such evidence may have on a jury. This combination makes evidence of identification particularly hazardous.

- Discuss the various mechanisms set out in Code D of PACE for police identification procedures, and assess their effectiveness in safeguarding against mistaken identification. Here you can make a distinction between those methods (such as ID parades and video identification) which provide the witness with a choice of individuals, and those (such as confrontation and dock identification) which suggest the likely outcome in advance.

▶

- Set out the requirements of the *Turnbull* direction and the three elements of the dircction, making clear that it is not required in all cases but is in those where the prosecution case relies 'wholly or substantially' on the identification evidence.

- Offer some evaluation/comment on how effective the current rules are in protecting defendants from conviction as a result of mistaken identification.

 Make your answer stand out

Emphasise the risk of an appeal being allowed on the basis of a defective judge's direction on identification, such as in *R* v *Pattinson*. This requires judges to be very careful over the precise form of words used, and misdirection may undermine an otherwise sound conviction. Make the wider point that defective judge's directions (on a number of topics) are a common source of successful appeals.

## READ TO IMPRESS

Bromby, M. (2007) An examination of criminal jury directions in relation to eyewitness identification in commonwealth jurisdictions. *CLWR*, 36(4): 303.

Lewis, P. (2006) A comparative examination of corroboration and caution warnings in prosecutions of sexual offences. *Crim LR*, 889.

Lucas, J.R. (2011) Turnbull turned turtle. *Archbold Review*, 3 March: 5.

Roberts, A. (2004) The problem of mistaken identification: some observations on process. *EvPro*, 8(2): 100.

Roberts. A. (2012) Expert evidence on the reliability of eyewitness identification – some observations on the justifications for exclusion: *Gage* v *HM Advocate*. *International Journal of Evidence & Proof*, 16(1): 93.

Sauerland, M. and Sporer, S.L. (2008) The application of multiple lineups in a field study. *Psychology, Crime and Law*, 14(6): 549–64.

Stone. M. (2012) Pre-trial defects in criminal evidence: scope for advocacy and judgment. *Criminal Law & Justice Weekly*, 176: 43.

Wolchover, D. (2009) VIPER and the vandalizing of PACE. *JPN*, 173: 5.

**www.pearsoned.co.uk/lawexpress**

 Go online to access more revision support including quizzes to test your knowledge, sample questions with answer guidelines, podcasts you can download, and more!

# Illegally and improperly obtained evidence

8

## Revision checklist

**Essential points you should know:**

- [ ] The relatively relaxed approach of the courts in England and Wales towards illegally obtained evidence
- [ ] The concept of entrapment and the law of evidence
- [ ] Exclusion of evidence under section 78 PACE 1984
- [ ] Exclusion of evidence under section 82 PACE 1984

## ■ Topic map

Illegally/improperly obtained evidence

Exclusion under section 78 PACE

Exclusion under section 82 PACE

# ■ Introduction

## Does it really matter how we get the evidence?

As we saw earlier (in Chapter 6), the law of evidence allows for the exclusion of confessions, even when they are known to be true, because of the manner in which they were obtained. This chapter will consider other situations where evidence may be excluded by the court. This does not mean, however, that the court will readily hold evidence to be inadmissible because of the circumstances under which it was secured. We are used to courtroom dramas from the USA where rigid rules of admissibility are routinely applied, but things are very different here.

## ASSESSMENT ADVICE

### Essay questions

These may ask you to consider the approach of the courts towards the admissibility of evidence generally, including evidence obtained as a result of illegal searches, etc. before addressing the exclusionary rules under section 78 and section 82 PACE. This may also be combined with discussion of section 76 PACE as it applies to confession evidence.

### Problem questions

These may require you to apply section 78 and section 82 and, as with essay questions, this might include a confession which would also necessitate consideration of section 76. Other possible areas might include entrapment and illegal searches.

# ■ Sample question

Could you answer this question? Below is a typical problem question that could arise on this topic. Guidelines on answering the question are included at the end of this chapter, whilst a sample essay question and guidance on tackling it can be found on the companion website.

## PROBLEM QUESTION

Steve is a well-known local villain, with a string of convictions for burglary and other property offences. He is arrested on suspicion of handling stolen mobile phones and taken to a local police station for interview. At the beginning of the interview the investigating officer administers a caution to Steve, who requests a solicitor but is told that there isn't one available and that the officers do not have time to wait. The interview proceeds and Steve denies any involvement in the offences. After almost an hour, the investigating officer suggests a break and, 15 minutes later, resumes the interview. Steve, however, asks him not to turn on the tape recorder so they can talk 'off the record'. The officer agrees but forgets to repeat the caution before they begin talking. Steve tells him that he knows where more of the stolen phones are being kept but makes no admission of guilt and the interview ends so that police can investigate this information.

The following day, Steve is interviewed again, this time with a solicitor present. His information proved to be correct and the police have the phones. Before the interview, the investigating officer decides to tell Steve and the solicitor that Steve's fingerprints have been found on the phones (this is not true). On hearing this, the solicitor requests a private consultation with his client, after which Steve makes a full admission.

Assess the possibility of a challenge to the admission of the above evidence *ignoring* any application of section 76 PACE.

# ■ Admissibility generally

We saw earlier (in Chapter 1) that evidence which is relevant is admissible, though this raises the question of how the court will view evidence which is clearly relevant but which has been obtained unlawfully, for example by means of an illegal search.

The starting point to this discussion is the general principle that the courts will not ordinarily exclude evidence simply on the grounds that it has been improperly obtained.

### KEY CASE

*R* v *Leatham* (1861) 25 JP 468 (pre-SCJA 1873)

*Concerning: admissibility of evidence*

**Facts**

As part of an investigation into corruption surrounding the election of a Member of Parliament, a letter was sent between the parties involved, detailing sums of money paid.

The letter was not produced when requested and so secondary evidence of its contents was admitted.

**Legal principle**

Crompton J: 'It matters not how you get it; if you steal it even, it would be admissible in evidence.'

**KEY CASE**

***Jones* v *Owens* (1870) 34 JP 759**

*Concerning: admissibility of evidence*

**Facts**

A constable conducted what was later held to be an unauthorised search of the accused and found a number of salmon, leading to a charge of unlawful fishing.

**Legal principle**

Mellor J: 'It would be a dangerous obstacle to the administration of justice if we were to hold, because evidence was obtained by illegal means, it could not be used.'

Despite these historical decisions, however, it would be inaccurate to think of the law of evidence as a total free-for-all with no restrictions on the evidence which can be adduced. Instead, it is more accurate to think of a general principle of admissibility which is subject to exception, as for example with the exclusionary discretion of confession evidence under section 76 PACE. This chapter will concentrate on the other two key mechanisms for the exclusion of evidence under section 78 PACE and the power to exclude under the common law, preserved by section 82 PACE.

# Section 78 PACE 1984

It will be remembered from earlier **(see Chapter 6)** that section 76 PACE applies only to confession evidence. By contrast, section 78 applies to all forms of evidence, including confession evidence, and it is important to remember that both provisions may need to be considered, depending on the type of evidence in question.

> **!** Don't be tempted to . . .
>
> It is very easy to become confused between the application of section 76 PACE and section 78. Be careful to restrict consideration of section 76 to confession evidence but, equally, do not forget to address the possible application of section 78 in confession cases.

**KEY STATUTE**

**Police and Criminal Evidence Act 1984, s. 78**

**Exclusion of unfair evidence**

(1) In any proceedings the court may refuse to allow evidence on which the prosecution proposes to rely to be given if it appears to the court that, having regard to all the circumstances, including the circumstances in which the evidence was obtained, the admission of the evidence would have such an adverse effect on the fairness of the proceedings that the court ought not to admit it.

It is immediately obvious that this is much broader in scope than the exclusionary rule under section 76(2) which is confined to 'oppression' and 'unreliability'. Under section 78 evidence may be excluded if the court considers this necessary 'having regard to all the circumstances', and this gives the court considerable latitude to decide that evidence should not be adduced.

In considering the possible application of section 78, the following should be noted:

- this section only applies to evidence on which 'the prosecution *proposes* to rely' and so, like section 76, the power to exclude will only apply *before* the evidence is admitted;

- unlike section 76, this is a discretionary power to exclude. In this way, whereas section 76 states that the court '*shall not* allow the confession', section 78 merely states that the court '*may* refuse to allow evidence'.

Furthermore, as the test for exclusion is that the evidence has '*such* an adverse effect on the fairness of the proceedings', this suggests that the court is not required to exclude the evidence merely because it has *some* adverse effect, thereby increasing the court's discretion in applying the provision.

**KEY CASE**

*Re Saifi* [2001] 4 All ER 168 (DC)

*Concerning: application of s. 78 PACE*

**Facts**

The Indian government sought the extradition of S to face charges of murder and conspiracy to murder. S alleged that certain statements from him should be excluded under section 78 as they had been obtained by torture, intimidation and inducement. The stipendiary magistrate declined to exclude the evidence.

**Legal principle**

When considering whether to exclude evidence under section 78, there was no need to make a specific finding in relation to every issue raised. The absence from the section of words suggesting that facts were to be established or proved to any standard was deliberate, leaving the matter open and unrestricted by rigid evidential considerations. Rose LJ: 'The purpose of the section is to enable the court to achieve fairness in the conduct of its proceedings, not by reference to the particular character or type of evidence but by having "regard to all the circumstances". The exercise of the power is unlikely to achieve its aim if encased in a rigid framework.'

The existence of this deliberately wide discretion requires some examination of those factors which the courts *have* considered sufficient to warrant exclusion under section 78.

## Section 78 and breaches of PACE Codes

One key question is whether breaches of the Codes of Practice under PACE by the police will automatically justify exclusion under section 78.

**KEY CASE**

*R* v *Sanghera* [2001] 1 Cr App R 299 (CA)

*Concerning: s. 78 and breaches of PACE Codes*

**Facts**

S was a sub-postmaster who reported an armed robbery. During the investigation of this claim, police conducted a search of the Post Office premises which was not in accordance with the relevant Code of Practice. The search revealed a hidden box containing £4,390. Officers installed a hidden video camera and filmed S looking in the box. He was subsequently arrested and convicted of theft. He appealed on the grounds that the evidence obtained during the illegal search should have been excluded under section 78. ▶

---

**Legal principle**

Lord Woolf: 'In relation to section 78, it is of importance, in our judgment, that each particular case is considered on its facts and that no broad generalisation is made as to its application. . . . There are situations where a serious breakdown in the proper procedures has taken place in the whole of the prosecution process. In such a situation, the courts may well take the view that the nature of the breakdown is so significant that it would not be appropriate to allow the evidence to be admitted. There are also situations lower down the scale where there has been a breach of the Code which can be regarded as being significant but not serious. That is not of the same gravity [and] . . . the court will almost inevitably come to the conclusion that there has been no injustice or unfairness involved and will exercise its discretion in favour of allowing the evidence to be given.'

---

This does, however, acknowledge that some breaches will be sufficiently serious to justify exclusion of the evidence.

**KEY CASE**

*R* v *Samuel* **[1988] 2 All ER 135 (CA)**

*Concerning: s. 78 and breaches of PACE Codes*

**Facts**

S was arrested on suspicion of robbery and questioned by police on a number of occasions. His requests for a solicitor were refused, in breach of section 58 PACE and the relevant Codes of Practice. He finally confessed and was convicted.

**Legal principle**

It was held that the refusal of access to a solicitor had been unjustified and the interview should not have taken place. This was one of the most important rights of the accused and so the evidence should be excluded. Hodgson J: 'Any officer attempting to justify his decision to delay the exercise of this fundamental right of a citizen will, in our judgment, be unable to do so save by reference to specific circumstances.'

## Bad faith and police malpractice

A related issue is whether bad faith on the part of the investigating officers is required to justify exclusion under section 78. It has repeatedly been stated by the courts that the purpose of section 78 is not to punish the police.

**KEY CASE**

*R* v *Delaney* (1988) 153 JP 103 (CA)

*Concerning: exclusion of evidence*

**Facts**

D, a 17-year-old educationally subnormal youth, was interviewed by police in connection with an alleged indecent assault on a three-year-old girl. He admitted the offence but there were irregularities in the recording of the interview which breached the relevant Codes of Practice.

**Legal principle**

Lord Lane CJ: 'the mere fact that there has been a breach of the Codes of Practice does not of itself mean that evidence has to be rejected. It is no part of the duty of the court to rule a statement inadmissible simply in order to punish the police for failure to observe the Codes of Practice.'

This may apply even where the evidence has been the product of a deliberate trick or deceit on the part of the police.

**KEY CASE**

*R* v *Bailey* [1993] 3 All ER 513 (CA)

*Concerning: s. 78 exclusion*

**Facts**

B and another person were arrested on suspicion of robbery but gave 'no comment' interviews. Officers placed them in a cell together, falsely telling them that they had been forced to do so by the custody officer. The cell had been bugged and officers recorded incriminating conversations between B and the other person which were adduced in evidence. B was convicted and appealed on the ground that the taped conversation should have been excluded.

**Legal principle**

It was held that the trial judge had been correct to admit the evidence of the taped conversation as it did not breach the Codes of Practice. Brown LJ: 'where, as here, very serious crimes have been committed, and committed by men who have not themselves shrunk from trickery and a good deal worse, and where there has never been the least suggestion that their covertly taped confessions were oppressively obtained or other than wholly reliable, it seems to us hardly surprising that the trial judge exercised his undoubted discretion in the way he did.'

There are limits to this principle, however.

---

**KEY CASE**

*Matto* v *Wolverhampton Crown Court* (1987) *The Times,* 27 May (DC)

*Concerning: s. 78 exclusion*

**Facts**

M was suspected of driving with excess alcohol. An illegal (and positive) breath test was conducted by officers on M's property and he was arrested. On arrival at the police station a second positive test was obtained. M appealed against conviction on the basis of the illegality of the first test.

**Legal principle**

It was held that the officers had acted with mala fides in knowingly conducting an illegal breath test and, as the result of this first test had led directly to the second test, the evidence should have been excluded. Lord Woolf: 'The Crown Court clearly found that when that specimen was being requested the officers realised that they were acting illegally and were not entitled so to do.'

---

**KEY CASE**

*R* v *Mason* [1988] 1 WLR 139 (CA)

*Concerning: s. 78 exclusion*

**Facts**

M was arrested on suspicion of arson. The police had no direct evidence against M but told him and his solicitor that a fragment of a bottle had been found at the scene containing flammable liquid and bearing M's fingerprints. This was untrue but, on hearing this, M confessed and was convicted. He appealed on the grounds that the confession should have been excluded.

**Legal principle**

It was held that, unlike section 76 which required oppression or unreliability, the trial judge could use section 78 to exclude the confession on the basis of the unfairness it produced. The judge should have recognised the deceit of the police and excluded the confession. Watkins LJ: 'It is obvious from the undisputed evidence that the police practised a deceit not only on the appellant, which is bad enough, but also on the solicitor whose duty it was to advise him. In effect, they hoodwinked both solicitor and client. That was a most reprehensible thing to do.'

✎ EXAM TIP

When mentioning this decision, make clear that it may have been the fact that the solicitor was also lied to, which made the court take a particularly dim view of the actions of the police in this case. If legal advisers are not properly informed of the case against their clients by the police, it may adversely affect their ability to offer professional advice and so undermine the protection which they represent.

Therefore, as a general rule, in cases involving a breach of the Codes of Practice, it is the seriousness of the breach which matters more than whether the officers concerned have acted in good faith.

**KEY CASE**

*R* v *Walsh* (1989) 91 Cr App R 161 (CA)

*Concerning: s. 78 exclusion*

**Facts**

W was arrested on suspicion of robbery. He made a confession after being denied access to a solicitor and there were a number of other serious breaches of the relevant Codes of Practice. W was convicted and appealed on the grounds that his confession should have been excluded under section 78.

**Legal principle**

The appeal was allowed but the court made clear that the task of the court was to consider whether there would be such an adverse effect on the fairness of the proceedings that justice required the exclusion of the evidence and, while bad faith on the part of the officers concerned might make substantial and significant breaches which might not otherwise have been so, their good faith would not render breaches which were themselves significant and substantial no longer so. Saville J: 'the failure of the police officers to comply with the Code in the respects that we have categorised as significant and substantial, we consider that to admit the evidence would have such an adverse effect on the proceedings that the judge should have excluded it.'

 Make your answer stand out

Impress the examiner by citing the recent decision of the Supreme Court in *Beghal* v *Director of Public Prosecutions* [2015] UKSC 49 in which it was held that evidence obtained from a defendant by means of legal compulsion such as under Schedule 7 to ▶

the Terrorism Act 2000, which requires a person at a port or airport to answer questions asked by police officers, immigration officers and customs officers, is a classic case of evidence which it will be unfair to admit and which should be excluded under section 78.

## Entrapment and agents provocateurs

Another area where there have been attempts to exclude evidence under section 78 relates to allegations of entrapment by the police acting as **agents provocateurs**. In such cases the police provide the opportunity for the commission of the offence (typically by means of an undercover operation) and then arrest the accused. As part of this discussion the distinction must be made between those cases where the police merely provide an opportunity for the accused to commit an offence which they would have committed anyway and those cases where the police encourage the accused to commit an offence which is out of character and which they would not have committed except for the actions of the police. The fact that the defence of entrapment has not been available under the criminal law of England and Wales has traditionally placed great importance on section 78 as the principal mechanism for attempting to counter such evidence.

**KEY DEFINITION: Agent provocateur**

A person who unfairly instigates the commission of an offence by another person.

**KEY CASE**

*R v Christou* [1992] QB 979 (CA)

*Concerning: entrapment*

**Facts**

To counter an increase in burglary, police set up a fake shop which offered to buy jewellery with 'no questions asked'. The shop was equipped with video cameras and recording equipment. C, together with an accomplice, was arrested for burglary/handling stolen goods as a result of visiting the shop and offering stolen goods to the police officers posing as the shop owners. At trial, C challenged the admission of the evidence from the undercover operation but, when the judge allowed the evidence, he pleaded guilty. He subsequently appealed against the decision to admit the evidence.

**Legal principle**

The appeal was dismissed. Although the police had engaged in a trick which had produced evidence against the appellants, the trick had not as such been applied to them but rather they had voluntarily applied themselves to the trick and, for this reason, it had not resulted in unfairness. Lord Taylor CJ: 'the trick was not applied to the appellants; they voluntarily applied themselves to the trick. It is not every trick producing evidence against an accused which results in unfairness . . . a trick, certainly; in a sense too, a trick which results in a form of self-incrimination; but not one which could reasonably be thought to involve unfairness.'

## KEY CASE

### *Williams* v *DPP* [1993] 3 All ER 365 (DC)

*Concerning: entrapment*

**Facts**

Police officers left an unlocked van parked with cartons of cigarettes visible in the back of the van. W was observed removing cartons from the van and was arrested. Having been convicted under the Criminal Attempts Act 1981, W appealed on the grounds that the police had enticed the commission of the offence by providing an 'irresistible temptation'.

**Legal principle**

The appeal was dismissed. W had voluntarily taken the goods in the absence of any pressure from the police and with full understanding of the dishonesty of his actions. Wright J: 'In my judgment it is an entirely legitimate enterprise on the part of the police and of a permissible character for the detection of crime.'

## KEY CASE

### *R* v *Bryce* [1992] 4 All ER 567 (CA)

*Concerning: entrapment*

**Facts**

During a telephone conversation, B offered to sell a car at well below the market price to an undercover police officer and, when the two men later met, B stated that the car had been stolen 'two or three days previously'. On arrest, he also made other incriminating statements after the police interview tape had been turned off and without a caution being administered. On conviction for handling stolen goods, B appealed on the grounds that both conversations should have been excluded.

**Legal principle**

The appeal was allowed. The telephone conversation about the car had been at the instigation of the police officer and the incriminating statement by B went directly to the question of guilt. Also, the discussion was disputed and there was no contemporary record of the conversation. Similarly, the statement made after the recorded interview had ended should have been preceded with a caution (as required by the Codes of Practice) or B may have concluded that the statement was 'off the record' and so would not be used in evidence. Lord Taylor CJ: 'One of the main purposes of the Code is to eliminate the possibility of an interview being concocted or of a true interview being falsely alleged to have been concocted. If it were permissible for an officer simply to assert that, after a properly conducted interview produced a nil return, the suspect confessed off the record and for that confession to be admitted, then the safeguards of the code could readily be bypassed.'

---

**KEY CASE**

### *DPP* v *Marshall* [1988] 3 All ER 683 (DC)

*Concerning: entrapment*

**Facts**

M was licensed to sell alcohol but only by the case, rather than individual bottles and cans. Plainclothes police officers posed as customers and were sold individual bottles of wine and cans of beer. M was charged under the Licensing Act 1964 but contended that the evidence of the police officers should be excluded under section 78. This was accepted by the Magistrates and the case was dropped. The DPP appealed by way of case stated.

**Legal principle**

It was held that the officers' evidence did not have an adverse effect on the fairness of the proceedings and so had been wrongly excluded. Woolf LJ: 'there is no question of there being any defence of entrapment under English law and merely knowing that the police officers obtained the evidence by taking part themselves in a sale which contravened the law does not mean that the evidence must be excluded under section 78 of the 1984 Act.'

---

**KEY CASE**

### *R* v *Looseley, Attorney-General's Reference (No. 3 of 2000)* [2001] UKHL 53 (HL)

*Concerning: entrapment*

**Facts**

Both appellants had been convicted of supplying Class A drugs (heroin) as a result of an undercover police operation which saw officers pose as buyers in order to purchase drugs. Both appellants appealed on the basis that the evidence of the drug purchases should have been excluded under section 78 or the proceedings should have been stayed as an abuse of process.

**Legal principle**

Although English law does not recognise a defence of entrapment, where a defendant can show entrapment the court may stay the proceedings as an abuse of process or exclude evidence under section 78 of PACE. Lord Nicholls: 'The greater the inducement held out by the police, and the more forceful or persistent the police overtures, the more readily may a court conclude that the police overstepped the boundary.'

In deciding *Looseley,* the House of Lords clarified the current position on the use of such 'entrapment' evidence, both in relation to section 78 and applications to stay proceedings as an abuse of process. In particular:

- although the Lords declined to recognise entrapment as a substantive defence under the criminal law, there remains the possibility of either exclusion under section 78 or a stay (as abuse of process) in such cases. Where entrapment can be shown, a stay of proceedings will be the usual outcome, rather than exclusion under section 78;

- the presence or absence of a predisposition to commit the offence on the part of the accused is not the deciding factor in determining the propriety of police conduct. Such a predisposition will not render acceptable what would otherwise be unacceptable police conduct;

- the court should consider whether the police did no more than present the accused with an unexceptional opportunity to commit a crime or, alternatively, whether they actually caused the commission of the offence;

- this will not necessarily be determined by whether the officers adopt an 'active' or 'passive' role in the events leading to the commission of the offence, as officers may have to adopt an 'active' role to overcome the suspicions of those engaged in criminal activity. This will, in part, depend on the nature of the offence under investigation;

- the court will also consider the degree of police inducement offered to the accused and the probable effects of this inducement, including the circumstances and vulnerability.

**✎ EXAM TIP**

The House of Lords in *Looseley* also stated that the ability to exclude evidence under section 78 and to stay proceedings as an abuse of process in cases of alleged entrapment was compliant with Article 6 of the European Convention on Human Rights. You might also wish to mention the decision of the European Court of Human Rights in *Teixeira de Castro* v *Portugal* (1998) 28 EHRR 101, which had seen the Strasbourg

▶

court find actions of the police in inciting the commission of an offence to be a breach of Article 6. For more recent judicial consideration of entrapment in the UK, see *R* v *Harmes & Crane* [2006] EWCA Crim 928, *R* v *Moore* [2013] EWCA Crim 85 and *R* v *Palmer (Tre) and others* [2014] EWCA Crim 1681.

# ■ Exclusion under the common law

In addition to the general power to exclude under section 78 and the power to exclude confession evidence under section 76, there remains a residual power under the common law which was expressly preserved by PACE.

---

**KEY STATUTE**

**Police and Criminal Evidence Act 1984, s. 82(3)**

Nothing in this Part of this Act shall prejudice any power of a court to exclude evidence (whether by preventing questions from being put or otherwise) at its discretion.

---

The current scope of this common law discretion is based on the following leading case.

---

**KEY CASE**

*R* v *Sang* [1980] AC 402 (HL)

*Concerning: common law exclusion of evidence*

**Facts**

S was charged with conspiracy to supply forged banknotes. At trial, the defence sought to argue that the events arose from the entrapment of S by a police informer acting as an agent provocateur and that the evidence should be excluded. The trial judge ruled that he had no such general power to exclude the evidence and this prompted a guilty plea from S. His appeal against the judge's ruling was dismissed by the Court of Appeal.

**Legal principle**

It was held that the judge always retained the discretion to exclude evidence where in his opinion its prejudicial effect outweighed its probative value. However, because the court was not concerned with how evidence was obtained, but instead with how it was used by the prosecution at trial, a judge had no discretion to refuse to admit relevant admissible

---

evidence simply because it had been obtained by improper or unfair means, except in the case of admissions, confessions and evidence obtained from the accused after the commission of the offence. Roskill LJ: 'The modern discretion is a general one to be exercised where fairness to the accused requires its exercise.'

In this way, the judge must balance the 'prejudicial effect' of the evidence on the accused against the 'probative value' of the evidence to the case being advanced.

# ■ Putting it all together

## Answer guidelines

See the problem question at the start of the chapter.

### Approaching the question

The question requires a clear grasp of the various exclusionary powers, most notably section 78 and section 82(3) PACE. A competent answer also requires you to make use of the supporting case law which has indicated the manner in which the courts will apply these, largely, discretionary principles.

### Important points to include

- Consider the general discretionary power to exclude under *R* v *Sang,* as preserved by section 82(3). This requires the judge to consider whether the 'prejudicial effect' of the evidence on the accused outweighs its 'probative value' to the case being advanced. This is extremely broad and, because the test is *subjective,* depends largely on the opinion of the judge hearing the case.

- In considering section 78, we can see that there has been a breach of section 58 PACE and the Codes of Practice in denying Steve access to a solicitor. This may justify exclusion but remember that section 78 requires '*such* an adverse effect' and it might be argued that, as a seasoned criminal, Steve is more than capable of dealing with the questioning and, therefore, that the absence of a solicitor has not seriously undermined his position. You might wish to cite *Samuel* and *Walsh* on this.

- The lies by the police to both Steve and (perhaps more seriously) his solicitor echo the facts of *Mason,* and this may be cited in support of the view that the admission should be excluded under section 78.     ▶

Make your answer stand out

- Emphasise the subjective nature of the test in *Sang*.
- Point out that breaches of the Codes of Practice do not, of themselves, render the evidence inadmissible under section 78.

## READ TO IMPRESS

McKay, S. (2009a) Approaching allegations of entrapment (Part 1). *JPN*, 173: 11.

McKay, S. (2009b) Approaching allegations of entrapment (Part 2). *JPN*, 173: 33.

Ormerod, D. and Roberts, A. (2002) The trouble with *Teixeira*: developing a principled approach to entrapment. *EvPro*, 6(1): 3.

Robertson, B. (1989) The looking-glass world of Section 78. *NLJ*, 139: 1223.

Sanders, A. (1990) Access to a solicitor and s 78 of PACE. *LS Gaz*, 87(31 October):17.

**www.pearsoned.co.uk/lawexpress**

 Go online to access more revision support including quizzes to test your knowledge, sample questions with answer guidelines, podcasts you can download, and more!

# Privilege, disclosure and public interest immunity

## Revision checklist

**Essential points you should know:**

- [ ] The meaning of 'privilege' within the law of evidence
- [ ] The forms of privilege
- [ ] Disclosure under the Criminal Procedure and Investigations Act 1996
- [ ] Public interest immunity

# ■ Topic map

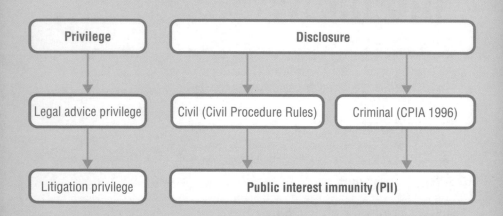

# ■ Introduction

**There is some information that you just don't want the other side to know.**

As a general principle, a witness must answer any questions put to them during their testimony and each party to the proceedings must make available any documents in their possession for inspection by their opponents. Failure to do so may constitute contempt of court and is punished severely. For this reason, any mechanism which allows a party to avoid answering questions or divulging documents is of particular interest. This chapter will consider both of the principal ways in which information can be withheld – privilege and public interest immunity – together with the disclosure process which facilitates the exchange of information between the parties.

## ASSESSMENT ADVICE

**Essay questions**

Essay questions on privilege or public interest immunity generally require you to outline the key provisions in each area and offer some assessment of their effectiveness and/or desirability. Essay questions on disclosure are less common and require you to chart the development of the principles through the operation of the Attorney General's Guidelines and then CPIA 1996.

**Problem questions**

These typically ask you to consider a number of scenarios, each of which highlights a different aspect of privilege or public interest immunity.

# ■ Sample question

Could you answer this question? Below is a typical essay question that could arise on this topic. Guidelines on answering the question are included at the end of this chapter, whilst a sample problem question and guidance on tackling it can be found on the companion website.

ESSAY QUESTION

The disclosure of material to the defence is an essential due process safeguard within the criminal justice system.

Discuss.

# ▉ Privilege

As has already been stated, there is a general requirement on witnesses to answer questions in court and on the litigants to make available documentation in their possession. The principal means of avoiding this obligation is **privilege**, which comes in a number of different forms.

**KEY DEFINITION: Privilege**

The ability to refuse to disclose certain information as part of litigation.

## Privilege against self-incrimination

It has long been established that a person may refuse to answer questions or reveal documents under the circumstances outlined by Goddard LJ in *Blunt* v *Park Lane Hotel* [1942] 2 KB 253 (CA):

> The rule is that no one is bound to answer any question if the answer thereto would, in the opinion of the judge, have a tendency to expose the deponent to any criminal charge, penalty, or forfeiture which the judge regards as reasonably likely to be preferred or sued for.

## Witnesses generally

To claim privilege, the witness must reasonably apprehend incrimination.

**KEY CASE**

*R* v *Khan* [2007] EWCA Crim 2331 (CA)

*Concerning: privilege against self-incrimination*

**Facts**

K had pleaded guilty to terrorism offences but gave evidence for a co-accused. K's evidence was that he was solely responsible for the offences for which both men had been charged. During his evidence, K claimed privilege and refused to answer some questions. The judge indicated that any attempt to claim privilege in relation to matters which he had already admitted by virtue of his previous guilty plea would constitute contempt of court. Despite this warning K continued to refuse to answer questions relating to such matters and was found in contempt. He appealed.

**Legal principle**

The appeal was dismissed. Privilege could only be invoked where it created no material increase to an existing risk of incrimination. In this case, K had already admitted his involvement in the offences by means of his guilty plea, therefore answering the questions would present no increased risk of prosecution to him. Moses LJ: 'we reject this appeal, on the basis that the questions he refused to answer did not expose him to any increased danger of incrimination. On the contrary, any danger to which he was exposed already existed as a result of his plea of guilty.'

## Statutory exceptions

There are a number of statutory exceptions to the general privilege against self-incrimination.

**KEY STATUTE**

**Road Traffic Act 1988, s. 172**

**Duty to give information as to identity of driver, etc. in certain circumstances**

(1) Where the driver of a vehicle is alleged to be guilty of an offence to which this section applies –

   (a) the person keeping the vehicle shall give such information as to the identity of the driver as he may be required to give by or on behalf of a chief officer of police, and

   (b) any other person shall if required as stated above give any information which it is in his power to give and may lead to identification of the driver.

**KEY STATUTE**

### Children Act 1989, s. 98

Self-incrimination

(1) In any proceedings in which a court is hearing an application for an order under Part IV or V, no person shall be excused from –

    (a) giving evidence on any matter; or

    (b) answering any question put to him in the course of his giving evidence, on the ground that doing so might incriminate him or his spouse [or civil partner] of an offence.

**KEY STATUTE**

### Theft Act 1968, s. 31

**Effect on civil proceedings and rights**

(1) A person shall not be excused, by reason that to do so may incriminate that person or the [spouse or civil partner] of that person of an offence under this Act –

    (a) from answering any question put to that person in proceedings for the recovery or administration of any property, for the execution of any trust or for an account of any property or dealings with property; or

    (b) from complying with any order made in any such proceedings;

(2) but no statement or admission made by a person in answering a question put or complying with an order made as aforesaid shall, in proceedings for an offence under this Act, be admissible in evidence against that person or (unless they [married or became civil partners] after the making of the statement or admission) against the spouse [or civil partner] of that person.

## Self-incrimination privilege and Article 6

The question of whether such statutory provisions could contravene the right to a fair trial under Article 6 ECHR was considered in the following decision.

**KEY CASE**

*Saunders* v *United Kingdom* (1996) 23 EHRR 313 (ECtHR)

*Concerning: privilege against self-incrimination*

## Facts

As part of an investigation by DTI inspectors into fraudulent share dealings, S was questioned under section 434 Companies Act 1985, which compelled S to answer questions or face being held in contempt of court. The answers provided by S were subsequently used in criminal proceedings against S who was convicted. S appealed on the grounds that this contravened his right to a fair trial under Article 6.

## Legal principle

It was held that the right not to incriminate oneself was central to the notion of a fair trial. This right had been contravened in this case. Bernhardt J: 'The Commission considered that the privilege against self-incrimination formed an important element in safeguarding individuals from oppression and coercion, was linked to the principle of the presumption of innocence and should apply equally to all types of accused.'

## KEY CASE

*Beghal* v *Director of Public Prosecutions* [2015] UKSC 49 (SC)

*Concerning: privilege against self-incrimination*

## Facts

The appellant was questioned at an airport under Schedule 7 to the Terrorism Act 2000 which requires a person at a port or airport to answer questions asked by police officers, immigration officers and customs officers. She refused to do so and, although not detained, she was subsequently convicted of wilfully failing to answer questions. One of the issues for determination was whether Schedule 7 was compatible with the privilege against self-incrimination.

## Legal principle

Held –The risk of prosecution based upon answers to Schedule 7 questioning was not real and appreciable. Even if a prosecution did follow, the evidence would inevitably be excluded under section 78 PACE, in which case, the risk which the privilege against self-incrimination existed to guard against was not present. Lord Hughes: 'The appellant was at no stage a defendant to a criminal charge and no question of a breach of a right to a fair trial arises. For those reasons, there was . . . neither a wrongful denial of the common law privilege against self-incrimination nor a breach of Article 6 ECHR.'

**Make your answer stand out**

Point out that, in his dissenting judgment, Lord Kerr concluded otherwise, stating: 'I consider therefore that the requirement in Schedule 7 that a person questioned under its provisions must answer on pain of prosecution for failing to do so is in breach of that person's common law privilege against self-incrimination.'

# The accused in criminal cases

Statute has also altered the position in relation to the accused in criminal cases.

**KEY STATUTE**

**Criminal Evidence Act 1898 (as amended), s. 1(2)**

A person charged in criminal proceedings who is called as a witness in the proceedings may be asked any question in cross-examination notwithstanding that it would tend to incriminate him as to the offence charged.

**□ REVISION NOTE**

When considering this provision, you may also wish to read the section on the 'right to silence' in Chapter 2 and, in particular, section 35 Criminal Justice and Public Order Act 1994 which applies where the accused refuses to give evidence in their own defence at trial.

# Legal professional privilege

The second key category of privilege is that which extends to communications between lawyer and client, known as 'legal professional privilege'. The justification for such privilege is that it enables the client to speak openly and honestly to their lawyer without fear that their conversation may later be made public. There are three types of legal professional privilege.

## 1 Legal advice privilege

This protects communication between lawyer and client. This does not have to be connected with litigation or even the possibility of litigation and this test has been broadly interpreted.

*Three Rivers District Council* v *Bank of England* [2004] UKHL 48 (HL)

*Concerning: legal advice privilege*

**Facts**

After the collapse of the Bank of Credit and Commerce International (BCCI), an independent inquiry was set up into the Bank of England's supervision of BCCI. Subsequently, legal proceedings were commenced against the Bank of England for losses caused by the BCCI collapse. In the course of those proceedings, the question arose whether communications between the bank and its lawyers for the purpose of the earlier inquiry qualified for legal professional privilege. The trial judge ruled that only 'advice concerning the bank's rights and obligations' qualified for privilege. The Court of Appeal held that, for legal advice privilege purposes, the advice being sought had to be advice as to legal rights or liabilities.

**Legal principle**

The appeal would be allowed. Lord Brown: 'I would go so far as to state as a general principle that the process by which a client seeks and obtains his lawyer's assistance in the presentation of his case for the purposes of any formal inquiry – whether concerned with public law or private law issues, whether adversarial or inquisitorial in form, whether held in public or in private, whether or not directly affecting his rights or liabilities – attracts legal advice privilege.'

That does not mean, however, that any communication between lawyer and client will automatically be subject to privilege. As Lord Scott commented in *Three Rivers*, 'If a solicitor becomes the client's "man of business", and some solicitors do, responsible for advising the client on all matters of business, including investment policy, finance policy and other business matters, the advice may lack a relevant legal context.'

## 2 Litigation privilege

This second type of privilege extends to communications between the client (or their lawyers) and a third party, such as witnesses, including expert witnesses. The limitation on this form of privilege is that the communication in question must have come into existence for the 'dominant purpose' of pending or contemplated litigation.

> **KEY CASE**
>
> *Waugh* v *British Railways Board* [1980] AC 521 (HL)
>
> *Concerning: the 'dominant purpose' test*
>
> **Facts**
>
> W was the widow of a British Railways Board employee killed in a workplace accident. It was the standard practice of the BRB in such cases to prepare an 'internal enquiry report' to consider the circumstances of the incident. Internal BRB documents showed that the report was prepared to review safety procedures and also in preparation for any litigation which would follow. The BRB document suggested that both justifications ranked equally (and so there was no 'dominant purpose' for the report). W sought disclosure of the document but BRB resisted, claiming litigation privilege.
>
> **Legal principle**
>
> It was held that a document could only attract legal professional privilege if the dominant purpose for which it was prepared was for pending or contemplated litigation. Since litigation was merely one of the stated purposes for preparing this report, the board's claim of privilege failed and the report would have to be disclosed. Lord Edmund-Davies: 'I would certainly deny a claim to privilege when litigation was merely one of several purposes of equal or similar importance intended to be served by the material sought to be withheld from disclosure.'

## 3 Items referred to in types 1 and 2 privileged documents

This privilege extends to documents referred to in documents which are themselves subject to privilege under 1 and 2 above, providing that such documents have also been created in connection with the provision of legal advice. This distinction can be illustrated by reference to the following case.

> **KEY CASE**
>
> *R* v *King* [1983] 1 All ER 929 (CA)
>
> *Concerning: privilege*
>
> **Facts**
>
> As part of a prosecution for fraud, the defence were required to produce certain documents which they had sent to a handwriting expert for analysis in order to verify the signature. The defence refused, citing litigation privilege.
>
> **Legal principle**
>
> It was held that, although the expert's report on the documents would attract privilege, this did not extend to the documents which had been sent to the expert and on which he

had based his opinion. These existing documents had not been created for the purposes of the litigation and so were not subject to privilege. Dunn LJ: 'no privilege will attach to exhibit 257. It was one of the documents examined by Mr Radley, on which he based his opinion, and the court was entitled to have it adduced in evidence.'

## Fraud

As might also be expected, such privilege does not protect documents created for the purposes of committing a crime or fraud.

**KEY CASE**

*R* v *Cox and Railton* (1884) 14 QBD 153 (CCR)

*Concerning: privilege and fraud*

Facts

C and R sought advice from their solicitor over a bill of sale which, unknown to the solicitor, was to be used to fraudulently avoid payment to a creditor who had obtained a judgment against them.

Legal principle

It was held that such communication was not subject to privilege. Grove J: 'no such privilege exists. If it did . . . a man intending to commit treason or murder might safely take legal advice for the purpose of enabling himself to do so with impunity, and that the solicitor to whom the application was made would not be at liberty to give information against his client for the purpose of frustrating his criminal purpose.'

In criminal proceedings PACE 1984 provides a definition of 'items subject to legal privilege'

**KEY STATUTE**

**Pace 1984, s. 10**

(1)  Subject to subsection (2) below, in this Act "items subject to legal privilege" means –

    (a)  communications between a professional legal adviser and his client or any person representing his client made in connection with the giving of legal advice to the client;

    (b)  communications between a professional legal adviser and his client or any person representing his client or between such an adviser or his client or ▶

> any such representative and any other person made in connection with or in contemplation of legal proceedings and for the purposes of such proceedings; and
>
> (c) items enclosed with or referred to in such communications and made –
>
>     (i) in connection with the giving of legal advice; or
>
>     (ii) in connection with or in contemplation of legal proceedings and for the purposes of such proceedings,
>
> (a) when they are in the possession of a person who is entitled to possession of them.
>
> (2) Items held with the intention of furthering a criminal purpose are not items subject to legal privilege.

It should also be noted that attempts to extend legal advice privilege to professionals other than lawyers have recently been rejected by the Supreme Court.

## KEY CASE

*R (on the application of Prudential plc)* v *Special Commissioner of Income Tax* [2013] UKSC 1 (SC)

*Concerning: legal advice privilege*

### Facts

HMRC asked Prudential to disclose documents relating to a tax avoidance scheme it had entered into. Prudential argued that the documents, which had been produced by the firm's accountants, contained legal advice on tax matters and so were covered by LAP. In doing so, Prudential asserted that the status of the adviser, whether lawyer or accountant, was less important than the legal nature of the advice being provided.

### Legal principle

Lord Neuberger: 'I reach this conclusion for three connected reasons. First, the consequences of allowing Prudential's appeal are hard to assess and would be likely to lead to what is currently a clear and well understood principle becoming an unclear principle, involving uncertainty. Secondly, the question whether LAP should be extended to cases where legal advice is given from professional people who are not qualified lawyers raises questions of policy which should be left to Parliament. Thirdly, Parliament has enacted legislation relating to LAP, which, at the very least, suggests that it would be inappropriate for the court to extend the law on LAP as proposed by Prudential.'

# Inadvertent disclosure of privileged documents

Where a privileged document is disclosed to the opposing party by mistake, it can be used only with the permission of the court.

---

**KEY CASE**

*Rawlinson and Hunter Trustees SA (as trustee of the Tchenguiz Family Trust) and another v Director of the Serious Fraud Office* **[2014] EWCA Civ 1129 (CA)**

*Concerning: privilege and inadvertent disclosure*

**Facts**

During a complex fraud trial, over 10,000 documents were disclosed by the SFO to the opposing side as part of the standard discovery process. It emerged that a small number of sensitive documents had been inadvertently included and the opposing party made an application to use these documents in evidence. The SFO resisted the application on the basis that the release of the documents had been an 'obvious mistake.'

**Legal principle**

Held – The documents could be used by the opposing party as it was not obvious that they had been disclosed inadvertently. Moore-Bick LJ: 'once it is accepted that the person who inspected a document did not realise that it had been disclosed by mistake, despite being a qualified lawyer, it is a strong thing for the judge to hold that the mistake was obvious.'

---

# 'Without prejudice' correspondence

Another category of privileged material is 'without prejudice' correspondence. This refers to the negotiations which typically take place between the parties in a civil dispute. In order to encourage out of court settlement of such disputes, their correspondence (which may contain both offers and admissions) is privileged and cannot be produced in evidence should the negotiations fail and the case ultimately come to trial.

---

**KEY CASE**

*Rush & Tompkins Ltd v Greater London Council* **[1989] AC 1280 (HL)**

*Concerning: 'without prejudice' communications*

**Facts**

The appellants were two building firms which had been employed by the Greater London Council which found itself in dispute with both firms. The dispute with one of the firms ▶

was settled before trial, but the other came to court and, as part of their case, the builder sought access to 'without prejudice' correspondence between the other firm and the GLC, which they felt might be relevant to the case.

**Legal principle**

It was held that the 'without prejudice' rule made proof of any admissions made with a genuine intention to reach a settlement inadmissible in any subsequent litigation connected with the same subject matter. Balcombe LJ: '[otherwise] nothing would be put on paper but this is in itself a recipe for disaster in difficult negotiations which are far better spelt out with precision in writing.'

Note, however, that the document in question must constitute a 'genuine intention to reach a settlement' in order to qualify under the rule.

# Privilege and journalists' sources

A related area is the protection for journalists' sources provided by the Contempt of Court Act 1981.

**KEY STATUTE**

**Contempt of Court Act 1981, s. 10**

Sources of information

No court may require a person to disclose, nor is any person guilty of contempt of court for refusing to disclose, the source of information contained in a publication for which he is responsible, unless it be established to the satisfaction of the court that disclosure is necessary in the interests of justice or national security or for the prevention of disorder or crime.

The justification for this provision is the protection of individuals who provide valuable information to journalists which may be in the public interest but which may place their jobs, or even their safety, in jeopardy. There is, therefore, a desire to protect such sources in order to encourage the freedom of the press to publicise matters of public interest.

Looking at section 10, however, it is clear that the protection provided by the statute is not unqualified and may be overridden where revealing the identity of the source is 'necessary in the interests of justice or national security or for the prevention of disorder or crime'.

*Secretary of State for Defence* v *Guardian Newspapers Ltd* [1984] 3 WLR 986 (HL)

*Concerning: s. 10 Contempt of Court Act 1981*

Facts

A classified document belonging to the Ministry of Defence, outlining arrangements for the deployment of nuclear missiles in the UK, was copied and sent to the *Guardian* newspaper. The Government sought the return of the document and the name of the source but the newspaper refused, citing section 10.

Legal principle

It was held that, although the newspaper was entitled to the protection of section 10, the Government had adduced sufficient evidence that disclosure of the source was necessary in the interests of national security. Lord Bridge: 'There is no ambiguity in the phrase "necessary in the interests of national security".'

*Ashworth Hospital Authority* v *MGN Ltd* [2002] UKHL 29 (HL)

*Concerning: s. 10 Contempt of Court Act 1981*

Facts

Mirror Group Newspapers (MGN) published extracts from the confidential medical records of convicted murderer Ian Brady, who was a patient at the Ashworth Psychiatric hospital. The information could only have come from an employee of the hospital, which demanded that the source be identified. The newspaper cited section 10.

Legal principle

It was held that the care of patients at the hospital was fraught with difficulty and danger and that the unauthorised disclosure of patients' records increased that difficulty and danger. In order to deter similar wrongdoing in the future, it was essential that the source should be identified and that made an order to disclose in the instant case necessary, proportionate and justified. Lord Woolf: 'The fact that Ian Brady had himself disclosed his medical history did not detract from the need to prevent staff from revealing medical records of patients. Ian Brady's conduct did not damage the integrity of Ashworth's patients' records. The source's disclosure was wholly inconsistent with the security of the records and the disclosure was made worse because it was purchased by a cash payment.'

# ■ Journalists' sources and Article 10

It has been argued that compelling journalists to reveal their sources in this way may constitute an infringement of their right to freedom of expression under Article 10 of the European Convention.

---

**KEY STATUTE**

**European Convention on Human Rights, Article 10**

(1) Everyone has the right to freedom of expression. This right shall include freedom to hold opinions and to receive and impart information and ideas without interference by public authority and regardless of frontiers. This article shall not prevent States from requiring the licensing of broadcasting, television or cinema enterprises.

(2) The exercise of these freedoms, since it carries with it duties and responsibilities, may be subject to such formalities, conditions, restrictions or penalties as are pre-scribed by law and are necessary in a democratic society, in the interests of national security, territorial integrity or public safety, for the prevention of disorder or crime, for the protection of health or morals, for the protection of the reputation or the rights of others, for preventing the disclosure of information received in confidence, or for maintaining the authority and impartiality of the judiciary.

---

It can be seen, however, that Article 10(2) makes clear that this is not an absolute right and provides a lengthy series of criteria which may justify some restriction on the right. This has been interpreted by the courts in terms of 'necessity and proportionality'.

---

**KEY CASE**

*Goodwin* v *United Kingdom* (1996) 1 BHRC 81 (ECtHR)

*Concerning: Art. 10 and journalists' sources*

**Facts**

A journalist received information from a company employee which had been taken from the company's corporate plan and which detailed its previously unknown financial difficulties. The company sought to prevent publication of the commercially damaging information and to compel the journalist to reveal the source. The journalist resisted, citing section 10 of the Contempt of Court Act, but both the Court of Appeal and House of Lords ordered the disclosure of the source and fined the journalist for contempt of court. The journalist argued that this infringed his rights under Article 10.

---

**Legal principle**

It was held that there had been an infringement of the journalist's Article 10 right and that the company's arguments of commercial sensitivity were not sufficient to outweigh this. Article 10 required that any compulsion imposed on a journalist to reveal his source had to be restricted to exceptional circumstances where vital public or individual interests were at stake, and that was not established in this case. Ryssdal J: 'the residual threat of damage through dissemination of the confidential information otherwise than by the press, in obtaining compensation and in unmasking a disloyal employee or collaborator were, even if considered cumulatively, sufficient to outweigh the vital public interest in the protection of the applicant journalist's source.'

# Disclosure

As indicated in the introduction to this chapter, the notion of hiding information from the other side is increasingly out of place within the modern trial process, where sharing information is seen as encouraging settlement in civil cases and reducing the possibility of miscarriages of justice in criminal cases. This process is known as '**disclosure**' or 'discovery' and is an essential part of the litigation process. It has also proved to be the cause of many of the most notorious miscarriages of justice in the criminal justice system.

## Disclosure in civil cases

The disclosure obligations in civil trials are addressed by the Civil Procedure Rules.

**KEY STATUTE**

**Civil Procedure Rules (Part 31), r 31.6**

Standard disclosure – what documents are to be disclosed

Standard disclosure requires a party to disclose only –

(a)  the documents on which he relies; and

(b)  the documents which –

    (i)  adversely affect his own case;

    (ii)  adversely affect another party's case; or

    (iii)  support another party's case; and

(c)  the documents which he is required to disclose by a relevant practice direction.

Disclosure in civil cases is generally relatively straightforward, although there are issues surrounding the exchange of expert reports.

Note that this topic should be revised alongside the relevant sections in Chapter 5 on expert evidence.

It will be remembered that a party who has instructed an expert to prepare a report for the purposes of pending litigation will be able to claim litigation privilege for that document, but this must be balanced against the ethos underlying the Civil Procedure Rules, which is to streamline and expedite the trial process. Therefore, a party will usually only be able to adduce an expert report which they have disclosed to their opponents. Similarly, once disclosed, such reports are also available to the other side as evidence.

**KEY STATUTE**

**Civil Procedure Rules (Part 35), r. 35.11**

**Use by one party of expert's report disclosed by another**

Where a party has disclosed an expert's report, any party may use that expert's report as evidence at the trial.

**KEY STATUTE**

**Civil Procedure Rules (Part 35), r. 35.13**

**Consequence of failure to disclose expert's report**

A party who fails to disclose an expert's report may not use the report at the trial or call the expert to give evidence orally unless the court gives permission.

# Disclosure in criminal cases

In criminal cases, the role of disclosure is slightly different. Rather than making material available to the other side to encourage them to settle, the purpose of disclosure in criminal cases is to provide protection for the accused by making him aware of any material held by the prosecution which has the potential to either undermine the prosecution case or assist the defence. Obviously, in the course of a criminal investigation, the police will amass a large number of statements and other evidence which is never adduced at trial. It is this so-called 'unused material' which must potentially be made available to the defence.

## Disclosure and miscarriages of justice

The non-disclosure of material by the prosecution to the defence is a key aspect of the majority of the most famous miscarriages of justice in the UK. In all cases, vital documents were withheld from the defence with disastrous consequences and the result was a string of successful appeals in the early 1990s.

---

### ✎ EXAM TIP

In discussing this point, remember to mention that, in its first annual report, the Criminal Cases Review Commission identified defective disclosure as a factor in 23 of its first 80 referrals. As such, this was the third most common reason for referring convictions.

*(Annual Report, 1999–2000, London, CCRC, p. 11)*

---

### KEY CASE

*R* v *Maguire and others* **[1992] QB 936 (CA)**

*Concerning: non-disclosure*

**Facts**

In 1976, following explosions in two public houses, the appellants were each convicted on a charge of possession of explosives. The case against them was based on scientific evidence that traces of explosive had been found on their hands. Contradictory scientific evidence had been known to the prosecution but had been withheld from the defence.

**Legal principle**

It was held that the failure to disclose the material which undermined the prosecution case was a material irregularity in the trial which rendered the convictions unsafe. The convictions would therefore be quashed. Stuart-Smith LJ: 'the test and the trials which were not disclosed constituted material which ought to have been disclosed.'

---

### KEY CASE

*R* v *Kiszko* **(1992)** *The Times*, **18 February (CA)**

*Concerning: non-disclosure* ▶

## Facts

Stefan Kiszko was convicted of the rape and murder of an 11 year-old girl. Although 23 years old he was assessed as having a mental age of 12 and was interviewed without a solicitor. Having been told by police that he would be allowed to go home if he admitted the crime, he made a confession which was the only evidence against him. He was convicted and served 16 years in prison before a review of the case found a medical report on Kiszko showing that he was incapable of producing the sperm found at the scene and so could not have committed the crime. He was released in 1992 but died of a heart attack within months.

## Legal principle

The failure to disclose details of the medical condition had led to a wrongful conviction and miscarriage of justice.

---

**KEY CASE**

*R* v *Taylor (Michelle); R* v *Taylor (Lisa)* (1993) *The Times*, 15 June (CA)

*Concerning: non-disclosure*

## Facts

The Taylor sisters were convicted of the murder of a woman in her home (Michelle Taylor had been having an affair with her husband). A witness originally claimed that he may have seen a black woman leaving the victim's house at the time of the killing but later changed his statement to say that the woman was white (as were the Taylor sisters). The existence of the earlier inconsistent statement was not disclosed to the defence. The same witness had also claimed a reward offered for information leading to the conviction of the murderer.

## Legal principle

The statement should have been disclosed and the failure to do so rendered the convictions unsafe. McCowan LJ: 'Neither prosecuting counsel at the trial nor the Crown Prosecution Service had any idea of the existence of that document. However, the detective sergeant in charge of the case did know of its existence and also its significance but decided there was no need to disclose it to the prosecuting legal team. He was plainly wrong in so thinking.'

**R v Ward [1993] 2 All ER 577 (CA)**

*Concerning: non-disclosure*

**Facts**

W was convicted of involvement in an IRA bombing campaign in which 12 people were killed. She was convicted largely on the basis of a confession and scientific evidence which linked her to explosives. At trial, contradictory scientific evidence and evidence that she suffered from a severe personality disorder which rendered her confessions unreliable was not disclosed to the defence.

**Legal principle**

Her conviction was quashed. Both the contradictory scientific evidence and the evidence of her mental condition severely undermined the safety of the conviction and this material should have been disclosed to the defence. Glidewell LJ: 'in the failure to disclose evidence, some in the possession of the police, some in the possession of the scientists and some in the possession of the Director, there were material irregularities at the trial.'

Concerns over the failure of the prosecution to disclose valuable material to the defence influenced the deliberations of the Royal Commission on Criminal Justice (1993) which led to the introduction of a statutory procedure for disclosure in criminal cases.

# The Criminal Procedure and Investigations Act 1996 (CPIA)

The 1996 Act imposes a duty on the prosecutor to disclose material to the defence.

**Criminal Procedure and Investigations Act 1996, s. 3**

**Initial duty of prosecutor to disclose**

(1) The prosecutor must –

    (a) disclose to the accused any prosecution material which has not previously been disclosed to the accused and which might reasonably be considered capable of undermining the case for the prosecution against the accused or of assisting the case for the accused, or

    (b) give to the accused a written statement that there is no material of a description mentioned in paragraph (a).

## ✎ EXAM TIP

When discussing the section 3 test, point out that this single stage of disclosure was only introduced by the Criminal Justice Act 2003. The original CPIA included a two-stage process of 'primary' and 'secondary' disclosure which was later abandoned. You should also mention that the current objective test of 'which might reasonably be considered capable' replaced the previous subjective test of 'in the prosecutor's opinion'.

It should be noted, however, that this duty only applies to 'prosecution material'.

## KEY STATUTE

**Criminal Procedure and Investigations Act 1996, s. 3(2)**

For the purposes of this section prosecution material is material –

(a) which is in the prosecutor's possession, and came into his possession in connection with the case for the prosecution against the accused, or

(b) which . . . he has inspected in connection with the case for the prosecution against the accused.

There is, therefore, no disclosure obligation on the prosecution in relation to material in the possession of third parties. Similarly, only material which satisfies the test for 'relevance' falls to be disclosed.

## KEY STATUTE

**Criminal Procedure and Investigations Act 1996, Codes of Practice 2.1**

Material may be relevant to an investigation if it appears to an investigator, or to the officer in charge of an investigation, or to the disclosure officer, that it has some bearing on any offence under investigation or any person being investigated, or on the surrounding circumstances of the case, unless it is incapable of having any impact on the case . . .

Clearly the relevance test is very wide and so should (in theory, at least) capture any material which may be of use to the defence. It should be remembered, however, that it is still up to the police to identify any material and make its existence known – which does not always happen.

*R v Tucker* [2008] EWCA Crim 3063 (CA)

*Concerning: non-disclosure*

**Facts**

T was convicted of robbery. The principal evidence against him came from M, a drug dealer whom T had been informing on to the police. A statement made by another witness, providing a possible alibi for T and suggesting an alternative suspect, had been given to police but not disclosed to the defence. Also, a statement from M's partner, recounting a conversation where M had admitted to 'setting up' T, was similarly not disclosed.

**Legal principle**

The appeal was allowed. The information which had not been disclosed suggested that M had his own reasons for giving false evidence against T. Moses LJ: 'The failure of disclosure was a significant irregularity. It is not possible to say precisely what impact it would have had on the jury. But it is likely that the information would have provided powerful support for the suggestion that the accomplice had reasons of his own for giving false evidence against the appellant.'

 Make your answer stand out

Point out that defective disclosure continues to be a problem in criminal cases. In *R v DS and another* [2015] EWCA Crim 662 the trial judge had stayed the proceedings after serious failings in disclosure, commenting: 'The officer in the case was ignorant of the duties and responsibilities of disclosure and even lacked basic training. The CPS had been no better placed and failed to treat disclosure with the respect and importance it deserved.'

## Defence disclosure

Although CPIA imposes a duty on the prosecution to disclose potentially useful material to the defence, it also requires the defence to make more limited disclosure to the prosecution, not of specific documents but, instead, of the general nature of the defence which is to be put forward at trial. This is by means of a 'defence statement'.

**Criminal Procedure and Investigations Act 1996, s. 6A**

**Contents of defence statement**

(1) For the purposes of this Part a defence statement is a written statement –

    (a)    setting out the nature of the accused's defence, including any particular defences on which he intends to rely,

    (b)    indicating the matters of fact on which he takes issue with the prosecution,

    (c)    setting out, in the case of each such matter, why he takes issue with the prosecution, and

    (d)    indicating any point of law (including any point as to the admissibility of evidence or an abuse of process) which he wishes to take, and any authority on which he intends to rely for that purpose.

The obligation on the defence to make known their proposed case represents a significant inroad into the principle in *Woolmington* by, in effect, requiring the defence to assist the prosecution by revealing their case in advance, rather than the traditional tactic of 'keeping the powder dry' until trial. There are parallels with the inroads into the 'right to silence' under the Criminal Justice and Public Order Act 1994 discussed earlier (see Chapter 2) and, as with those provisions, the sanction for non-compliance is adverse inference at trial.

**Criminal Procedure and Investigations Act 1996, s. 11**

**Faults in disclosure by accused**

(1) This section applies where section 5 applies and the accused –

    (a)    fails to give a defence statement under that section,

    (b)    gives a defence statement under that section but does so after the end of the period which, by virtue of section 12, is the relevant period for section 5,

    (c)    sets out inconsistent defences in a defence statement given under section 5,

    (d)    at his trial puts forward a defence which is different from any defence set out in a defence statement given under section 5,

(2) Where this section applies –

    (a)    the court or, with the leave of the court, any other party may make such comment as appears appropriate;

    (b)    the court or jury may draw such inferences as appear proper in deciding whether the accused is guilty of the offence concerned.

As has already been noted, there is a potential overlap between the non-submission of a defence statement under CPIA and silence at interview. There is also the question of whether requiring the defence to outline their proposed defence in advance may breach the Article 6 right to a fair trial. All three issues arose in the following case.

---

**KEY CASE**

*R* v *Essa* [2009] EWCA Crim 43 (CA)

*Concerning: adverse inference and s. 34*

**Facts**

E was accused of a robbery committed on a train and gave a 'no comment' interview to police. He also did not submit a defence statement. At trial he asserted that he had been mistakenly identified as, although he regularly took the train in question, he had not done so on the day of the alleged attack.

**Legal principle**

It was held that the trial judge had been correct to allow section 34 CJPOA inference to be drawn and in allowing comment on the failure to submit a defence statement. It was also held that the requirements of section 11 CPIA were compatible with the rights under Article 6. Hughes LJ: 'It is not open to those who advise Defendants to pick and choose which statutory rules applicable to the conduct of criminal proceedings they obey and which they do not.'

---

# Non-sensitive and sensitive material

Although CPIA imposes an obligation on the prosecution to disclose material to the defence, there are clearly categories of material which the prosecution will want to withhold (such as details of informants or covert methods). This is achieved by dividing prosecution material into 'non-sensitive' and 'sensitive'.

## Non-sensitive material

This is listed on a schedule which is made available to the defence.

## Sensitive material

This is listed on a separate schedule which is not passed to the defence but which is kept by the prosecutor. Disclosure of this material is usually opposed by the prosecution by means of an application for public interest immunity.

# ■ Public interest immunity (PII)

**Public interest immunity** is the mechanism by which the state can seek to avoid their obligation to disclose material to the other side in both civil and criminal litigation.

---

**! Don't be tempted to . . .**

When discussing public interest immunity, do not make the mistake of thinking that it prevents information being revealed in the press or published elsewhere. PII is confined to the courtroom where it prevents the disclosure of material to the other side. It is, therefore, 'immunity' from the duty of disclosure.

---

## The basic principle of PII

This was originally known as 'Crown privilege' and allowed the state to withhold documents where their disclosure was considered injurious to the public interest. You may have encountered this topic previously if you have studied constitutional and administrative law, where it is sometimes studied from a constitutional perspective. Here, we are solely concerned with its application as a mechanism for restricting the disclosure of evidence.

---

**KEY CASE**

*Duncan* v *Cammell Laird & Co. Ltd* [1942] AC 624 (HL)

*Concerning: public interest immunity*

**Facts**

Ninety-nine sailors were drowned when an experimental submarine failed to surface during sea trials. The families of the deceased brought an action for negligence against the shipbuilders, alleging that design faults in the vessel had caused the deaths. In support of their claim they requested access to various documents relating to the construction of the submarine. The Admiralty objected to their disclosure and claimed Crown privilege.

**Legal principle**

It was held that a valid objection to the disclosure of the documents by the Minister on the grounds that this would be injurious to the public interest was conclusive. Therefore, the documents would not be released. Viscount Simon LC: 'It seems to me that, if a public department comes forward and says that the production of a document is detrimental to the public service, it is a very strong step indeed for the court to overrule that statement by the department.'

---

This emphasised that the courts were unlikely to overrule a Minister's assessment that the documents should not be disclosed; however, a later decision marked a noticeable shift in responsibility for this decision.

## KEY CASE

*Conway* v *Rimmer* [1968] AC 910 (HL)

*Concerning: public interest immunity*

**Facts**

A probationary police constable sought disclosure of the reports written about him by his superiors in order to support a claim of malicious prosecution against the Chief Constable. The Home Secretary claimed Crown privilege for the documents in question.

**Legal principle**

It was held that, rather than accept the Minister's assessment of the likely harm which would follow disclosure of the documents, it was for the court to examine the documents and decide whether or not they should be withheld.

Following this decision, it has long been accepted that it is for the court to consider the claim for PII and decide whether or not to order disclosure. As might be expected, the most important examples of PII arise in the criminal law and frequently concern the use of covert material.

## Different types of PII hearing

Where the prosecution has such material, there are three types of hearing in which an application for PII might be made:

- with notice to the defence of at least the general type of material in question and with the opportunity for the defence to make representations for disclosure;

- if, however, to reveal even the general type of material in question might, in effect, reveal what the prosecution argued must be kept secret in the public interest, then an *ex parte* hearing (without the defence being present) may be appropriate, although the defence should be informed that such a hearing is being sought;

- in extreme cases, where even to tell the defence that an application was being made would reveal too much, then an *ex parte* application might be made without notification to the defence.

As with other aspects of disclosure, the use of PII has raised questions over whether the procedures contravene the defendant's Article 6 right to a fair trial. This was addressed by the House of Lords in the following case.

**KEY CASE**

**R v H and C [2004] UKHL 3 (HL)**

*Concerning: public interest immunity*

**Facts**

The defendants were charged with serious drugs offences and, due to the nature of the police evidence in the case, applications for PII were made. An appeal was granted on the following question of law: 'Are the procedures for PII compliant with Article 6?'

**Legal principle**

It was held that, providing the existing procedures were implemented scrupulously, they were compliant with Article 6: 'There will be very few cases indeed in which some measure of disclosure to the defence will not be possible, even if this is confined to the fact that an *ex parte* application is to be made. If even that information is withheld and if the material to be withheld is of significant help to the defendant, there must be a very serious question whether the prosecution should proceed, since special counsel, even if appointed, cannot then receive any instructions from the defence at all.'

 Make your answer stand out

In reaching this decision, the House of Lords set out a detailed procedure to be followed by the court in considering such applications. For a discussion of this, see Taylor, C. (2004) 'Public Interest Immunity: *R v H & C, International Journal of Evidence and Proof,* 8(3): 179–85.

The fact that there is a PII hearing, however, does not automatically mean that there is material which will assist the defence.

**KEY CASE**

**R v Gray and others [2014] EWCA Crim 2372 (CA)**

*Concerning: public interest immunity*

**Facts**

The appellant was convicted of various burglary offences and sought disclosure of details of the police surveillance operation conducted prior to his arrest, arguing that this could be used to support his case.

**Legal principle**

Held – Hallett LJ: '[the] assertion that the fact that a PII hearing took place indicates material exists which might assist the defence or undermine the prosecution portrays a misunderstanding of how the PII system works. It does not follow from the fact of a hearing that the defence have been deprived of such material. The material may not even relate to the individual, let alone assist his case. If it does, it is the judge's task to analyse whether the material must be disclosed to ensure a fair trial, whatever the Crown's reservations.'

Note that, where the court concludes that the sensitive material must be disclosed to the defence in order for the defendant to receive a fair trial, it is then for the prosecution to decide whether to proceed with the case and reveal the material or to discontinue the case. Usually, in such cases, the charges will be dropped rather than risk endangering an informant or revealing covert information-gathering techniques.

# ■ Putting it all together

## Answer guidelines

See the essay question at the start of the chapter.

### Approaching the question

Disclosure is a fairly 'self contained' topic but one which demands a degree of evaluation. As one of the most important causes of miscarriage of justice, there are clearly reasons why the system should work properly and this wider debate can form a useful theme in an essay of this type.

### Important points to include

- Explain what disclosure is and the role it performs within the trial process.
- Consider some of the notorious miscarriages of justice which have been based on defective disclosure.
- Outline the key provisions of the Criminal Procedure and Investigations Act 1996 and the duty which it imposes on the prosecution.
- Discuss the imposition of a limited duty of disclosure on the defence under the 1996 Act.
- Consider the role of public interest immunity in protecting sensitive material. ▶

**Make your answer stand out**

Highlight that both CPIA 1996 and the Criminal Justice and Public Order Act 1994 were born of the same Conservative 'Law and Order' agenda which saw significant inroads into civil liberties in the name of 'rebalancing' the criminal justice system.

## READ TO IMPRESS

Copeman. J. (2013) A privileged position? *NLJ*, 163: 164.

Jones, A. (2012) Legal privilege – are you covered? *Cons.Law*, 23(8): 23.

McEvedy, V. (2006) The secret source of free expression. *NLJ*, 156: 444.

Miller, J. (2013) Privilege – legal professional privilege – scope, *NLJ*, 163: 109.

Redmayne, M. (2007) Rethinking the privilege against self-incrimination. *OJLS*, 27: 209.

Sandy, D. (2002) False sources and the freedom of the press. *NLJ*, 152: 856.

Taylor, C. (2005a) Advance disclosure and the culture of the investigator: the good idea that never quite caught on? *International Journal of the Sociology of Law,* 33: 118–31.

Taylor, C. (2005b) What next for public interest immunity? *JOCL*, 69(1): 75–83.

Taylor, C. (2010) The evolution of the defence statement. *JOCL*, 74(3): 214–22.

**www.pearsoned.co.uk/lawexpress**

 Go online to access more revision support including quizzes to test your knowledge, sample questions with answer guidelines, podcasts you can download, and more!

# And finally, before the exam . . .

## Check your progress

☐ Look at the **revision checklists** at the start of each chapter. Are you happy that you can now tick them all? If not, go back to the particular chapter and work through the material again. If you are still struggling, seek help from your tutor.

☐ Attempt the **sample questions** in each chapter and check your answers against the guidelines provided.

☐ Go online to **www.pearsoned.co.uk/lawexpress** for more hands-on revision help:

    ☐ Try the **test your knowledge** quizzes and see whether you can score full marks for each chapter.

    ☐ Attempt to answer the **sample questions** for each chapter within the time limit and check your answers against the guidelines provided.

    ☐ Listen to the **podcast** and then attempt the question it discusses.

    ☐ Evaluate sample exam answers in **you be the marker** and see if you can spot their strengths and weaknesses.

    ☐ Use the **flashcards** to test your recall of the legal principles of the key cases and statutes you've revised and the definitions of important terms.

Remember the areas of overlap within the law of evidence, such as with the 'right to silence' provisions and the law of disclosure and with section 76 and section 78 PACE 1984.

AND FINALLY, BEFORE THE EXAM . . .

# ◼ Linking it all up

Traditionally, examination questions in evidence tend to concentrate on a single area, rather than combining a number of topics within the same question. However, it is in the nature of the subject that a question on one topic may include reference to another, and being able to exploit this within the examination can help you to achieve higher grades. The examiner will want to see that you can approach the subject, not as a series of separate areas, but as a whole, pointing out where there is an overlap between different rules of evidence or where additional information might be required. Check where there are overlaps between subject areas. (You may want to review the 'Revision note' boxes throughout this text.) Make a careful note of these, as knowing how one topic may lead into another can increase your marks significantly. Here are some examples:

✔ section 76 and section 78 PACE;

✔ expert evidence and privilege;

✔ character evidence and witness testimony generally;

✔ hearsay evidence and witness testimony generally.

# ◼ Knowing your cases

Make sure you know how to use relevant case law in your answers. Use the table below to focus your revision of the key cases in each topic. To review the details of these cases, refer back to the particular chapter.

| Key case | How to use | Related topics |
|---|---|---|
| **Chapter 1 – Evidential issues within the trial process** | | |
| R v Spiby | To illustrate that human intervention is required if an electronic record is to be treated as hearsay | Forms of evidence/ hearsay |
| R v Daye | To define a 'document' for the purposes of the law of evidence | Forms of evidence/ documents |
| R v Harden | To outline requirements for expert testimony where the jury is required to compare handwriting | Forms of evidence/expert evidence |

| Key case | How to use | Related topics |
|---|---|---|
| *Bishop Meath* v *Marquis of Winchester* | To give an example of 'proper custody' principle for documents | Forms of evidence/ documents |
| *Doe d Arundel (Lord)* v *Fowler* | To give an example of 'proper custody' principle for documents | Forms of evidence/ documents |
| *Anderson* v *Weston* | To show the court accepting the date on a document (being unable to prove otherwise) | Forms of evidence/ documents |
| *Doe d Tatum* v *Catomore* | To provide guidance on presumed date of alteration of deeds and wills | Forms of evidence/ documents |
| *R* v *Grant* | To show judicial consideration of the circumstantial evidence of money found in the possession of the accused | Forms of evidence/ circumstantial evidence |
| *Holcombe* v *Hewson* | To demonstrate that evidence of good service in one contract is not relevant to the performance of another | Relevance |
| *Joseph Constantine Steamship Line Ltd* v *Imperial Smelting Corp. Ltd* | To demonstrate where the burden of proof lies in a claim for frustration | Burden of proof |
| *Soward* v *Leggatt* | To demonstrate that the burden of proof remains with the claimant in civil cases | Burden of proof |
| *Levison and Another* v *Patent Steam Carpet Cleaning Co. Ltd* | To demonstrate where the burden of proof lies in cases alleging fundamental breach of contract | Burden of proof |

▶

| Key case | How to use | Related topics |
| --- | --- | --- |
| *Woolmington* v *DPP* | To show that the burden of proof in criminal cases remains with the prosecution | Burden of proof |
| *Gatland* v *Metropolitan Police Commissioner* | To clarify the respective burden of proof of the parties | Burden of proof |
| *R* v *Hunt* | For judicial discussion of the reverse burden of proof in cases of drugs possession | Burden of proof |
| *R* v *Lambert* | For judicial discussion of the reverse burden of proof in cases of drugs possession | Burden of proof/Art. 6 |
| *R* v *Johnstone* | For judicial discussion of the reverse burden of proof | Burden of proof/Art. 6 |
| *Sheldrake* v *DPP; Attorney General's Reference (No 4 of 2002)* | For judicial discussion of the reverse burden of proof | Burden of proof/Art. 6 |
| *Chard* v *Chard* | For judicial discussion of the presumption of death | Presumptions |
| *Scott* v *London & St Katherine Docks Co.* | For an example of the concept of res ipsa loquitur | Presumptions |

### Chapter 2 – Witnesses

| Key case | How to use | Related topics |
| --- | --- | --- |
| *R* v *Valentine* | For a definition of 'recent complaint' | Recent complaint |
| *R* v *O* | For a definition of 'recent complaint' | Recent complaint |
| *R* v *Funderburk* | For judicial consideration of the effect of previous inconsistent statements | Previous inconsistent statements |

| Key case | How to use | Related topics |
|---|---|---|
| R v *Mukadi* | For discussion of YJCEA 1999, s. 41(3) | Questioning on sexual history |
| R v *Tahed* | For discussion of YJCEA 1999, s. 41(3) | Questioning on sexual history |
| R v *Hayes* | For judicial guidance on the competence of child witnesses generally | Competence/ compellability |
| R v *Barker* | Assessing the competence of child witnesses | Competence/ compellability |
| R v *Essa* | For an example of the right to silence and s. 34 CJPOA 1994 | Right to silence |
| R v *Moshaid* | For an example of the right to silence and s. 34 CJPOA 1994 | Right to silence |
| R v *Condron and Condron* | For an example of the right to silence and s. 34 CJPOA 1994 | Right to silence/effects of legal advice |
| R v *Beckles* | For an example of the right to silence and s. 34 CJPOA 1994 | Right to silence/effects of legal advice |

### Chapter 3 – Character evidence

| | | |
|---|---|---|
| *Hobbs* v *Tinling & Co. Ltd* | To confirm the admissibility of questioning witnesses on matters of character | Character evidence/ witnesses |
| R v *Butler* | As an example of the court allowing similar fact evidence to be admitted in relation to sexual conduct | Character/similar fact evidence |
| *Hales* v *Kerr* | As an example of the court allowing similar fact evidence to be admitted in a negligence case | Character/similar fact evidence |

▶

| Key case | How to use | Related topics |
|---|---|---|
| *Mood Music Publishing Co. Ltd* v *De Wolfe Publishing Ltd* | As an example of the court allowing similar fact evidence to be admitted in a copyright case | Character/similar fact evidence |
| *DPP* v *P* | As an example of the court allowing similar fact evidence to be admitted in relation to sexual conduct | Character/similar fact evidence |
| *O'Brien* v *Chief Constable of South Wales Police* | To clarify the different tests to be employed in admitting similar fact evidence in civil and criminal cases | Character/similar fact evidence |
| *R* v *Rowton* | For a judicial statement that only evidence of good character which related to general reputation was admissible | Character/evidence of good character |
| *R* v *Redgrave* | For a judicial statement that only evidence of good character which related to general reputation was admissible | Character/evidence of good character |
| *R* v *Vye* | For the decision which set out the requirements of a 'good character' direction | Character/evidence of good character |
| *R* v *Gray* | As an example of the application of a good character direction for those with past convictions | Character/evidence of good character |
| *R* v *Zoppola-Barraza* | As an example of the application of a good character direction for those who admit past misconduct | Character/evidence of good character |

| Key case | How to use | Related topics |
|---|---|---|
| *R* v *Speed* | Evidence of convictions for one type of offence disclosed to show no previous history of the offence in the present case | Character/evidence of bad character |
| *R* v *Edwards* | As an example of the admission of bad character evidence under CJA 2003 | Character/evidence of bad character |
| *R* v *Phillips* | As an example of the admission of bad character evidence under CJA 2003 | Character/evidence of bad character |
| *R* v *MP* | To provide evidence of previous violence to explain victim's fear of reporting offence | Character/evidence of bad character |
| *R* v *Chopra* | As an example of the admission of bad character evidence under CJA 2003 | Character/evidence of bad character |
| *R* v *Hanson* | As an example of the conditions under which evidence of bad character might be admitted | Character/evidence of bad character |
| *R* v *Brima* | As an example of the conditions under which evidence of bad character might be admitted | Character/evidence of bad character |
| *R* v *Conway (Patrick Peter)* | To provide evidence of propensity for violence | Character/evidence of bad character |
| *R* v *Campbell* | As an example of the conditions under which evidence of bad character might be admitted | Character/evidence of bad character |

▶

| Key case | How to use | Related topics |
|---|---|---|
| *R* v *Musone* | As an example of admissibility under CJA 2003 | Character/evidence of bad character |
| *R* v *Johnson* | For a discussion of the principles governing the admissibility of bad character evidence adduced by one defendant against another | Character/evidence of bad character |
| *R* v *Hesse* | To provide evidence of propensity for violence | Character/evidence of bad character |
| *R* v *Sutton* | To provide an example of the admission of bad character evidence to correct a false impression given by the accused | Character/evidence of bad character |
| *R* v *Garrett* | To provide an example of the admission of bad character evidence to correct a false impression given by the accused | Character/evidence of bad character |
| *R* v *Singh (James Paul)* | To provide an example of the admission of bad character evidence following an attack on character of a witness by the accused | Character/evidence of bad character |

## Chapter 4 – Hearsay

| | | |
|---|---|---|
| *R* v *Sharp* | For a definition of hearsay evidence in criminal cases | Hearsay |
| *Sparks* v *R* | For an example of the exclusion of hearsay evidence | Hearsay |

| Key case | How to use | Related topics |
|---|---|---|
| *Subramaniam* v *Public Prosecutor* | For an example of evidence which was not held to be hearsay | Hearsay |
| *Ratten* v *R* | For an example of a statement challenged as possible hearsay evidence | Hearsay |
| *R* v *Kearley* | For judicial discussion of the distinction between hearsay and implied assertion | Hearsay/implied assertion |
| *R* v *Castillo* | For judicial consideration of the admissibility of a statement from an unavailable witness | Hearsay/unavailable witnesses |
| *R* v *Marshall (Stewart)* | Determining the unfitness of a witness to give evidence | Hearsay/medical condition of witness |
| *R* v *Martin* | For consideration of how the court will treat a hearsay statement from an intimidated witness | Hearsay/witness intimidation |
| *R* v *Docherty* | For consideration of how the court will treat a hearsay statement from an intimidated witness | Hearsay/witness intimidation |
| *R* v *Harvey and others* | Definition of 'fear' under CJA 2003 | Hearsay/fear of witness |
| *R* v *Andrews* | For judicial consideration of the *res gestae* doctrine | Hearsay/*res gestae* |
| *Tobi* v *Nicholas* | For judicial consideration of the *res gestae* doctrine | Hearsay/*res gestae* |
| *R* v *Carnall* | For judicial consideration of the *res gestae* doctrine | Hearsay/*res gestae* |

▶

| Key case | How to use | Related topics |
|---|---|---|
| *Barnaby* v *DPP* | *Res gestae* | Hearsay/*res gestae* |
| *R* v *McCay* | For an example of hearsay considered in relation to identification evidence | Hearsay/identification |
| *R* v *Moghal* | For an example of hearsay evidence admitted to demonstrate state of mind | Hearsay/state of mind |
| *R* v *Gilfoyle* | For an example of hearsay evidence admitted to demonstrate state of mind | Hearsay/state of mind |
| *R* v *L* | Admission of hearsay evidence 'in the interests of justice' | Hearsay/interests of justice |
| *R* v *Ibrahim* | A case will be halted where it is based largely on unreliable hearsay evidence | Hearsay/unreliability |

**Chapter 5 – Opinion and expert evidence**

| | | |
|---|---|---|
| *Folkes* v *Chadd* | For clarification of the circumstances where expert testimony would be required | Opinion evidence/experts |
| *R* v *Turner* | For clarification of the circumstances where expert testimony would be required | Opinion evidence/experts |
| *R* v *Smith* | For clarification of the circumstances where expert testimony would be required | Opinion evidence/experts |
| *R* v *Land* | For clarification of the circumstances where expert testimony would be required | Opinion evidence/experts |

| Key case | How to use | Related topics |
|---|---|---|
| *R* v *Sliverlock* | For confirmation of the principle that an expert need not be formally qualified | Opinion evidence/experts |
| *R* v *Murphy* | For confirmation of the principle that a police officer could be an expert within the boundaries of their experience | Opinion evidence/experts |
| *R* v *Clare and Peach* | For confirmation of the principle that a police officer could be an expert within the boundaries of their experience | Opinion evidence/experts |
| *R* v *Edwards* | For an example of the court rejecting 'expert' evidence from persons with no relevant expertise | Opinion evidence/experts |
| *R* v *Abadom* | For confirmation of the principle that experts can rely on the accumulated literature within their field | Opinion evidence/experts/ hearsay |
| *DPP* v *A and BC Chewing Gum Ltd* | Expert evidence admitted on the central fact of the case | Opinion evidence/experts |
| *R* v *Cannings* | For an example of a miscarriage of justice based on flawed expert evidence | Opinion evidence/experts |
| *R* v *Clark* | For an example of a miscarriage of justice based on flawed expert evidence | Opinion evidence/experts |

▶

| Key case | How to use | Related topics |
|---|---|---|
| **Chapter 6 – Confession evidence** | | |
| *R* v *Garrod* | For a definition of a 'mixed' statement in the context of confessions | Confession evidence |
| *R* v *Hasan* | For clarification of the status of wholly exculpatory statements as outside PACE, s. 76 | Confession evidence |
| *R* v *Sliogeris* | To shoe definition of 'confession' for purposes of PACE | Confession evidence/ exclusionary rules |
| *R* v *Hayter* | For confirmation that a confession can be used in evidence against a co-accused | Confession evidence |
| *Li Shu-Ling* v *R* | To show definition | Confession evidence |
| *Parkes* v *R* | For an example of a confession by actions | Confession evidence |
| *R* v *Ward and others* | For judicial consideration of the principle that the confession must be made by the accused person | Confession evidence |
| *R* v *Cox* | For an example of a confession being excluded even where it is known to be true | Confession evidence/ exclusionary rules |
| *R* v *Fulling* | For judicial consideration of the scope of 'oppression' under PACE, s. 76(2)(a) | Confession evidence/ exclusionary rules |

| Key case | How to use | Related topics |
|----------|------------|----------------|
| *R* v *Emmerson* | For judicial consideration of the scope of 'oppression' under PACE, s. 76(2)(a) | Confession evidence/ exclusionary rules |
| *R* v *Paris* | For a clear example of 'oppression' under PACE, s. 76(2)(a) | Confession evidence/ exclusionary rules |
| *R* v *Seelig* | For confirmation that 'oppression' is partly dependent on the characteristics of the suspect | Confession evidence/ exclusionary rules |
| *R* v *Kenny* | To clarify the scope of 'unreliability' under PACE, s. 76(2)(b) | Confession evidence/ exclusionary rules |
| *R* v *Northam* | To clarify the scope of 'unreliability' under PACE, s. 76(2)(b) in relation to inducements | Confession evidence/ exclusionary rules |
| *R* v *McGovern* | To show the impact on a confession of refusal of legal advice | Confession evidence/ exclusionary rules |
| *R* v *Goldenberg* | As an example of the requirement for 'anything said or done' under PACE s. 76(2)(b) | Confession evidence/ exclusionary rules |
| *R* v *Walker* | To clarify the scope of 'unreliability' under PACE, s. 76(2)(b) | Confession evidence/ exclusionary rules |
| *R* v *Harvey* | For an example of the exclusion of confession evidence under PACE, s. 76(2)(b) even where there was no wrongdoing by the police | Confession evidence/ exclusionary rules |

►

| Key case | How to use | Related topics |
|---|---|---|
| R v Alladice | To show that the absence of a solicitor is viewed as less serious for a 'seasoned' criminal | Confession evidence/ exclusionary rules |
| R v Barry | For an example of numerous breaches of PACE Codes resulting in exclusion of a confession | Confession evidence/ exclusionary rules |
| R v J | To show the court emphasising the need for additional safeguards for vulnerable adults | Confession evidence/ exclusionary rules |
| **Chapter 7 – Hazardous evidence** | | |
| Nicholas v Penny | For an example of corroboration by speedometer | Corroboration |
| R v Makanjuola | For judicial discussion of the requirement for a care warning | Care warnings |
| R v Jones and Jenkins | To show the requirement for a care warning in cases of 'cut-throat' defence | Care warnings |
| Benedetto and Labrador v R | To illustrate the need for special care in cases of 'cell confession' | Care warnings |
| R v Lucas | To set out the procedure for dealing with evidence of lies by the accused | Care warnings |
| R v Barnett | For an example of the procedure for dealing with evidence of lies by the accused | Care warnings |

| Key case | How to use | Related topics |
|---|---|---|
| R v Sunalla (Adel Abdulwaheb) | To explain the treatment by the court of lies by the accused | Lies of the accused |
| R v Stott | For a discussion of police identification procedures | Identification |
| R v Kelly | For a discussion of police identification procedures | Identification |
| R v Pattinson | For an example of the application of the Turnbull direction in cases of identification evidence | Identification |

### Chapter 8 – Illegally and improperly obtained evidence

| Key case | How to use | Related topics |
|---|---|---|
| R v Leatham | To demonstrate the general admissibility of evidence | Admissibility of evidence |
| Jones v Owens | Confirmed the general admissibility of evidence | Admissibility of evidence |
| Re Saifi | Confirmed the general admissibility of evidence | Exclusionary rules |
| R v Sanghera | To demonstrate the relationship between PACE, s. 78, in relation to the Codes of Practice | Exclusionary rules |
| R v Samuel | To demonstrate the relationship between PACE, s. 78, and the denial of access to a solicitor | Exclusionary rules |
| R v Delaney | To demonstrate the relationship between PACE, s. 78, in relation to the Codes of Practice | Exclusionary rules |

▶

| Key case | How to use | Related topics |
|---|---|---|
| *R* v *Bailey* | For an example of the general application of PACE, s. 78 | Exclusionary rules |
| *Matto* v *Wolverhampton Crown Court* | For the principles governing the exclusion of an improperly obtained breath test | Exclusionary rules |
| *R* v *Mason* | For the principles governing the exclusion of evidence following police lies to both accused and solicitor | Exclusionary rules |
| *R* v *Walsh* | To demonstrate the relationship between PACE, s. 78, in relation to the Codes of Practice | Exclusionary rules |
| *R* v *Christou* | For judicial consideration of evidence obtained by alleged 'entrapment' | Exclusionary rules |
| *Williams* v *DPP* | For judicial consideration of evidence obtained by alleged 'entrapment' | Exclusionary rules |
| *R* v *Bryce* | For judicial consideration of evidence obtained by alleged 'entrapment' | Exclusionary rules |
| *DPP* v *Marshall* | For judicial consideration of evidence obtained by alleged 'entrapment' | Exclusionary rules |
| *R* v *Looseley* | For judicial consideration of evidence obtained by alleged 'entrapment' | Exclusionary rules |
| *R* v *Sang* | For judicial discussion of the residual common law exclusionary power | Exclusionary rules |

| Key case | How to use | Related topics |
|---|---|---|
| **Chapter 9 – Privilege, disclosure and public interest immunity** | | |
| *R* v *Khan* | For an example of the limits of the privilege against self-incrimination | Privilege/ self-incrimination |
| *Saunders* v *UK* | For judicial confirmation of the importance of the privilege against self-incrimination by the ECtHR | Privilege/ self-incrimination |
| *Beghal* v *Director of Public Prosecutions* | Assertion of privilege against self-incrimination | Section 78 of PACE Article 6 ECHR |
| *Three Rivers District Council* v *Bank of England* | For an example of the scope of legal advice privilege | Privilege/legal advice privilege |
| *Waugh* v *British Railways Board* | To show the court confirming the 'dominant purpose' requirement for litigation privilege | Privilege/litigation privilege |
| *R* v *King* | To show the court confirming that litigation privilege did not extend to documents consulted by experts in preparation of their reports | Privilege/litigation privilege |
| *R* v *Cox and Railton* | To show the court confirming that legal advice privilege did not extend to advice on how to commit illegal acts | Privilege/legal advice privilege |
| *R (on the application of Prudential plc)* v *Special Commissioner of Income Tax* | Rejection by the House of Lords of the suggestion that legal advice privilege should be extended to professionals other than lawyers | Legal advice privilege |

▶

| Key case | How to use | Related topics |
| --- | --- | --- |
| *Rawlinson and Hunter Trustees SA (as trustee of the Tchenguiz Family Trust) and another* v *Director of the Serious Fraud Office* | Privilege and inadvertent disclosure | Privilege |
| *Rush & Tompkins Ltd* v *Greater London Council* | For judicial discussion of the privilege attached to 'without prejudice' communications | Privilege/'without prejudice' communication |
| *Secretary of State for Defence* v *Guardian Newspapers Ltd* | For an application of the Contempt of Court Act 1981 on grounds of national security | Privilege/journalists' sources |
| *Ashworth Hospital Authority* v *MGN Ltd* | For an application of the Contempt of Court Act 1981 on grounds of patient confidentiality | Privilege/journalists' sources |
| *Goodwin* v *United Kingdom* | For an example of Art. 10 ECHR protecting the rights of journalists to protect their sources | Privilege/journalists' sources |
| *R* v *Maguire and others* | To show a successful appeal as a result of non-disclosure | Disclosure |
| *R* v *Kiszko* | To show a successful appeal as a result of non-disclosure | Disclosure |
| *R* v *Taylor* | To show a successful appeal as a result of non-disclosure | Disclosure |
| *R* v *Ward* | To show a successful appeal as a result of non-disclosure | Disclosure |

| Key case | How to use | Related topics |
|---|---|---|
| *R* v *Tucker* | To show a successful appeal as a result of non-disclosure | Disclosure |
| *R* v *Essa* | As an example of adverse inference following failure to submit a defence statement | Disclosure/Art. 6 ECHR |
| *Duncan* v *Cammell Laird & Co. Ltd* | For the leading decision on public interest immunity based on view of minister | Disclosure/PII |
| *Conway* v *Rimmer* | PII and police disciplinary records | Disclosure |
| *R* v *H and C* | For the current procedures to be followed in *ex parte* PII applications | Disclosure/PII |
| *R* v *Gray and others* | Defining the scope of public interest immunity | PII |

# Sample question

Below is an essay question that incorporates overlapping areas of the law. See whether you can answer this question, drawing upon your knowledge of the whole subject area. Guidelines on answering this question are included at the end of this section.

### ESSAY QUESTION

'The law of evidence makes considerable effort to ensure the quality of witness evidence in criminal cases.'

Critically evaluate any two restrictions on witness testimony.

# Answer guidelines

## Approaching the question

As the question concentrates on witness evidence in criminal (rather than civil) trials, there are potentially more areas to consider. In addition to general aspects of witness testimony, such as unfavourable and hostile witnesses and the use of previous statements, there are also areas such as character evidence and hearsay, which are of greater application in criminal cases. As with any law essay, the key is to provide a structured answer which is both descriptive (in setting out the relevant legal rules) and also analytical (offering some reflection and evaluation of the various principles).

## Important points to include

- Explain the basic principles of the trial process and the relationship between the concepts of relevance, admissibility and weight.
- Indicate the particular strengths and weaknesses of witness testimony (e.g. it can be tested by cross-examination and it reveals the demeanour of the witness but it is prone to emotion, exaggeration and untruth).
- Consider any of the key areas controlling witness testimony. These might include the rules governing character evidence, hearsay, the rules against compellability of spouses, the use of previous statements (both consistent and inconsistent), confession evidence, expert evidence or the rules governing unfavourable and hostile witnesses.

 **Make your answer stand out**

- Emphasise the role of witness testimony as but one part of the evidential 'picture', with a valuable role also played by real and circumstantial evidence.
- Be objective and even-handed in your answer – do not simply put forward one side of the argument.
- Always include a conclusion which offers some genuine reflection on the question.

# ■ Further practice

To test yourself further, try to answer these three questions, which also incorporate overlapping areas of the law. Evaluate your answers using the answer guidelines available on the companion website at **www.pearsoned.co.uk/lawexpress**

## Question 1

David, Simon, Peter and Michael are arrested, following the discovery of a woman's body on wasteland near the city centre. They are interviewed by DC Keen and DC Eager. Each is interviewed under caution.

David refuses to answer any questions, simply replying 'no comment'. At trial his defence is that he was abroad when the murder occurred.

Simon also refuses to answer any police questions and at trial he refuses to give evidence. In addition he does not present any evidence in his defence.

Peter answers some of the questions put to him in interview, but, when asked to explain how he came to have recent injuries to his face, he declines to answer.

At the outset, Michael requests a solicitor but is told that 'no-one is available at the moment'. Instead, he is questioned for six hours without break by DC Keen, who is aggressive throughout, repeatedly banging the table with his fist and pointing his finger into Michael's face. Unknown to both officers, Michael suffers from mild learning difficulties which make him particularly suggestible, although he still makes no admissions in relation to the offence.

After a short break the interview resumes. This time, Michael is accompanied by David, a duty solicitor. Frustrated by the lack of progress, DC Eager tells Michael and David that they have found Michael's fingerprints on the murder weapon and that an eyewitness has identified him as being with the victim earlier that evening (both statements are untrue). After a short consultation with David, Michael makes a full confession to the murder.

Advise Michael.

## Question 2

Anwar is known to the police as someone who buys cannabis for his own use but will sell some of it on to friends. He is not regarded as a significant drug dealer.

As part of an undercover police operation, DS Smart meets with Anwar, posing as a drug dealer. He asks Anwar whether he could get £5,000 worth of cocaine and promises him £500 if he can provide the drugs. Anwar has never seen any cocaine before but wants to make the money and remembers that another local man Sid deals in the drug. Martin promises DC Smart that he will get the cocaine and arranges to meet him the next day.

Anwar manages to obtain the drugs from Sid and arrives at the meeting, only to be arrested by DC Smart. Anwar violently resists the arrest and DC Smart is badly injured.

At trial, Anwar wishes to adduce the following evidence as part of his defence:

✔ Evidence from Dr Smith, a consultant psychologist. She will testify that Anwar would be likely to be suffering from depression and anxiety, following the injury of his close friend in a car accident the week before the alleged incident which may have impaired his judgement.

✔ Evidence from Sam, who monitors the CCTV cameras which captured the alleged assault. The quality of the images is poor but Sam will testify that the person filmed committing the assault is not Anwar.

✔ Evidence from Sally who is on the same university course as Anwar. She will testify that Anwar could not have committed the assault as he is a peaceful person who would not have the physical strength to inflict the injuries which DC Smart suffered in the attack.

Advise Anwar.

# Question 3

Critically evaluate the impact of the Criminal Justice Act 2003 in relation to the admissibility of both hearsay and character evidence.

# Glossary of terms

The glossary is divided into two parts: key definitions and other useful terms. The key definitions can be found within the chapter in which they occur as well as in the glossary below. These definitions are the essential terms that you must know and understand in order to prepare for an exam. The additional list of terms provides further definitions of useful terms and phrases which will also help you answer examination and coursework questions effectively. These terms are highlighted in the text as they occur but the definition can only be found here.

## ■ Key definitions

| | |
|---|---|
| Agent provocateur | A person who unfairly instigates the commission of an offence by another person. |
| Corroboration | A requirement for supporting evidence from another source on the same point. |
| Credibility | The degree to which a witness or a piece of evidence is likely to be believed. |
| Hearsay | A statement originally made out of court, repeated in court for the purpose of proving the truth of the statement. |
| Leading question | A question which indicates the desired answer or which suggests the acceptance of facts as yet unproved. |
| 'Mixed statement' | A statement which is partly in favour of the person making it and partly against them. |
| Privilege | The ability to refuse to disclose certain information as part of litigation. |
| Propensity | The likelihood of the accused having engaged in a particular course of conduct based on their history of having engaged in such conduct previously. |
| Rebuttable presumption | A fact which the court will accept without evidence but which can be disputed. |

## GLOSSARY OF TERMS

**Res ipsa loquitur**

'The thing speaks for itself' – passes the burden of proof to the defendant to show that the events were not their responsibility.

**Reverse burden**

A situation where the burden of proof lies not with the prosecution but with the defence.

**Similar fact evidence**

Evidence which seeks to highlight a similarity between previous conduct of the accused and the events forming the subject of the present charge.

**'Ultimate issue' rule**

A rule which has, traditionally, prevented an expert witness from giving an opinion on the central question of guilt in the case.

# ■ Other useful terms

**Admissibility**

Whether the court will allow the evidence to be heard.

**Burden of proof**

General requirement that the person making the point has an obligation to prove it.

**Circumstantial evidence**

Background and supporting evidence.

**Disclosure**

The process of exchange of documents between the parties as part of the litigation process.

**Documentary evidence**

Evidence contained in a document.

**Evidence**

Information put forward to support the case being advanced.

**Facts in issue**

The key assertions which must be proved.

**Hostile witness**

A witness who, with malice, opposes the party which called them.

**Public interest immunity (PII)**

Ability of the state to avoid disclosure of documents which are injurious to the public interest.

**Real evidence**

Evidence which is physical in nature.

**Relevance**

The link between the evidence and the point being made.

**Standard of proof**

The level to which the party has to prove the issue.

**Unfavourable witness**

A witness who, without malice, does not say what was expected of them.

**Weight**

How persuasive the evidence is.

# Index

Note: **Emboldened** entries refer to those appearing in the glossary

access to legal advice
  adverse inferences from silence 50–2, 53
  confessions 134, 145–6, 148–9, 180, 183, 189
  illegally and improperly obtained evidence 176, 180, 183, 189
**admissibility**
  character evidence 11, 55–83
  confessions 24, 131–4, 139–52
  criminal proceedings 11, 12, 24
  cross-examination 35
  documentary evidence 6
  expert and opinion evidence 11, 116–25
  hearsay 11, 24, 88–110
  illegally and improperly obtained evidence 173–90
  relevance 4, 11, 12, 24
  trial process 4, 6, 10, 11–12, 24
  weight 4, 12, 24
adverse inferences from silence 10, 30, 48–52, 138–9, 214–15
**agents provocateur** 184–8
anonymity orders for witnesses 47–8
appropriate adult 144, 151

bad character evidence 57–63, 66, 67–81
bad faith and police malpractice 180–3
**burden and standard of proof** 12–21, 40
  confessions 150
  evidential burden 12–13
  fair hearing, right to a 18–21
  golden thread 15

legal burden 12
**reverse burden** 16–21

care warnings 157, 158, 160–2
character evidence 55–83
  admissibility 11, 55–83
  attacks by defendants on another person's character 79–81
  bad character 57–63, 66, 67–81
  civil proceedings 58–63
  co-defendants 75–7
  credibility 35, 57–9, 65–6, 72, 74–5
  criminal proceedings 60, 62–82
  cut-throat defence 76–7
  defendants 67–81
  explanatory evidence 70–1
  false impressions, correcting 77–9
  gateways 57–8, 62–3, 68–81, 82
  good character 57, 58, 63–7, 77–9, 81
  hearsay 82, 100
  previous convictions 58–60, 66–7, 68–75, 80
  probative value 63, 68, 75–6
  **propensity** 60–6, 69, 71, 72–5
  relevance 11, 71–2
  similar fact evidence 60–3, 75, 82
  *Vye* directions 65–7
children
  infant deaths and miscarriages of justice 125–7
  maturity and understanding 42
  special measures directions 44, 46
  unsworn evidence 43–4
  witnesses 42–4, 46
**circumstantial evidence** 9–10

# INDEX

civil proceedings
   burden and standard of proof 12, 13–15
   character evidence 58–63
   disclosure 207–8
   expert and opinion evidence 116–17, 122–5
   facts in issue 4
   hearsay 88–9, 93
   relevance 11
   self-incrimination, privilege against 196
   similar fact evidence 60–3
   witnesses 44
co-defendants 75–7, 137, 149–50, 161
compellability/competence of witnesses 29,
   39–44
computer printouts 4–5
confession evidence 129–53
   access to legal advice 134, 145–6, 148–9,
      180, 183, 189
   admissibility 24, 131–4, 139–52
   appropriate adult 144, 151
   bugging cells 181
   burden and standard of proof 150
   co-defendants 137, 149–50
   conduct 138–9
   definition 134–9
   drugs, withdrawal from 146–7
   exculpatory statements 135–6
   external events causing unreliability 146–7
   hearsay 100
   illegally and improperly obtained evidence
      175–8, 180–3, 189
   inculpatory statements 135–6
   inducements 145
   mental disabilities, persons with 143–8,
      150–1
   **mixed statements** 135–6
   oppression 139, 141–4, 178, 182–3
   PACE and codes 131–7, 139–52
   partly adverse statements 134
   silence, inferences from 138–9
   unreliability 140–1, 144–9, 152, 182
**corroboration** 157, 158–62
costs 115, 119
**credibility**
   character evidence 35, 57–9, 65–6, 72, 74–5
   lies by defendants, evidence of 162
   witnesses 35, 36–7, 58

criminal proceedings
   burden and standard of proof 12, 15–21
   character evidence 60, 62–82
   child witnesses 43–4
   circumstantial evidence 9
   corroboration 157, 158, 160–1
   disclosure 207, 208–15, 219–20
   documentary evidence 6–7
   evidence, admissibility 11, 12, 24
   expert and opinion evidence 116–27, 159
   facts in issue 4
   fraud 9, 201–2
   hearsay 89–110
   memory, refreshing 30–1
   public interest immunity 217
   relevance 10–11
   similar fact evidence 60, 62, 75, 82
   witnesses 31, 32–44
   see also confession
cross-examination 32, 35–9, 59, 92
Crown privilege 216–17
cut-throat defence 76–7, 161

death, presumption of 22
deeds, alteration to 7, 8–9
defendants
   character evidence 67–81
   co-defendants 75–7, 137, 149–50, 161
   compellability as witnesses 40
   lies, evidence of 9, 162–4
   witnesses 40
directions see jury directions
**disclosure** 192, 193, 207–15
   advance disclosure 214–15
   civil proceedings 207–8
   criminal proceedings 207, 208–15, 219–20
   defence statements 213–15
   due process 194
   experts, reports of 208
   fair hearing, right to a 215
   faults in disclosure 214–15
   litigation privilege 208
   miscarriages of justice 207, 209–11, 219
   non-sensitive and sensitive material 215
   primary disclosure 212
   prosecutor, duty of 211–13, 215, 219
   public interest immunity 192, 193, 216–19

relevance 212
secondary disclosure 212
silence, adverse inferences from 214–15
standard disclosure 207
third parties 212
unused material 209
discretionary care warnings 157, 158, 160–2
**documentary evidence** 5–9
    copies and originals 6
    date created, presumption of 7, 8
    document, definition of 5–6, 98–9
    execution 6–7
    expert evidence 6–7
    hearsay 98–9
    physical condition 4
    proper custody, presumption of 7–8

entrapment and agents provocateur 175, 184–8
examination in chief 30–5
expert and opinion evidence 113–28
    admissibility 11, 116–25
    basis of opinion 122
    civil proceedings 116–17, 122–5
    corroboration 159
    costs 115, 119
    criminal proceedings 116–27, 159
    definition of expert evidence 116–17, 127
    disclosure 208
    documentary evidence 6–7
    fact distinguished from opinion 116
    handwriting 6–7, 119
    hearsay 100
    infant deaths and miscarriages of justice 125–7
    legal professional privilege 199, 200–1
    medical evidence 116, 127
    miscarriages of justice 125–7
    opinion evidence, definition of 116, 127
    psychiatric evidence 116, 118
    qualifications 117, 119–21
    real evidence 4
    reform 124–5
    relevance 11
    reports 115, 124, 208
    requirement for expert 117–19
    single experts 125, 128
    ultimate issue rule 122–3
    weight 12

fabrication 33, 92
**facts in issue** 4
fair hearing, right to a
    adverse inferences from silence 51
    burden and standard of proof 18–21
    disclosure 215
    entrapment and agents provocateur 187–8
    hearsay 109
    presumption of innocence 18, 197
    public interest immunity 217–19
    self-incrimination, privilege against 196–8
    special measures directions for vulnerable
        witnesses 46
fraud 9, 201–2
freedom of expression 206–7

good character evidence 57, 58, 63–7, 77–9, 81

handwriting 6–7, 119
hazardous evidence 155–71
    corroboration 157, 158–62
    discretionary care warnings 157, 158, 160–2
    identification evidence 157, 164–70
    lies by defendants 162–4
**hearsay** 85–111
    admissibility 11, 24, 88–110
    age, date or place of birth 100
    agreements on admissibility 94
    business and other documents, definition of
        98–9
    character evidence 82, 100
    civil proceedings 88–9, 93
    common enterprise 100
    confession evidence 100
    credibility 107–9
    criminal proceedings 89–110
    definition 87–92
    expert evidence 100
    fear, definition of 96–8
    and human rights 109
    implied assertions 92–3
    interests of justice 94, 104–5, 110
    misleading impressions 92
    multiple statements 107
    oaths 92
    previous statements 105–6
    public documents 100

**hearsay** (*continued*)
  public nature, works of a 99
  purpose of evidence 90–1
  real evidence 5
  records 100
  relevance 11
  *res gestae* statements 100–4, 110
  state of mind, evidence of 103–4
  statement, definition of 89
  truth of statement, proof of 88–91
  unavailability of witnesses 95–8
  witness statements 93–7, 99–100
**hostile witnesses** 31, 32, 35

identification evidence 157, 164–70
  appeals 168, 170
  confrontations 164, 166–7, 169
  dock identification 167, 169
  group identification 166
  hierarchy of procedures 165
  mistakes 164, 168
  PACE Code D 164–7, 169
  parades 165, 169
  *Turnbull* direction 167–9, 170
  unreliability 164, 167–8
  video identification 165, 169
illegally and improperly obtained evidence 173–90
  access to legal advice 176, 180, 183, 189
  admissibility 175–90
  agents provocateur and entrapment 184–8
  bad faith and police malpractice 180–3
  bugging cells 181
  cautions 176
  common law, exclusion under 177, 188–9
  confessions 175–8, 180–3, 189
  immunity *see* public interest immunity (PII)
  infant deaths and miscarriages of justice 125–7
  oppression 178, 182–3
  PACE and codes 175–90
  police malpractice 180–3
  probative value 188–9
  searches 175–7, 179
insanity and M'Naghten Rule 16
interests of justice 94, 104–5, 110, 204–5

journalists' sources and privilege 204–7
judicial notice 21–3

jury directions
  adverse inferences from silence 52, 53
  character evidence 65–7
  identification evidence 167–9, 170
  Judicial Studies Board 52, 53, 65
  *Lucas* directions 162–4
  *Turnbull* directions 167–9, 170
  *Vye* directions 65–7

**leading questions**, rule against 31, 35
legal advice *see* access to legal advice
legal professional privilege 198–207
  dominant purpose test for litigation 199–200
  experts 199, 200–1
  fraud 201–2
  inadvertent disclosure of privileged documents 203
  legal advice privilege 192, 198–9, 200–2
  litigation privilege 192, 199–200, 208
  other professions 202
  types 1 and 2 privileged documents 200
  without prejudice correspondence 203–4
legitimacy, presumption of 22
lies by defendants, evidence of 9, 162–4
live links 46
*Lucas* directions 162–4

marriage, presumption of 21
mechanical devices, presumption of working order of 23
memory, refreshing 30–1
mental disabilities, persons with 44–5, 143–8, 150–1
miscarriages of justice 125–7, 164, 168, 207, 209–11, 219

national security 204–5
  *see also* public interest immunity (PII)
negligence 4, 23

oaths 42–4, 92
official capacity, individuals acting in an 23
opinion evidence *see* expert and opinion

perjury, corroboration 159
police malpractice and bad faith 180–3
presumptions 7–9, 16, 18, 21–3, 197

previous convictions 58–60, 66–7, 68–75, 80
previous statements 29, 32–5
    consistent statements 32–5, 106
    inconsistent statements 35–6, 105–6
**privilege** 192, 193, 194–207
    contempt of court 193, 197, 204–6
    journalists' sources 204–7
    self-incrimination 185–6, 194–8
    *see also* legal professional privilege
probative value 12, 104, 188–9
public from court, removal of 46
**public interest immunity (PII)** 192, 193, 216–19

racial discrimination 18
re-examination 39
**real evidence** 4–5
regularity, presumption of 23
**relevance** 10–11, 24, 71–2, 212
reliability 140–1, 144–9, 152, 164, 167–8
religious discrimination 18
*res gestae* statements 100–4, 110
res ipsa loquitur 23

screens 46
searches 175–7, 179
self-incrimination, privilege against 185–6, 194–8
sexual offences, complainants in
    corroboration 158
    previous sexual history, cross-examination on
        36–8
    recent complainants 33–5
silence, right to 10, 30, 48–52, 138–9, 214–15
**similar fact evidence** 60–3, 75, 82
special measures directions for vulnerable
        witnesses 44–6
speeding offences 158–9
spent convictions 59–60
spouses or partners of defendants, compellability
        of 40–1
**standard of proof** *see* burden and standard of
        proof
survivorship in relation to property claims,
        presumption of 22

trial process 11–24
    admissibility 4, 6, 10, 11–12, 24
    burden and standard of proof 12–21

circumstantial evidence 9–10
documentary evidence 5–9
facts in issue 4
forms of evidence 4–10
judicial notice 21–3
presumptions 7–9, 21–3
real evidence 4–5
relevance 4, 10–11, 24
weight 4, 10, 12, 24
*see also* witnesses

**ultimate issue rule** 122–3
**unfavourable witnesses** 32–3, 35
unsworn evidence 43–4
unused material 24, 209

video-recorded evidence 46

**weight** 4, 12, 24
wigs and gowns, removal of 46
wills, alteration to 7, 9
without prejudice correspondence 203–4
witnesses 10, 27–54
    anonymity orders 47–8
    cell witnesses 161
    character evidence 58
    children 42–4, 46
    civil proceedings 44
    compellability 29, 39, 40–1
    competence 29, 39–44
    credibility 35, 36–7, 58
    criminal proceedings 31, 32–44
    cross-examination 32, 35–9, 59, 92
    defendants 40
    examination in chief 30–5
    hostile witnesses 31, 32, 35
    leading questions, rule against 31, 35
    memory, refreshing the 30–1
    oaths 42–4
    previous consistent statements 32–5
    previous inconsistent statements 35–6
    previous statements 29, 32–6
    re-examination 39
    self-incrimination, privilege against 194–8
    sexual offences 33–9
    silence, right to 30, 40, 48–52
    special categories 40–4

witnesses (*continued*)
    special measures directions for vulnerable
        witnesses 44–6
    spouses or partners of defendants,
        compellability of 40–1

stages 30–9
unavailability 95–8
unfavourable witnesses 32–3, 35
unsound mind, persons of 44
*see also* expert and opinion evidence